More praise for
Bloody Business . . .

"JEFFERS IS A SUPERIOR CRIME WRITER AND JOURNALIST . . . flows like a good crime novel . . . highly recommended." —*The Coast Book Review Service*

"OFFBEAT . . . IRRESISTIBLE." —*Booklist*

"JEFFERS CHRONICLES THE BIRTH AND GROWTH OF LONDON'S METROPOLITAN POLICE . . . in a book that has the extra appeal of recalling some of London's most famous crimes." —*Sacramento Bee*

"FASCINATING!" —*Fresno Bee*

"READERS OF BRITISH MURDER MYSTERIES . . . will devour this history of the world's most famous police agency." —*Publishers Weekly*

BLOODY BUSINESS

SCOTLAND YARD'S MOST FAMOUS AND SHOCKING CASES

H. Paul Jeffers

BERKLEY BOOKS, NEW YORK

BLOODY BUSINESS

A Berkley Book / published by arrangement with
Pharos Books

PRINTING HISTORY
Pharos Books edition published 1992
Berkley edition / January 1994

ISBN: 0-425-14054-7

BERKLEY®
Berkley Books are published by
The Berkley Publishing Group, 200 Madison Avenue,
New York, New York 10016.
BERKLEY and the "B" design are trademarks of
Berkley Publishing Corporation.

PRINTED IN THE UNITED STATES OF AMERICA

10 9 8 7 6 5 4 3 2 1

This book is dedicated to my niece
Virginia Detwiler,
who shares my delight in London
and a zest for murder most English.

"I have been down to see friend Lestrade at the Yard. There may be an occasional want of imaginative intuition down there, but they lead the world for thoroughness and method."

Sherlock Holmes,
"The Adventure of the Three Garridebs"

CONTENTS

INTRODUCTION

"Good Evening, Inspector."

"DON'T YOU FEEL THE NEED TO GIVE YOUR OLD ARCHENEMY Inspector Plodder of the Yard a run for his money?" asks tax-poor mystery novelist Andrew Wyke in Anthony Shaffer's devilishly ingenious play *Sleuth*.

The proposition is criminal. Wyke has enticed his tiresome and extravagant wife's lover to Wyke's stately English manor in order to engage hairdresser Milo Tindle in a complex scheme to defraud an insurance company. Wyke promises to divorce his unfaithful wife if Milo makes off with a trove of jewels in a fake burglary. Sale of the gems will finance Milo's marital bliss. Wyke then collects the insurance on the gems. Everyone lives happily ever after.

Milo is dubious. "The police are always stupid in the kind of books you write, aren't they?" he asks. "They never solve anything."

For generations of readers the keystone of English detective fiction has been the notion that a representative of the Criminal Investigation Department of London's Metropolitan Police, known the world over as Scotland Yard, is so dumb that he needs the assistance of an outsider to solve a crime.

Since Sherlock Holmes first described the smartest Yarder as the pick of a bad lot, amateur sleuths have been stalking British criminals in books, films, and television programs while the man from Scotland Yard lags a few paces and several clues behind, waiting for the puzzle to be unraveled and the culprit handed over.

For Holmes it is Gregson, Lestrade, and others of varying capability. For Agatha Christie's Hercule Poirot it's Inspector

Jimmy Japp who is greeted with "Good evening, Inspector!" when he appears at the scene of a crime that Poirot and his "little gray cells" already are well on the way to solving.

"That good inspector believes in matter in motion," says Poirot of Japp in *The Plymouth Express*. "He travels; he measures footprints; he collects mud and cigarette-ash! He is extremely busy! He is zealous beyond words." In Poirot's view, Japp is "the younger generation knocking at the door," but he is so busy knocking that he does not notice that the door is open.

This superior attitude is evident in Miss Jane Marple when she chats with Chief Inspector Fred Davy at Bertram's Hotel, with Inspector Slack as he deals with the body in the library and the murder at the vicarage, with Chief Inspector Craddock concerning a murder observed on the 4:50 from Paddington and with others from the Murder Squad. All play second fiddle while the little old lady from St. Mary Mead obligingly solves baffling homicides through a mixture of spinsterly snooping, eavesdropping, woman's intuition, and flashes of odd but instructive anecdotes she drags from memories of a lifetime in the flowery English countryside.

Through the years there has been a banquet of amateurs for readers to feast upon with the hapless Yarder for dessert. In stories by Margery Allingham the Cambridge-educated aristocrat Albert Campion unlocks the mystery, first for Inspector Stanislaus Oates and then Superintendent Charlie Luke. The gentleman-adventurer Captain Hugh (Bulldog) Drummond, as created by H. C. McNeile, has his Colonel Neilsen of the Yard. Inspector Hanslet and Inspector Waghorn could be counted on to bring their most perplexing puzzles to Dr. Lancelot Priestley, in the novels of John Rhode. The word's bookshelves bulge with the genre.

In the century since Sherlock Holmes looked down his hawkish nose and declared, "I am the last and highest court of appeal in detection," there has been no shortage of outsiders prepared to explain the case to Inspector Plodder.

For devotees of these detective stories the impression has been left that the British police are inept bunglers who never solve a crime by themselves. It's an especially indelible image for Americans whose primary knowledge of the British police has crossed the Atlantic Ocean in books, films, and television shows featuring portrayals of the Scotland Yard detective as supporting player, antagonist, and pupil. It is a reputation that has been reinforced in the United States on Public Television's "Mystery!" series.

There have been exceptions. Although the giants of English mystery writing, Sir Arthur Conan Doyle and Dame Agatha Christie, promulgated the image of the plodding Scotland Yard detective, other writers have chosen to illuminate the work of competent Scotland Yard professionals. The earliest to do so was Charles Dickens, bringing to life the first professional detective in English literature—Inspector Bucket in *Bleak House*. Soon after in *The Moonstone*, Wilkie Collins described Sergeant Cuff as being preceded by a reputation as the finest police detective in England. Collins based his creation on a real-life Scotland Yarder, Jonathan Whicher, whose most notable investigation is recounted in this book.

In this century John Dickson Carr created Colonel March as head of the Department of Queer Complaints. Roy Vickers invented the Department of Dead Ends and Freeman Wills Crofts gave mystery readers Inspector Joseph French, a man with a twinkle in his eyes and an uncanny ability to destroy so-called unbreakable alibis. In twenty-one books John Creasey, using the pseudonym of J. J. Marrick, recorded cases of Commander George Gideon of Scotland Yard, a role subsequently translated from book to screen by Jack Hawkins in the 1958 *Gideon of Scotland Yard*, directed by John Ford. Hawkins also provided a realistic portrait of a Scotland Yard detective in the 1956 movie *The Third Key*. As Superintendent Tom Halliday, he diligently pursued a safe-cracking case clue by clue until he got his man.

In the 1950s American television went further, presenting a "Fabian of Scotland Yard" series based on the exploits of the flesh-and-blood Inspector Robert Fabian.

Over the past several years the viewers of "Mystery!" have followed fictional investigations by Inspector Morse, Sergeant Cribb, and Commander Adam Dalgliesh. Yet, despite portrayals of capable and successful official detectives, it's the fictional image of the inept and ineffectual Yarder that persists.

The truth is, as Milo Tindle warns smug Andrew Wyke in *Sleuth*, "There's no such animal as Inspector Plodder. It'll probably be some sharp-eyed bloke who knows his job down to the last detail."

This book is a record of many of those sharp-eyed blokes who were called upon to solve intricate true-life mysteries, singular daring crimes, and the bloodiest of murders since the formation of the most romanticized detective department in the world, the CID of the Metropolitan Police. But the story of Scotland Yard that unfolds in these pages is more than a tapestry of cops, robbers, and killers. It is also a record of two centuries of efforts to balance a need for law and order in an increasingly complex and evermore dangerous society with Britain's ancient and jealously guarded freedoms.

Weaving true cases of crime and murder into a fascinating history of the police department that is arguably the most famous and admired in the world, *Bloody Business* looks beyond the blue beehive helmet of the Bobby on his beat and the Murder Squad detective's trench coat to cut through the fiction and reveal dramatic portraits of real detectives wrestling with the most notorious crimes in British history to bring the culprits to the bar of justice. And frequently to the gallows.

ONE

The Body in the Boot

THE TALL, YOUNG BLACK MAN BOARDING WAYNE ROLLAND'S shuttle bus at the long-term auto parking lot of the North Terminal of Gatwick Airport on Thursday morning, May 30, 1991, appeared to be terribly nervous. "Is this the bus that goes to the Continental Airlines terminal?" he asked, adjusting the shoulder straps of a knapsack, his only luggage.

"This is it, sir," answered Rolland.

"Will it take long?" The young man's American-accented voice trembled. "I can't afford to miss my flight. I have to get back to Boston right away. I just learned that my father has died."

"I'm very sorry about your trouble, sir," Rolland said as he started the bus. "I'll have you at the terminal in a jiffy."

At Gatwick there are two terminals, South and North. Handling more than 16 million passengers a year, they constitute the third busiest international airport in the world. It was opened in 1958 just in time for the dawn of the era of jetliners, when London's only airport, Heathrow, was already swamped with air traffic.

Unlike Heathrow, which sprawls inside the boundaries of the Metropolitan Police headquartered at New Scotland Yard in London, the airport at Gatwick lies in the jurisdiction of the county of Sussex. Therefore, it was officers of the Sussex Police Department patrolling the parking lots at 10:30 Saturday morning who were attracted to a car that seemed oddly out of place.

A two-door green Montego sedan, it had registration plates of a rental car. Wondering why it had been left in a long-term lot rather than being returned to the auto leasing company, the officers investigated. Finding the doors locked, they peered in through the windows.

Immediately, they saw what appeared to be bloodstains. Reporting the discovery to headquarters by radio, one of the officers said, "I think we'd better have somebody out here to have a look in the boot."

Curled into the trunk, the body of a young woman had been stabbed and slashed several times. Beside her lay a knife with a four-and-a-half-inch folding blade.

Clearly, such a brutal murder could not have been carried out in the busy parking lot at Gatwick. Accordingly, investigating the homicide would have to be a nationwide undertaking. Such cases were referred to the Criminal Investigation Department of the Metropolitan Police. Commonly known as Scotland Yard, the CID coordinated a national network of regional crime squads whose task was to investigate serious crimes, such as murder, involving more than one police jurisdiction. It also brought to a case the resources of the Metropolitan Police Forensic Science Laboratory and the Scene of the Crime officers to provide expertise in biology, chemistry, crime-scene photography, fingerprints, and other technologies of modern criminology.

Investigation began with the most significant clue, the car. Detectives traced its registration to a rental firm in Stoke-on-Trent, a small town north of Birmingham and some 200 miles northwest of London. Records of the auto rental firm showed that the Montego had been hired on Wednesday, May 29, by a tall black American who had listed his address as the Holly Tree Hotel.

"The gentleman stayed here five nights," reported hotel co-owner Zara Harriman. He had checked in with only a rucksack for luggage, had been well behaved, and had seemed to have plenty of money, although he left without paying his bill.

While the automobile was being traced, the dead woman was being identified. She was Catherine Ayling. A humanities student at Crewe and Alsager College not far from Stoke-on-Trent, she had been reported missing on Thursday, May 30, after she did not show up for a final examination. The next day her bloodstained car was found on campus.

Examination of her Citroën left no doubt in the detectives' minds that she had been murdered in it and had struggled with her killer, probably on the evening of Wednesday, May 29.

Attention turned next to identifying the audacious man who had rented the car at Stoke-on-Trent and then driven it with Ayling's body in the boot some 250 miles from Crewe to Gatwick on a route that included some of England's major highways. Who was he? What was his relationship to Ayling? Why did he kill her?

Convinced that answers to these questions would be found in the details of the victim's life, the detectives centered their investigation on Catherine. Born in 1967, she had been raised in the village of Littlehampton in Sussex on the south coast of England, best known for its quaint hotels, good sands, and a golf course at the mouth of the Arun. Interviewing Catherine's older sister, Sylvia, and her brother, Christopher, at Littlehampton, the police heard a story of a vivacious and intelligent young woman who had worked at a local pub to earn money for tuition and who had had everything to live for.

"She planned to earn a master's degree," Sylvia explained. "In pursuit of that goal she joined a student exchange program that took her to the United States in 1989. She enrolled at Bridgewater State College in Massachusetts."

"That's where the trouble began," said Christopher. "She had the bad luck of meeting Curtis Howard. He was obsessed with her. She told him that she was not interested. She was terrified of him. When she returned home she was relieved to have gotten away from him. But he wouldn't give up. He came over here looking for her."

Could Christopher describe him?

"A black man," he said. "Very tall."

"It was as if he was stalking Catherine," said Sylvia.

"When was that?"

"Last June," Sylvia replied. "I remember as if it were only yesterday. It was terrible. When he found out she was not here he went on a rampage through the house."

"He tore up the bed with a knife," Christopher said, "and then he gouged pagan symbols in the wall."

"After that he went to the cemetery where our father was buried," Sylvia continued. "Dad died at Christmas 1989. Catherine was very close to Dad, so I suppose that's why Curtis Howard did what he did. He vandalized the headstone and then left the knife sticking in the grave. A few days later Catherine received an anonymous letter. It said that a contract had been taken out on her."

"The police arrested Howard and the government deported him," Christopher went on. "His passport was stamped with an order that he was not to be allowed back into England. But it appears that he managed it, doesn't it?"

"You don't know that for a fact, do you?" asked a detective.

"Catherine's dead," Christopher answered. "Who would want to murder her, if not him?"

With the events described by Catherine's brother and sister confirmed, and certain that if Howard had entered England he had to have done so with a false passport, another department of the CID was called in. Specializing in the apprehension of fugitives, the Extradition, Illegal Immigration, and Passport Squad asked the U. S. government for information concerning Curtis Howard's passport records and any other data on him that might be on file.

The response was alarming. The State Department reported that following his expulsion from England, Howard had attempted to obtain a U.S. passport under the name of Kevin Dion Bell, a Boston native who died in 1975 at the age of nine. When the ruse was detected, an arrest warrant was issued for Howard in March 1990, but it had never been executed because Howard could not be located. Neither the State Department nor the FBI could provide an immediate explanation as to how he had obtained the passport he had used to return to England in May 1991. Neither could they provide the name on the passport which Howard was using.

Uncertain as to Howard's whereabouts but convinced that he had murdered Ayling, investigators informed the press of their manhunt. "Obviously, the police in Britain want to speak to Curtis Howard quite quickly," said Chief Inspector Anne Pyke of the Cheshire constabulary, the jurisdiction where the murder had occurred. CID Detective Superintendent Bryan Grove admitted that authorities were still investigating how Howard had been able to enter England. Jill Nichols of the Sussex Police Department said no one could say if Howard had left the country. "He could have gone straight onto a plane," she said.

"Other people have said they have seen him around the airport since then."

For London's tabloid newspapers, notorous for sensationalizing murder cases, the story was irresistible. It had all the elements for eyecatching headlines. "Wanted for Murder in England," blared *News of the World* above a photograph of Howard and offering a $40,000 reward. Others carried similar headlines. "Fears for Love-Pest Beauty." "Bloody Car Horror." Stories told of the white English college woman stalked by a love-crazed black American who was described as "hulking," a "6-foot, 4-inch giant," "obsessed with white women," and pacing the Holly Tree Hotel "like a tiger."

Meanwhile, painstaking examination of departure records and questioning of employees at Gatwick Airport persuaded investigators that Howard had left the country immediately after abandoning his rental car and that his destination had been Boston.

As a result of this information, the British government filed a request with the U.S. government for Howard's arrest on a fraudulent immigration charge with the understanding that an application for extradition on the charge of murdering Catherine Ayling would be forthcoming.

Because there already was an arrest warrant for Howard based on his passport application under the name of Kevin Bell, agents of the FBI's Boston office, led by Special Agent-in-Charge Tron Brekke and joined by troopers of the Massachusetts State Police and detectives of the Boston police, set out to pick him up.

Measured against most suspects, Curtis Howard was far from typical. Many aspects of his life were exemplary. For thousands of black youths struggling to overcome obstacles that confronted them everyday, Howard seemed to be an outstanding role model. A 1984 graduate of Boston Technical High School, he had worked for PepsiCo, Inc., where his design of a new management computer program so impressed his employer that he was awarded a $2,000 scholarship. Four years later, he had received a second scholarship from the New England Mutual Life Insurance Company. Described as a "computer whiz," he enrolled at Bridgewater State College.

Suddenly, things went wrong. He dropped out of Bridgewater and then was arrested by college police and charged with trespassing for unauthorized presence in a dormitory. When he did not appear in court to answer that charge, an arrest warrant was issued. In October 1989, Bridgewater police arrested him on that warrant and for outstanding charges of car theft and armed robbery in Boston.

There also had been trouble with women. While a freshman at Northeastern University he had met a woman at a church. When she rebuffed him he stabbed himself. Following the breakup of another relationship, he slashed the woman with a razor and then was briefly sent to a state mental hospital. "When girls tell him they're leaving," said a perplexed relative, "Curtis goes crazy."

His last known address was a post office box in Mattapan. And Bridgewater State College records listed the address of a single-family home on Blake Street in Mattapan. Although neighbors said the family had moved away two years ago, someone recalled that there was a brother, Tim, who lived in the Mission Hill neighborhood of the Roxbury section of Boston.

Answering the knock on his door, Tim was not surprised to see the police. He had been expecting trouble since Curtis had shown up at the apartment on Thursday with several duffel bags. He had not seen his brother in two years. "Can I stay here for a while?" Curtis had asked. "I'm in big trouble."

Nothing Tim could do could persuade Curtis to talk about the trouble, but with State Trooper William Gorman and other detectives at the door, Tim recognized that his brother was in serious difficulty. "Is Curtis here?" Trooper Gorman asked.

Before Tim could answer, Curtis emerged from an adjoining room to surrender without a struggle.

In less than half a day since the discovery of Catherine's body, Scotland Yard detectives had positively identified her, determined the name and likely whereabouts of a suspect, and had provided authorities in America with reasonable cause for police in Massachusetts to make an arrest.

By that time a charge of murder had been brought against Howard in England and steps were being taken to extradite him for trial. Whether he would be turned over to the British legal system would be determined under provisions of an Anglo-American treaty on extradition. It was a process that would require many months before a judge ruled that he could be extradited.

Meanwhile, troublesome questions were raised by Howard's attorney, Jeffrey Denner. Was it possible for a black man from America to receive a fair trial in England? Referring to coverage of the case by British newspapers and expressing doubts about Howard's chances for an unprejudiced jury if he were tried in England, Denner cited a provision in the extradition treaty that forbids extradition of an individual if it would result in punishment "on account of his race, religion, nationality, or political opinions."

Were these objections valid? In England, was justice blind? Was there a presumption of innocence? Or was it assumed in an English courtroom that the individual in the prisoner's dock was guilty until proved innocent, especially if he were black? What rights could someone accused of a crime claim?

And what of those who leveled the charge of murder against Curtis Howard? What about the police? Could they be trusted to be fair? Might police in a sensational murder case have twisted the evidence? Had they rushed to judgment? Who were these men from Scotland Yard?

In raising these issues Denner was asking questions that, long before they heard of Catherine Ayling and Curtis Howard, had been posed by the English themselves.

TWO

A Perfect System of Police

THE VAUNTED LEGIONS OF JULIUS CAESAR MARCHED NORTH and west from Rome to subdue Europe. Britain proved rather more difficult. Impossible, actually. Faced with fierce opposition from its Celtic warriors who painted their faces blue and showed no inclination to bend their knees and bow their heads to *Pax Romana*, Caesar withdrew to Gaul and decreed that the western boundary of his empire would be the east side of the Channel. Julius's successor, Augustus, never having set foot on British soil, could be more optimistic. Reading the auguries in the safety of Palatine Hill, he said, "I can see Britain becoming as civilized as France." The Emperor Claudius shared his grandfather Augustus's high hopes for imposing a Roman peace on *Insulae Britanicae*. During a six-day visit to the troublesome island so as to demonstrate his military capabilities and qualify for a triumphal procession back home, he said, "The mission of Rome is to civilize the world. Where in the whole world would you find a race worthier of the benefits which we propose to confer upon it than the British race? The strange and pious task is laid upon us of converting these fierce compeers of our ancestors into dutiful sons of Rome." He must have impressed some Britons. In Colchester they named him a god. The deification of a Roman emperor notwithstanding, the daunting task of attempting to tame the stiff-necked British and bring them into the Roman fold of law-abiding citizens went on for four centuries until Emperor Honorius finally gave up the challenge and left the civilizing of the British to someone else.

The next invaders were Angles and Saxons. Seafarers, they flooded in from Germany and Frisia. Although taming the locals was not their prime motivation, over the next century and a half they imposed two concepts that would take root and flourish in Britain—Christianity and monarchy. Where the Twelve Tables of laws of the Roman Republic failed, the Book of Laws of King Albert gained a foothold and then flourished. "What ye will that other men should not do to you, that do ye not to other men," he decreed. He also proposed to the people another new but simple concept—one that Britons grabbed onto. If they pledged loyalty to the monarch, behaved themselves and kept his laws, he would guarantee them security from foreign invaders and tranquillity at home.

To achieve this, Albert set up a system of law enforcement with himself as the chief magistrate whose duty was to keep "the King's Peace." While making the Scripture's Golden Rule the basic law of the land, he sagely took into consideration that times and circumstances would change and so would rulers. "I have not dared to presume to set down in writing many laws of my own," he explained, "for I cannot tell what will meet with the approval of our successors."

By the time his great-grandson Edgar put on a crown (A.D. 959–975), times and circumstances had, indeed, changed. The king's dominion had grown. There were more people who had to be persuaded to keep the King's Peace. Edgar's answer was to modernize King Albert's system of policing by organizing the country into manageable regions called shires. Responsible for maintaining law and order was the "shire reeve." This system and these men, who eventually were called sheriffs, were ideal for a rural agrarian country and a population that had always been innately wary of strong central authority.

As those who have read of the adventures of Robin Hood or have seen the many movies based on the legend of a man who "took from the rich and gave to the poor," following the conquest of Britain by the Normans, the office of sheriff (in Robin's case, the Sheriff of Nottingham) was ripe for abuse. The result was rebellion (à la Robin) and a descent into fresh lawlessness. The consequence was reform of the manner of policing that returned the keeping of the peace to local authorities, as in the Anglo-Saxon system. The person invested with the police power was now the constable (from the Roman-Frankish term *comes stabuli*, or Master of the Horse). As the phrase suggests, the constable of this period was a military job. The Bobby in the beehive helmet and blue uniform as the embodiment of a local police authority was centuries in the future.

Meanwhile, successive kings grappled with the problem of policing in various ways. In 1195, Richard I appointed knights as "Conservators of the Peace" who were to be superior to the local sheriffs. Henry III (1251) established a system of high and petty constables under the conservators. As well-intentioned as these attempts at enforcing law and order were, the police power was still centered on the monarch and his minions rather than local authorities. Crime remained rampant. By 1285, it was clear to Edward I that "to abate the power of felons" radical reform was needed. His answer was the Statute of Winchester. It returned the power to police to the people themselves. All men were obliged to carry arms so as to preserve the peace and secure felons. Towns and cities were required to employ watchmen for nighttime patrolling. Suspicious persons were to be brought before the peace officers for questioning. Towns and cities with walls were to close their gates from sundown to sunrise.

In the centuries since Julius Caesar confronted blue-faced warriors who wanted no part of his Roman peace, and during the reigns of many kings whose realms were rural, some villages had become towns. A few of them swelled into centers of commerce. The greatest of these cities was London.

On the north shore of the Thames River at the head of the tidewater, it was called Londinium by the Romans. King Albert had ruled from there, followed by the Normans, Plantagenets, and Tudors. All were plagued by what the Tudor statute book described as "rogues, vagabonds and sturdy beggars."

The first of the Tudors, Henry VII, brooked no leniency for malefactors. By his order anyone found guilty of murder was to be marked with an *M* branded onto the left thumb. Two hundred years later an Act of Parliament provided that, instead of the thumb brand, a convict was to be branded on the most visible part of the left cheek nearest the nose. Still later, it was decreed that in place of burning a convict could be transported to colonies in America, to stay there for seven years.

Despite the harsh punishments, by the time Elizabeth I, the last of the Tudors, had ascended to the throne, Britain still was a long way from fulfilling Caesar Augustus's prediction that it would be as civilized as France. Guaranteeing the Queen's Peace was as difficult for Elizabeth as it had been for her male ancestors to ensure the King's Peace. It would remain so for monarchs for another two centuries.

Following the overthrow and beheading of Charles I, when Oliver Cromwell ruled from London as Lord General Protector of the Commonwealth, the work of the constabulary was taken over by a mounted cavalry who kept battered English freemen in line with merciless savagery until 1660 and restoration of the monarchy, when Charles II resumed the night-watch system. Mostly elderly men, they were no match for the young and the lawless. Detractors called them Old Charlies. (A policy emulated in the British colony of New York, the police were also called Old Charlies until the late 1820s, when they wore hard leather helmets and were given the double-meaning sobriquet "Leatherheads".)

In London, the Old Charlies held sway for two hundred years with no effect on curbing the growth of crime. With thieves in such abundance, the government in 1692 created a Parliamentary Reward System that offered a bounty of forty pounds for capturing a thief. This led to a thriving business among thieves who had no qualms about turning in confederates. It also introduced the idea that the best way to catch a thief was by hiring a thief, as in the case of Jonathan Wild.

A professional criminal enlisted by the Under Marshal of London to collar thieves, Wild thrived for nine years (1716–1725) running an extortion and protection racket that demanded a payoff as well as a share of the loot from any crook unfortunate enough to be nabbed. Retrieved stolen items were then returned to owners who were happy to pay Wild a reward. To facilitate the procedure, he created the Office of Lost and Stolen Property and became a multimillionaire. Ultimately, the government grew embarrassed about his activities and sought to trim his sails with a law that was so obviously aimed at him that it was known as the Jonathan Wild Act. Using it against him in 1725, Sir William Thompson, a judge who had written the law, ordered Wild arrested on the charge of bilking a blind woman who had solicited his aid in catching the person who had robbed her drapery shop. He was accused of pocketing the money "without discovering, apprehending, or causing to be apprehended, the felon who had stolen the lace." For this offense he was carted off to the gallows.

"By the eighteenth century," observed David Ascoli in *The Queen's Peace*, "there was no city in Europe more urgently in need of a preventive police force than dissolute, disorderly London."

Into this maelstrom stepped two remarkable men: Thomas de Veil, a soldier; and Henry Fielding, a playwright.

Appointed a court justice for Middlesex and Westminster in 1729, de Veil set up his office at No. 4 Bow Street, so-named for its geography, running in the shape of a bent bow. Serving for seventeen years as a magistrate, de Veil sent to prison or the gallows, in his words, "above nineteen hundred of the greatest malefactors that ever appeared in England." He was, in effect, the first commissioner of police of the metropolis of London.

Filling his shoes at Bow Street in 1748 was Henry Fielding. Twelve years earlier, an already accomplished novelist and playwright, he had formed a theatrical company to put on the comedies he wrote parodying official corruption and lawlessness in the city, only to have his enterprise shut down by an Act of Parliament. Censored, he abandoned the stage and went into the practice of law. Probably as a reward from political friends who appreciated his theatrical barbs aimed at their enemies, he was given the job of magistrate. It's likely that they expected him to use Bow Street to enrich himself through graft. While he did find time to write a novel about a rakish youth named Tom Jones, he made Bow Street Court a landmark on the path to effective and honest law enforcement.

Immediately upon taking the oath of office, he began hiring men to assist him, starting with his brother John and a former high constable of Holborn, Saunders Welch. He then picked seven others, all but one ex-constables who were "actuated by a truly public-spirit against Thieves" whose purpose was to go out from Bow Street and catch criminals. Outfitted in red vests and armed with pistols and for the pay of a guinea a week, supplemented by whatever could be picked up under the Parliamentary Reward Act, known as "blood money," they were ready for action within fifteen minutes of a call. Because of their reputation for being quick to respond and fleet of foot, these precursors of modern police became known as the Bow Street Runners.

For nine decades they were the only "thief takers" in all of London. But they were few in number. Never more than fifteen at a time, they were severely limited in effect. By 1822 there was one criminal for every 822 inhabitants of

London and some 30,000 people making their living by burglary and theft.

Thrust into this crisis of crime was one of the bright lights of the Tory party-Robert Peel. Born in 1788, the middle-class son of a selfmade man, he had been the secretary for Ireland from 1812 to 1818 and had set up a regular Irish constabulary there. The anarchic Irish for whom the word *police* was anathema immediately called them "Peelers." As Roman Catholics, they called their Protestant chief "Orange Peel." But when he turned over the Irish problem to his successor, he departed the Emerald Isle having created an Irish constabulary that would be a firm foundation for continued law and order. Doing the same thing on the other side of the Irish Sea wasn't going to be quite so easy.

Appointed Home Secretary in 1822, Peel established a Select Committee to look into the policing of the unruly Metropolis of London, with the hope that it would come back with recommendations that would result in the fashioning of "as perfect a system of police as was consistent with the character of a free country." The committee disappointed him, returning with a report that looked upon creating a "perfect system of police" with as much alarm as the blue-faced Celtic warriors greeted the arrival of Julius Caesar. "It is difficult," it stated, "to reconcile an effective system of police with that perfect freedom of action and exemption from interference which are the great privileges and blessing of society in this country." "The forfeiture or curtailment of such advantages," the report went on, "would be too great a sacrifice for improvements in police, or facilities in detection of crime, however desirable in themselves."

Undaunted, Peel turned his talents to reforming the penal laws to make them a more effective deterrent. His goal was to let criminals appreciate that their misdeeds would be punished, but that the punishments would fit the crimes. Previously, if a thief knew that he could go to the gallows for stealing, he showed no reluctance in murdering his victim so as to eliminate a witness.

At the very least, Peel hoped that by reforming the laws the law itself would not compel crooks to become killers.

The problem of crime in London was rooted in the abysmal conditions under which people were forced to live. "A dirtier or more wretched place he had never seen," wrote Charles

Dickens in describing the London of the time through the eyes of youthful Oliver Twist.

> The street was very narrow and muddy, and the air was impregnated with filthy odours. There were a good many small shops; but the only stock in trade appeared to be heaps of children, who, even at that time of night, were crawling in and out at the doors, or screaming from the inside. The sole places that seemed to prosper amid the general blight of the place, were the public-houses; and in them, the lowest orders . . . were wrangling with might and main. Covered ways and yards, which here and there diverged from the main street, disclosed little knots of houses, where drunken men and women were positively wallowing in filth; and from several of the doorways, great ill-looking fellows were cautiously emerging, bound, to all appearance, on no very well disposed or harmless errands.

Poverty was at the root of crime and at the heart of riots that plagued Britain's new industrial age and which the government met, not with social reforms but with armed force. The consequence of this was a series of governmental upheavals that didn't subside until King William IV turned to a national hero to take the helm—the Duke of Wellington, vanquisher of Napoleon at Waterloo. In January 1828, he recalled Peel to government to take over again as Home Secretary. Even more significantly, Peel also held the most powerful position in Parliament, Tory leader of the House of Commons. In both these roles he was now able to take on the task of reforming the Metropolis police. "It is the duty of Parliament," he advised Commons on April 15, 1829, "to afford to the inhabitants of the Metropolis and its vicinity, the full and complete protection of the law and to take prompt and decisive measures to check the increase in crime which is now proceeding at a frightfully rapid pace."

His Metropolitan Police Improvement Bill became law on June 19, 1829. It created an Office of Police to be "under the immediate Authority of One of His Majesty's Principal Secretaries of State," who would direct and control "the Whole of such new System of Police" for the area of metropolitan London as measured from Charing Cross bridge. Exempted from the authority of the Home Secretary was the one-square-mile City of London bounded by the ancient Roman walls, an independence retained by "the City" ever since.

To run the "New Police," the law empowered the Home Secretary to choose two commissioners. On July 6 Peel swore in forty-six-year-old Charles Rowan and thirty-three-year-old Richard Mayne. In the formation of the Metropolitan Police, they are comparable to J. Edgar Hoover of the U. S. Federal Bureau of Investigation—founding fathers who charted a course and set a tone. A century and a half after they set out to build their police force, Sir David McNee, commissioner of police of the Metropolis, wrote: "A great debt is owed to these two men for the outstanding contribution they made not only to the survival and development of policing but to the consequent good order and stability of society as a whole."

One of ten sons of a Northern Irish (Ulster) landowner, Rowan came from the military with experience in organizing and commanding a large body of men—just what was needed to create an effective police force. The son of an Irish judge, Mayne was a lawyer with the requisite knowledge of the intricacies of the criminal courts. Neither man was a slacker.

Within two weeks of their appointment they came back to Peel with a detailed plan for organizing the new police force into six divisions with a supervising headquarters, divisions broken down into sections and individual beats, a scale of pay, the locations of suitable station houses, a design for and a manufacturer of the force's uniforms, and 1,000 names of candidates for constables and superior officers.

For the crucial division encompassing the center of London (except the City), they recommended hiring 8 superintendents, 20 inspectors, 88 sergeants, and 895 constables.

They also handed Peel a *General Instruction Book* for the members of the force that remains a model of its kind. In defining the duties of their "New Police," they had some wise advice to draw upon. It was written by one of the original Bow Street Runners. A veteran constable before he'd joined Henry Fielding's little corps of red-vested lawmen at Bow Street, Saunders Welch had published a pamphlet entitled "Observations on the Office of Constable" that is as fine a definition of the role of the police now as it was then: "Let the service of the public be the great motive."

The general instructions also took into account the enduring reality of policing. A rule book cannot anticipate everything that may occur in an officer's performance of duty. "Something must necessarily be left to the intelligence and discretion of individuals," they wrote, "and according to the degree in which they show themselves possessed to these qualities and to their zeal, activity and judgment, on all occasions, will be their claims to future promotion and reward."

For the first time in English history, there was envisioned a *professional* police force. And Rowan and Mayne had no doubts concerning its purpose. "It should be understood at the outset," they noted, "that the principal object to be attained is the Prevention of Crime." The officers and police constables were "to distinguish themselves by such vigilance and activity, as may render it extremely difficult for any one to commit a crime within that portion of the town under their charge."

The uniform, designed to be "quiet" and not distinguishable from ordinary civilian livery, was a blue swallowtail coat with white buttons, blue peg-top trousers (white was optional in the summer), a collar worn over a stiff leather stock and fastened with a brass buckle, a broad leather belt, half-Wellington boots, and a tall chimneypot hat with reinforced sides and a flat top that was sturdy enough that a constable could stand on it. A blue and white armlet noted when a man was on duty. A letter and a number sewn onto the collar designated the division to which the officer was assigned. The outfit was standard for the next thirty years.

Equipment consisted of a rattle for summoning help and a truncheon. Because they were meant to be servants of the people, they were not authorized to carry firearms. Their power was to be based on the respect of the people, not on fear. "No gun" would be the rule for the constable on patrol during the entire history of the Metropolitan Police.

Discreet in their blue suits and stovepipe hats, they set out to walk their "beats." The term was as new as they were. Rowan had coined and defined it—as much space as one man could cover in fifteen or twenty minutes at a pace of two-and-one-half miles an hour. However, those who kept that cadence and carried out their duty to prevent crime were not universally welcomed. The popular names for them—Bobbies, Peelers, coppers—were not spoken with affection. Physical abuse of them was frequent. And on August 18, 1830, P. C. Long

of G Division was stabbed to death as he questioned three
suspicious characters.

When a tide of civilian complaints about police conduct
engulfed Commissioners Rowan and Mayne, they investigated
all charges. It was a nineteenth-century precursor to civilian
complaint review boards established after considerable opposition and controversy by many police departments in the United
States in the 1960s and by the Metropolitan Police in 1976.

In many ways the Londoners of the mid-1830s were very
much like Americans of the 1990s. Criminals seemed to be
all around them. They didn't feel safe in the streets. And
they saw a gallant but overwhelmed police force struggling
to cope with the mounting crime wave. Yet crime fascinated
them. Just as 1990s Americans cannot get a sufficiency of
"true crime" books and "reality-based" television programs
that luridly recreate the most monstrous of crimes, 1830s
Londoners scooped up sensational literature and flocked to
theatrical melodramas based on the latest outrages.

On June 12, 1833, a Londoner who could afford the price of
a ticket at the Surrey Theatre could take in *Jonathan Bradford;
or The Murder at the Roadside Inn*. It was but one of hundreds
of theatrical thrillers. "Nineteenth-century melodrama was as
voracious a consumer of scripts as is modern television," wrote
Richard D. Altick in *Victorian Studies in Scarlet*, "and no subject was drawn on more heavily by playwrights with impatient
managers at their door than the incomparably dependable one
of murder."

If stage thrills were too transitory, the Londoner crime buff
who wished to linger over bloody deeds had only to visit the
"Separate Room" at Madame Tussaud's Wax Museum at the
Bazaar near Portman Square in Baker Street, which opened in
1835. The room was a chamber of horrors, although it did not
take on that name officially until 1846, when it was suggested
by the magazine *Punch*.

A new genre of books also appeared in the 1830s—the
Newgate novel, so-named for Newgate Prison and its dreaded gallows where the criminal in the book invariably paid
the price for his crime by being led from his cell, through the
Debtor's Door, onto the scaffold, all to the tolling of the
prison's bell. In 1900, the site of Newgate Prison was taken
over for construction of the Central Criminal Court. Topped by

a bronze statue of Justice, the court is commonly known as the Old Bailey and has become familiar to readers of twentieth-century crime fiction by Agatha Christie (*Witness for the Prosecution*) and John Mortimer's books and TV programs fea turing the indomitable defense attorney Horace Rumpole. Despite the preachings of the authors of Newgate novels that "crime does not pay but leads only to the hangman," the popular, inexpensive novels dealing realistically with 1830s crime were denounced by officialdom for making criminals appear glamorous. Ironically, it was a government official who first capitalized on crime by writing about criminals. In 1776, the Reverend John Vilette, chaplain at Newgate Prison, published four volumes of *The Annals of Newgate or, the Malefactors' Register*, containing vivid accounts of murderers, thieves, and other scoundrels whose misdeeds had landed them in Newgate or on the gallows. Soon, accounts of evil men written by others were being sold for a penny apiece as broadsheets.

The best-known of these authors was James Catnach, whose *Last Dying Speech of William Corder* sold more than a million copies in 1828, with the tale of the culprit in a sensational case known as the Red Barn Murder. Corder killed young Maria Martin, buried her under the floor of her father's barn, and then carried on a year-long deception, including a claim that Maria was alive, well, happy, and on the Isle of Wight as Mrs. Corder.

Among more respectable writers accused of pandering to a sensation-seeking public was newspaperman-turned-novelist Charles Dickens, who described life among London's criminal class in his 1837 *Oliver Twist*. For an insight into the conditions that fostered the crime that the Metropolitan Police were struggling against in the 1830s, there is no better example than the hard and perilous adventures of Oliver as he stumbles into a den of thieves lorded over by Fagin. Running a school for young boys, Fagin offered lessons on how to lift wallets and dodge the coppers lest the boys swing for their crimes—although a public hanging, so long as it wasn't Fagin's, could be lucrative. "What a fine thing capital punishment is," he tells Oliver. "Ah, it's a fine thing for the trade!"

Despite the expectation that public hangings would serve to deter crime, pickpockets and cutpurses like Fagin eagerly listened for the tolling of the Newgate Prison bell announcing that there was to be an execution, and then joined the onlookers to snatch wallets or other valuables while everyone's attention was fixed on "the drop."

When Oliver was caught stealing, Dickens used the incident to note the common opinion of the constabulary: "a police officer (who is generally the last person to arrive in such cases) at that moment made his way through the crowd. . . ." The officer was implored not to hurt the boy. " 'Oh no, I won't hurt him,' he replied, tearing his jacket half off his back, in proof thereof."

Oliver's offense, wrote Dickens, had been committed within the district, and indeed in the immediate neighborhood of, "a very notorious" Metropolitan Police office. "In our station-houses," he wrote, "men and women are every night confined on the most trivial charges in dungeons, compared with which those in Newgate . . . are palaces." Oliver was detained in a cell that was "in shape and size something like an area cellar, only not so light."

Later in the novel, Dickens introduced a pair of Bow Street Runners, detectives Blathers and Duff, accompanied by constables Brittles and Giles. Summoned to investigate an apparent robbery, Blathers carried handcuffs that he played with carelessly "as if they were a pair of castanets." Duff, "who did not appear quite so much accustomed to good society," wrote Dickens, "or quite so much at his ease in it— one of the two— seated himself, after undergoing several muscular affections of the limbs, and forced the head of his stick into his mouth, with some embarrassment." The pair then "held a long council together, compared with which, for secrecy and solemnity, a consultation of great doctors on the knottiest point in medicine, would be mere child's play."

Dickens's low opinion of Bow Street Runners was evident also in *Great Expectations*, when "they took up several obviously wrong people, and they ran their heads very hard against wrong ideas, and persisted in trying to fit the circumstances to the ideas, instead of trying to extract ideas from the circumstances."

In the face of such widespread ridicule and disrespect from the public, low pay, difficult working conditions, and the dangers of the job, many of Peel's new police officers quit. Others, who didn't measure up, were dismissed. Turnover was high. But there was also persuasive evidence that the force was having some positive effect. Reports of theft were on the decline. Within the first five years of operations, it would be reported in 1834, losses through theft and robbery in the Metropolis dropped from nearly half-a-million pounds per year to 20,000 pounds.

How were they doing? In April 1833 a Select Committee was appointed to investigate "the State of the Police of the Metropolis within the Metropolitan District, and the State of Crime therein." Its report was a glowing endorsement, stating that "the Metropolitan Police Force, as respects its influence in repressing crime and the security it has given to persons and property, is one of the most valuable modern institutions."

Further evidence of effectiveness exhibited itself in the complaints of authorities outside the metropolitan region, who charged that criminals were fleeing London and becoming a problem for them. Beyond the Metropolis, policing continued as it had for centuries. The organization and control of the police was in the hands of local officials until 1839, when Parliament enacted the Permissive Act to allow counties to form police forces. When compliance turned out to be less than universal, permissiveness gave way to compulsion in the County and Borough Police Act of 1856. It provided for one-fourth of the costs of the police to be paid by the central government and set up a system of Inspectors of Constabulary. These institutions were not (and are not today) under the direct control of the Home Secretary. However, in the process of organizing their police, the counties and boroughs were encouraged to choose the Metropolitan Police as their model.

When Rowan and Mayne presented Robert Peel with their master plan for the New Police, they'd also suggested an address for the central police office: no. 4 Whitehall Place. Tradition held that it had been the site of a palace for visiting Scottish royalty. In 1829, it was a residential area whose stylish homes surrounded a narrow court called, logically, considering its regal history, Great Scotland Yard. Although the tenant of no. 4 was known officially as the Metropolitan Police Office, those who came and went through its doors soon found a more convenient name for it.

THREE

Scotland Yard

IN THE SAME YEAR IN WHICH PEEL, ROWAN, AND MAYNE invented a police department, George Shillibeer was introducing metropolitan London to an idea of his own—the omnibus. Offering horse-drawn coaches with a capacity for seating several foot-weary persons who had to get from one part of a sprawling, ever-expanding city to another, and who wished to spare themselves the expense of engaging a hansom cab, Shillibeer began what was the forerunner of the ubiquitous red doubledeckers that ply today's London. In December 1836, the police and the bus were brought together in the case of James Greenacre, a murderously ingenius forty-four-year-old cabinet maker from Lambeth, just across the Thames.

That Christmastide, Greenacre was betrothed to Hannah Brown, a widowed, fortyish washerwoman. The wedding was announced for Christmas Day at St. Giles's Church. In anticipation of their nuptials, Hannah moved out of her residence on the day before and into Greenacre's digs, where they celebrated with tea spiked with rum. Presently, James brought up the subject that was his real reason for marrying—Hannah's money. On several occasions she'd assured him that should he take her as his bride he would be rewarded with three or four hundred pounds. For his part, James had led her to believe that he had property. Both were liars.

Pressed to produce the dowry, Hannah laughed. With a sneer, she told him there was no money and, noting that he'd deceived her concerning his property, she cackled, "You're just as bad as I am."

Not amused, James grabbed a rolling pin. Although she was

struck so hard that an eye was knocked out, Hannah struggled for several agonizing minutes before collapsing. She seemed to be dead, but James made certain by slitting her throat. Having done so, he faced the immediate problem of concealing his deed. In view of the fact that Hannah's many friends were expecting to watch her marching down the aisle at St. Giles's Church the next day, he appreciated that he would have to provide a plausible explanation for calling off the wedding. He decided to tell the truth—the part about Hannah having deceived him about the money. Making the rounds of their customary drinking spots, he told the tale convincingly and not without receiving a great deal of sympathy.

Confident that Hannah's absence would be construed by their friends as her wishing to avoid the understandable embarrassment of being left at the altar (well, almost), James returned home to answer the question that confronts every murderer: How to get rid of the body?

Taking up the tools of his cabinet-making trade, he began sawing.

Finished with his bloody dismemberment, James now had to dispose of the parts—the limbs, the torso, and the head. Bundling them up separately, he set out on a Christmas Day odyssey beginning with an omnibus ride. The first of his gruesome packages was the head wrapped in Hannah's big silk handkerchief. Cradling it in his lap, he crossed the Thames to Gracechurch Street in the City, where he transferred to a second bus to Mile End in Stepney, one of the worst crime areas in all of the notorious East End. From there he walked to Regent's Canal to toss the head into the water, and then calmly reversed his itinerary back to Lambeth to dispose of the arms and legs in a Camberwell marsh. With the assistance of an unsuspecting carter and finally by hiring a cab, he was able to dump the weighty sack containing the torso at a construction site near a tollgate on Edgeware Road.

Three days later, an inquisitive policeman discovered it. Ten days after that gruesome find, the head was fished from the Ben Jonson lock of the canal. Presently, the arms and legs were found. In the meantime, Hannah's brother had reported her missing. From his description of her, police suspected that the reassembled body in the morgue was Hannah's. The brother's identification was positive.

After questioning him and Hannah's friends about Hannah's

last days on earth, the police learned of the abrupt, mysterious cancellation of the wedding. Suspicious, the men of Scotland Yard crossed the Thames to Lambeth to question the jilted groom. In due course, James confessed, not once but three times as he tried to get the charge of murder reduced to manslaughter and in a bid to exonerate another woman, Sarah Gale, who'd been his lover even while he was courting Hannah and to whom he'd presented Hannah's earrings. There was no deal. Sarah was tried and convicted and sentenced to life imprisonment as an accessory. Greenacre went to the gallows on May 2, 1837, in what the press described as one of the most popular hangings in the history of Newgate.

Children skipped through the streets chanting:

> Oh! Jimmy Greenacre!
> You shouldn't have done it, Greenacre;
> You knocked her head with a rolling pin,
> You wicked Jimmy Greenacre.

Macabre jokes circulated. The most popular told of Greenacre boarding the bus with Hannah's neatly wrapped head under his arm, asking "What's the fare?" and nearly fainting as the conductor replied: "Six pence a head." Another joke had it the other way around, with Greenacre leaving the bus and telling the conductor, "By right I ought to have paid for two passengers."

A much-needed success for the Metropolitan Police, the swift arrest of Greenacre occurred on the eve of the coronation of the monarch whose name would identify a new era that was to be the zenith of the British Empire. A period of civility and manners that was a veneer for scandals and social and sexual hypocrisy, it was also a time of burgeoning revolution and a series of bloody murders that would test Scotland Yard for as long as Victoria reigned.

When Princess Victoria of Kent succeeded her uncle William IV and ascended to the throne in 1837 at the age of eighteen, the monarchy was by no means a unanimously popular institution. A fervor of revolution threatened to sweep royalty from power in Europe while anarchists and socialists across the Channel were agitating among the lower classes of Britain to bring an end to their monarchy in favor of the revolutionists' idea of utopian, classless society. In this atmosphere some subjects of the fledgling Queen went so far as to hiss her on public occasions. Others resorted to an even greater extreme, with physical assaults and attempts upon her life.

As a breeding ground for revolutionists, London was an ideal hothouse. Among the early bloomers were Francis Place and William Lovett, authors of the "People's Charter." A document that came on the heels of the failure of the Reform Bill of 1832, it was a protest against the oppressive "poor laws" of 1834 and advocated universal suffrage and other radical political ideas. Nurtured by leaders of another form of protest, labor unions, Chartism took hold and flourished in industrial cities such as Birmingham. Some ninety-eight miles northwest of London, it was chosen in the summer of 1839 as the site of a Chartist national convention. Fearing disorders and with no local police force, the city magistrates appealed for help from the Metropolitan Police. Ninety men were sent.

The assembled Chartists interpreted the arrival of Bobbies from London as an affront and a provocation. Ordered to disperse, they refused. Wielding batons, the police charged into the crowd. Outnumbered, they fell back in full retreat and had to be rescued by the army. The next day the police did better but the Chartists rallied once more, sacking the central city. Again, the army came in and, with the help of a large body of hastily recruited special constables, restored order. For the Metropolitan Police, the entire affair was a humiliation. But it was also a lesson that would not be forgotten: Stay at home!

Nine years would go by before Chartists challenged the men of Scotland Yard on their own ground. They announced that on April 10, 1848, they would assemble at Kennington Common and then march on Parliament to present a petition for working-class rights. Duly alerted, the government under Liberal leader Lord John Russell, and the police under Home Secretary Sir George Gray and Commissioner Rowan, took steps to head off any possibility of a repeat of Birmingham. Rowan's police were detailed to guard all the bridges, 150,000 special constables were recruited, and the military was ordered into reserve. Supreme commander of this mighty force was to be none other than the hero of Waterloo, the Duke of Wellington.

The leaders of the Chartists may have been revolutionists

but they weren't fools. Rather than tangle with the arrayed power of the government, they hired three hansom cabs, directed their drivers to take them to Parliament, alighted from the coaches and delivered their petitions with all the excitement of postmen.

This was hardly the revolution that was being advocated by a German emigré who'd spent a great deal of his time during the 1840s in the Main Reading Room of the British Museum, composing a master plan for freeing the workers of the world from the bondage of capitalism. "A spectre is haunting Europe—the spectre of communism," warned Karl Marx. "Let the ruling classes tremble at a Communistic revolution. The proletarians have nothing to lose but their chains. They have a world to win." *The Communist Manifesto* was published in London in February 1848, with no noticeable effect.

The following month, Queen Victoria bestowed knighthood on Charles Rowan. In poor health, he continued as commissioner until January 5, 1850, and lived on for another two years. He died of cancer on May 25, 1852. In his twenty-three years at Scotland Yard he saw Robert Peel's New Police grow in numbers from a thousand to 5,625 and in esteem from ridicule and suspicion to admiration and respect. His partner in this enterprise had been Richard Mayne. While many expected Mayne to be given sole command of the police as the only commissioner following Rowan's retirement, it was not until 1856 that the Police Act put a single commissioner in charge at Scotland Yard.

In the midst of the social and political rumblings of the 1840s, the crime rate continued to rise. Policemen in uniform had succeeded in making the streets safer from thugs and pickpockets but, as Jürgen Thorwald noted in *The Century of the Detective*, within a few years it became apparent "that policemen in uniform were scarcely able to prevent crime, still less to solve crimes once committed. The wave of criminality receded only to the extent that robbers, thieves and murderers did not operate quite so brazenly. But in a thousand different guises and ways they continued their work from hiding places. And the only force that could track them to their lairs was the handful of Bow Street Runners—more corrupt than ever, a butt for journalists and caricaturists."

Of course, the Runners had never been envisioned in the role of ferreting out unknown criminals. They were not detectives, although occasionally a Runner demonstrated some genius in that direction. In 1835 Henry Goddard noticed that a bullet taken from the body of a murdered man bore a peculiar marking. Investigating a likely suspect, he spotted a mold used for making bullets and observed that it bore the same distinctive mark. In matching the bullet and the mold, Goddard became the granddaddy of twentieth-century ballistics. Confronted with the damning bullet, the man promptly confessed. Episodes such as this prompted a contemporary of the Runners to write, "Neither their numbers nor their organization were calculated to prevent crime, but as a detective police they seldom failed." If there were to be a reorganization of the police, he hoped, "recourse must be had to them again."

The question of the future of the Runners had been placed in the hands of a Select Committee appointed by Home Secretary Lord John Russell, in March of Victoria's coronation year—1837. The broad purpose of the committee was to evaluate the state of the police in the growing Metropolis, "including the City of London." In its report and in the Metropolitan Police Act that followed in 1839, an independent City police force was allowed to survive. The Bow Street Runners were not.

With their passage into history, London was left without a detective force. However, the need for one became evident in the brutal murder of a young girl on April 6, 1842. The name of the killer was known—Daniel Good, a familiar character to police. Yet it took ten days before they were able to track him down. The public was outraged. So was the press. The police, thundered the *Weekly Dispatch*, had been "marked with a looseness and want of decision which proves that unless a decided change is made in the present system, it is idle to expect that it can be an effective detective force."

Stung by the criticism, Commissioners Rowan and Mayne proposed to Home Secretary Sir James Graham a plan "relative to the Detective Powers of the Police." Authority for a detective force was granted on June 20, 1842. It consisted of a senior detective inspector (Nicholas Pearce, a Bow Street veteran), an assistant (John Haynes), and six sergeants, including Jonathan Whicher who would play a key role in one of the most celebrated murder cases of the ensuing decade, as would another of this new-style lawman, Dick Tanner.

When the new detectives set out from Scotland Yard to go about their duties in plain clothes, some citizens found cause for alarm. From their innate and historical suspicion of police, they looked on these nonuniformed representatives of the law and saw a potential for spying of the variety employed by the detested police force of France. And at least one magistrate expressed misgivings about plainclothesmen making arrests. "Now, although the police might wear plain clothes to detect crime," the judge declared, "yet when they are not dressed as officers they should not act as policemen themselves, but have the aid of some of the force who were on duty." Otherwise, he reasoned, how could a citizen appreciate that he was not being victimized by a criminal? He was, he made it clear, "against policemen assuming such disguises."

There was also resentment over the plainclothes detectives on the part of the policemen in uniforms, owing in no small measure to the fact that the detectives were paid more. Those in uniform referred bitterly to the detectives as "the commissioners' men." In an effort to dispel this ill will, Commissioner Rowan in 1846 issued a directive requiring two constables in each division to be trained in detective work. Despite this opportunity to enter the detective force, the numbers did not go up. Working out of three small rooms in Scotland Yard, there were twelve detectives in 1842 and fifteen in 1868.

Although the detectives were regarded with skepticism and suspicion by many, the sleuths of Scotland Yard had the good luck to find a booster whom historian Richard Altick called the best public relations man any police force was ever blessed with. "He had a lifetime love affair with the Metropolitan Police and in a number of journalistic articles, based on many excursions with his officer friends, in uniform or plain clothes, he describes their work, particularly in the slums and on the Thames," wrote Altick in *Victorian Studies in Scarlet*. His name was Charles Dickens, and anyone who has ever read or viewed a detective story owes him a debt, for it was Dickens who introduced England's first fictional detective.

His name was Bucket. We do not know his first name. He is an Inspector. Modeled on real-life Inspector Field of Scotland Yard, Bucket is a stout, middle-aged figure who wears a hat and carries a walking stick. "Otherwise mildly studious in his observation of human nature, on the whole a benignant philosopher and not disposed to be severe upon the follies of mankind," wrote Dickens, Mr. Bucket pervades a vast number of houses and strolls about an infinity of streets: to outward appearances rather languishing for want of an object. He is stolid, composed, honest, thoughtful, polite, hard-working, confident, and dauntless. "I am damned if I am going to have my case spoilt by any human being in creation," declares this tenacious bloodhound in *Bleak House*. "Do you see this hand, and do you think that I don't know the right time to stretch it out and put it on the arm that fired the shot?"

An avid follower of crime news, especially murder, Dickens relished acting out the knife murder of an oil-paint manufacturer by his artist-son in 1843. Six years later, in 1849, he rushed to Norfolk to examine the scene where James Blomfield Rush murdered Isaac Jermy, his son, and a maid and seriously wounded Mrs. Jermy—a killing rampage that soon became an exhibit in Madame Tussaud's gallery of evil deeds. And he joined with everyone in England in consuming newspaper accounts of a daring crime that took place in 1855: history's first robbery of a train.

The mastermind was William Pierce, a professional thief. His chief accomplice was Edward Agar. By bribing an employee of the South Eastern Railway, they obtained keys to strongboxes filled with 20,000 pounds in gold bullion. A payoff to another employee got them into the car where the boxes were stored. On route from London, Pierce and Agar rifled the boxes, substituted lead for the gold, locked the boxes, and threw the gold bars to other confederates stationed along the railway. By the time the theft was discovered at the train's destination, Boulogne, France, the booty had been divided and the gang dispersed. Unfortunately, Agar found himself under arrest on a charge of passing a forged check. To assure Agar that his share of the loot was safe, Pierce visited him in jail where he promised to turn over Agar's gold to Agar's mistress. It was a thief's promise. The woman received only a small portion of the proceeds. Outraged and hungry for revenge, Agar spilled the beans. In short order, detectives from Scotland Yard rounded up the gang. Preceding the first train stickup in America by eleven years, the heist would be known as the "Great Train Robbery" for a century, when that title was awarded to an even more daring group of railway bandits for whom 20,000 pounds would have been pocket change.

Two years after Pierce and his friends were sentenced to long prison terms, Dickens took up his pen to provide readers of *The Uncommercial Traveller* with what he titled "The Chopped-Up Murdered Man." The subject of the article had been found on the morning of October 9, 1857.

It was half-past five but the Thames was already alive with commerce. Through the dark, murky waters and between vessels, barges, and boats of all kinds, shape, and size, young James Barber and his friend were guiding a rowboat toward Waterloo Bridge. Always on the lookout for interesting things, Jim spied a bulky shape on the ledge of the third abutment. It was a sack of some kind and heavy looking. "Looka that, mate," he said to his friend, pointing to the object. "What do you think it is? Maybe it's the loot from some great robbery."

"Oh, right," scoffed his friend.

Heaving to, they noticed a cord hanging from the sack. It was a carpetbag, Jim realized. Grabbing the cord, he dragged it down into the boat. Opening it, the youths gaped in horror at its contents. Quickly closing the bag, they rowed to shore to report their find to the police. A constable promptly escorted them and the bag to the Bow Street police station.

Stuffed into the sack, the body of a man had been cut into at least twenty pieces. Only the head was missing. A surgeon was called to examine the body parts. "I fitted the bones together," he subsequently told a jury at an inquest, "and found that they must have all belonged to the same person." Asked whether he could state positively whether injuries to the body prior to its being carved up had been inflicted upon a living person, he said, "I can." So it *was* murder.

But who was this chopped-up man? Articles of clothing had been found in the bag but gave no clue.

Who killed and butchered him? To attempt to answer that question, detectives first sought to ascertain who had attempted to dump the bag into the river. In order to cross Waterloo Bridge it was necessary to pay a toll and pass through a turnstile, all under the watchful eyes of a tollkeeper named Evrington.

"I remember seeing a person dressed as a woman come up from the Strand side," he said. It was around half-past eleven. "She was alone, at least I did not notice anyone with her. She had a carpetbag with her. She laid a halfpenny on the iron plate and took the bag with her longways. In trying to get it through with her she turned the stile twice."

By double-turning the stile, the woman had registered two tolls but had paid only one. " 'Why did you not ask someone to help lift your bag up for you?" demanded Evrington. "See what you have done. You have caused me to lose a half-penny toll."

The woman grunted an unintelligible reply.

"I stooped down and took the bag by the handles," continued the tollkeeper for the benefit of detectives. "I particularly noticed the bag, as there was a strong gas-light from the lamp, and on the side of the bag I noticed there was a bright flower in the pattern."

There was no doubt that the bag Evrington had helped push through the turnstile was the one found by James Barber. What of the woman? "Her hair seemed plastered down on her forehead," said Evrington. "I particularly remarked that she seemed agitated, as if she was hurrying to go by the train from Waterloo, which starts at 11:45. She spoke rather gruffly; it was certainly in a masculine tone of voice. Her height might have been about five feet three inches. She was a short woman and rather stout."

Was this the testimony of a remarkably observant individual, or had Evrington invented the woman? The answer to that came from a man named Ball, a merchant who lived on Waterloo Road and was crossing the bridge between eleven and twelve o'clock. "As soon as I had passed the turnstile," he said, "I turned back to beg a light from Evrington. When I got there, I saw a short party who was dressed in female attire, and about five feet three inches in height, passing through the turnstile." Verifying Evrington's story concerning the woman's difficulty in getting the bag through the stile, Ball continued, "I then caught sight of her full face. She had a sallow complexion, with rather sunken eyes, and a mark on the left cheek, near the nose, which I took to be a mole. The hair was a kind of white, but it did not look a natural color. I saw her features distinctly, but did not take any notice of her dress. She proceeded along the bridge about half way, and then I overtook her and passed her."

To avoid the possibility of someone hearing the splash if the bag with its gruesome contents were dropped from the bridge, the detectives surmised, the woman must have lowered her horrible burden with the cord which Jim Barber had found and used to drag the bag into his boat in gleeful expectation of finding abandoned booty. Thinking she'd accomplished her task, the men from the Yard reasoned, she continued on her way believing that the bag and its contents were at the bottom of the river.

Who was she? Despite the vivid descriptions provided by Evrington and Ball, no one knows. She was never found. Lacking a head, her victim was never identified.

Although the Carpetbag Mystery was not solved, some theories were put forward, including speculation that it was a hoax by a newspaperman with a reputation as "the most audacious and enterprising penny-a-liner"and an "impudent boaster of his exploits," who stuffed the bag with parts that he'd collected from city morgues. But this was dispelled by the testimony from a well-known authority on what then was called "medical jurisprudence." Dr. Alfred Taylor testified that "the body has not been used for dissections for the purposes of anatomy." "On the contrary, he said, the remains had been rendered useless by a person or persons quite ignorant of the anatomical relations of parts." Furthermore, he told the inquest, they'd been cut and sawn and "partially boiled and salted."

Another version of the murder was offered in *Blackwood's Magazine* years after the mystery was filed as "unsolved." It held that the victim had been an Italian spy. The story is interesting because it was told by Sir Robert Anderson, whose distinguished name looms large in the history of the Metropolitan Police as the boss of detectives in the most famous unsolved murder case of all time—Jack the Ripper.

But before Saucy Jack stalked and slaughtered prostitutes in the dismal alleys and streets of the Whitechapel area of London's impoverished, lawless, and rebellion-minded East End, murder had reared its head in the idyllic countryside of green acres, clear streams, woodland, and meadows of Somersetshire.

FOUR

Is Constance a Killer?

"IT IS MY BELIEF, WATSON, FOUNDED UPON MY EXPERIENCE," said Sherlock Holmes, addressing his trusty traveling companion as he gazed from the window of a train on route to investigate strange doings at a place called Copper Beeches, "that the lowest and vilest of alleys in London do not present a more dreadful record of sin than does the smiling and beautiful countryside." In the city, he went on, there was no lane so vile that the scream of a tortured child, or the thud of the drunkard's blow, did not beget sympathy and indignation among neighbors. In the city, he said, it was but a step between the crime and punishment. "But look at these lonely houses," he mused, "each in its own fields, filled for the most part with poor ignorant folk who know little of the law. Think of the hellish cruelty, the hidden wickedness which may go on, year in, year out, in such places, and none the wiser."

The inspiration that prompted the creator of Sherlock Holmes to convey the world's first private consulting detective and Dr. Watson from Baker Street into the country is believed to have been a notorious case that unfolded in Penge, in the county of Kent, in 1877. It involved the cruel, scheming Staunton family. For sheer avarice and brutality, Louis Staunton, his mistress Alice Rhodes, his brother Patrick, and his wife are without par in the annals of English crime. Object of their devilish plot was a young woman named Harriet Richardson. Of weak mind and in faltering health, Harriet possessed some wealth and property. Though she believed it was love that evoked a proposal of marriage from Louis, what he and his relatives had in mind was inheriting Harriet's estate by starving her to death.

While there was ample evidence introduced at their murder trial that Harriet may have died from tubercular meningitis, there was no doubt that starvation hastened her demise. A jury found them guilty.

Arthur Conan Doyle was not alone among writers in lamenting the hideous crimes of the Victorian years, and the apparent easy acceptance of and even delight in them by the public. In 1849 *Chambers' Edinburgh Journal* observed: "In former times, a truly 'terrific murder' was the opprobrium of the epoch, and a landmark of history: now, one succeeds another with such rapidity, that the mind becomes deadened to the sense of the horror." Noting that this horrible taint in the national mood occurred in the midst of what it deemed a social, moral, and religious soundness, the paper called the public's thirst for blood the shadow of our refinement."

Charles Kingsley, writing in *The Christian Socialist*, saw "the most brutal, the most cowardly, the most pitiless, the most barbarous deeds done in the world" as the work of the "lower classes of the English people—once held to be by their birth, however lowly, generous, brave, merciful, and civilized." A later historian of Victorian Britain was not so quick to blame lower classes. "If one seeks the closely-guarded, authoritarian, almost sealed community," wrote W. L. Burn, "the mid-Victorian family can provide it; in practice it did not always possess the enchantment which the distance of a century lends it." The crime Burn was referring to shocked Britons in 1860. It was murder, not in the sordid slums of London's impoverished, crime-ridden, and rebellion-minded East End, but in an idyllic setting a hundred miles southwest of London.

In a spacious, airy, mansionlike home called Road Hill House resided Samuel Savile Kent and his large family, the offspring of two wives. The first Mrs. Kent had given him four children (two of whom died in infancy). Although her physical and mental health deteriorated after these births and deaths, she produced two more offspring. Constance was born in 1844 and William in 1845. To assist her in caring for the four surviving children, Kent brought in a young, attractive governess—a Miss Pratt.

Soon, she was more than a governess. After the death of the wife in 1852, she became the second Mrs. Kent. Bridesmaids at the wedding ceremony were Kent's eldest daughters, who were in their twenties, and nine-year-old Constance. Over the next eight years, the second Mrs. Kent bore three children. Born into this brood in 1857 was Francis Savile Kent. Mrs. Kent doted on the boy.

A typical Victorian father, Kent was sure of his position and himself. Domineering, didactic, demanding, and selfish, he was a tyrant—well meaning, perhaps, but a tyrant nonetheless. Nor was he a charmer outside his home. As Her Majesty's Inspector of Factories in the region, he was officious, gruff, and abrupt and was thoroughly disliked by the managers of the cloth-making firms he inspected. To neighbors he was downright unfriendly. To shut out their prying eyes he built a tall fence around his house. Those who trespassed with the intention of poaching trout from the stream that cut through his land were likely to be greeted with a blast from his shotgun.

While Road Hill House was roomy, with all those people under its roof, it was crowded. Mr. and Mrs. Kent occupied a bedroom on the second floor but shared it with the crib for their youngest girl. The two grown daughters of the first marriage had a room on the third floor. Fifteen-year-old William and sixteen-year-old Constance had separate rooms on the same floor. A cook and housemaid had small rooms above. In 1860, because his wife was again pregnant, Kent hired a nurse, Elizabeth Gough, who slept across the hall from the Kents' second-floor bedroom in a nursery with a one-year-old daughter and three-year-old Francis.

As was her custom, early in the morning of Saturday, June 29, Elizabeth arose to have a look at the baby. Finding her soundly asleep and turning to look at Francis, she saw that the boy was not in his cot. Because Mrs. Kent occasionally came into the room at night to take her favorite child to her bedroom, Elizabeth returned to her own bed and went back to sleep. Arising again about an hour later, she crossed the hall and tapped quietly on the door. Mrs. Kent answered. "Should I take Master Francis now?" asked Elizabeth.

Puzzled, Mrs. Kent replied, "But he's not here."

A quick search of the house left no doubt that the boy was gone. A window in the drawing room that Kent had closed the previous night was now open. Kent suspected a kidnapping by resentful poachers. Elizabeth Gough blurted, "It's revenge." Asked by Mrs. Kent to explain her meaning, Elizabeth shook her head and said nothing more.

"As Kent hurried to nearby Trowbridge to inform the police, a group of villagers from Road began a search of the grounds and the surrounding woods. It didn't last long. A pair of fishermen who'd joined the hunt, despite their resentment at having been run off the property by Kent, investigated a disused outhouse that had been a servants' privy. Immediately upon opening the door, they found bloodstains. A moment later, crammed into the vault, they found Francis. Dressed in his nightshirt, he was slashed across the throat so deeply that the head was nearly severed. He'd also been stabbed in the chest.

Presently, thundering from Trowbridge police station to take center stage in this terrible drama, arrived the local police in the persons of Inspector John Foley and a handful of officers. Like most provincial lawmen of the period whose encounters with crime and those who perpetrated them had been confined to robbery and burglary and the occasional rows that ended in fisticuffs at the public house, Foley was untrained in the complexities and nuances of a murder investigation. In a society that drew class distinctions, he was of common stock. He knew his place and never more so than on that warming summer day as he doffed his hat and entered the Kent mansion. With deference, he asked Kent for permission to search the house.

Within minutes two possible clues were discovered. The first was a woman's shift. Stuffed into a boiler hole, it contained bloodstains. "Put it back," Foley growled at the officer who had found the garment. Wagging an admonishing finger under the man's nose, he advised the officer that they had no cause nor right to disturb personal property. Next, Foley's attention was called to the open window in the drawing room. Clearly visible on the pane was a handprint in blood. "Good lord, man," grumbled Foley, "have you no feelings for the family? Do you want to scare them out of their wits?" Taking out his handkerchief, he wiped off the blood.

Despite the family's speculation that the youngster was the victim of resentful outsiders, Foley suspected the perpetrator was a member of the household. The thing to do, he surmised, was to search them for the murder weapon. Frisking Kent was out of the question. Searching son William, the fifteen-year-old half-brother of the dead boy, was no problem. The rest were servant women, Elizabeth Gough, Mrs. Kent, and the daughters. To handle this embarrassing task he sent to town for the wife of one of his officers. It was an exercise in futility. So much time had gone by since the murder that if the killer were in the household he or she had had ample opportunity to get rid of the weapon.

Foley's questioning of the occupants of the mansion was as inconclusive as the proceedings of a formal inquest that was convened a few days later. By then, town gossips had assembled a roster of suspects, chief of whom was Constance, largely because she'd never been very popular. A pretty girl— which was reason enough for some to suspect her—she stirred a great deal of resentment among townsfolk by spreading a story that she was a relative of the Queen, whom she resembled. In making this claim she also pointed to the family name, knowing very well that many in Road believed an old rumor that her father Samuel had been the illegitimate son of Victoria's father, the Duke of Kent. In fact, Samuel's dad was a carpet maker in London. Rumormongers also took note of the fact that a few years earlier Constance and brother William had run away, apparently out of unhappiness with their stepmother.

In that incident, they recalled, Constance had cut her hair short and dressed like a boy, believing that two wandering lads in a nation of vagabond waifs would not cause so much as one head to turn. The significance in this episode, whispered the wags of Road, was that in cutting her hair Constance had gone to the same outhouse in which Francis's throat was cut.

Adding to the speculation about Constance as the culprit was what her schoolmates said about her. From the boarding school a few miles from Road drifted unsettling tales concerning her strange attitude toward her family. "It may be nice for you to go home on holiday," she was reported to have said, "but not for me. My home is different." Asked her meaning, she answered with an enigmatic frown. In less guarded moments she had spoken critically about the favoritism shown by her father and stepmother to the progeny of the second marriage.

Unable to disregard the widespread public speculation about the girl, the magistrates at the inquest called her for questioning. With the same cool restraint she'd shown in answering the queries of Inspector Foley, she expressed amazement that anyone could harm the boy, least of all herself. "Everyone was

kind to Francis," she said. "I never heard of anyone wishing
him ill. I played with him often. I was very fond of him and
I believe he was very fond of me." Tearfully, she testified that
the first words she heard of Francis being missing came from
the nurse.

Accusations about Gough had been breezed about from the
start. Based on nothing more than public house and backyard
speculation and sheer imagination, they envisioned a sexual
relationship between Gough and Samuel Kent. After all, hadn't
he engaged in just such a liaison with Miss Pratt, the governess
he'd wasted no time in marrying after the death of his first
wife? The notion was so widely held that it reached the
ears of Charles Dickens. With scoffing tones, he wrote to
fellow novelist Wilkie Collins: "Mr. Kent intriguing with the
nursemaid, poor little child (Francis) awakes in crib and sits up
contemplating blissful proceedings. Nursemaid strangles him
then and there. Mr. Kent gashes body to mystify discoverers
and disposes of same."

The jury returned a verdict of murder by "some person or
persons unknown." But Inspector Foley believed otherwise.
In his mind, the culprit was Gough. Accordingly, although
there was not a shred of evidence against her, he arrested
the woman. It was a desperate act that could not hold up
in the face of the facts. She had an impeccable reputation
and, more important, she had no motive for killing the child.
Released from custody, she fled the area in embarrassment
and disgrace without ever being asked to explain what she'd
been thinking—or what she suspected—on the morning of the
murder when she exclaimed to Mrs. Kent, "Oh ma'am, it was
revenge."

For thrill-seeking Britons, the savage slaying of the boy was
a fresh sensation. Newspapers across the country played up the
murder as only they could. When the news spread that no one
was under arrest for the crime, public opinion was outraged. If
Inspector Foley were unable to bring the fiend to the dock, the
people cried, then the time had come for a surer hand to take
over the investigation. Clearly, this was a job for a detective
from Scotland Yard!

Tapped for the task was one of the Yard's original sleuths,
Jonathan Whicher. Brought into the incipient detective force
in 1842 along with ex-Bow Streeter Nicholas Pearce, John
Haynes, and Dick Tanner (whose great case would come four

years after the murder of Francis Kent), Whicher had proved to be a perceptive policeman with exactly the shrewd, incisive, and deductive mind required at the Kent mansion. However, his arrival on the scene on July 15, a little more than two weeks after the murder, was greeted frigidly by Inspector Foley and his men. If Whicher were expecting cooperation, he was disappointed. The locals clammed up—not a word about the bloody shift, no mention of the bloody handprint on the windowpane, no help at all. As far as Foley was concerned, the killer was Elizabeth Gough.

Whicher came to Road with no particular suspect. While there is no record of his saying so, it's reasonable to assume that he was thinking the words of latter-generation fictional detectives: "I suspect no one, I suspect everyone." Although she had been let go for want of evidence, he did not dismiss Gough from consideration. Reading in the local paper, the *Somerset and Wilts Journal*, that "a somewhat unusual number of servants" had been discharged from the Kent home, he sought them out. In interviewing them in Bristol and Frome, he listened intently to accounts of life in the Kent mansion. Particularly interesting was what they had to say about the relationship between Mr. and Mrs. Kent and Constance. Their portrait was of an unhappy girl who felt unappreciated, even ignored, especially by a stepmother who showered great affection on her own children, most especially little Francis.

Conversations with the villagers of Road sounded a like note. Again and again Whicher heard disturbing adjectives applied to Constance: resentful of her stepmother, cold, bitter, moody, troubled. They informed him that in the waning years of her unhappy life, the first Mrs. Kent's mind had gone. Their implication was that Constance might be mentally unstable.

Visiting Constance's school, he heard the stories that her classmates had voiced about her immediately after the murder, but it was when he inspected her room that Whicher found something tangible to bolster growing suspicions regarding her. Tucked under her mattress were copies of the London *Times*. Three years old, they contained reports of a trial in Scotland in which a Glasgow woman had been acquitted of killing her lover despite the popularly held belief that she was guilty. Why had Constance kept these papers? Why should a girl who was then only thirteen be so fascinated that she not only held onto them but hid them? When asked about the newspapers, Mr. Kent remembered them. He'd put them in a bureau drawer so that his children would not be exposed to such horrors.

Of course, possession of the newspapers was not proof that Constance murdered her stepbrother. Whicher had only his sense that the crime had been committed by someone in the house and a detective's instinct that it had been Constance. Experience and common sense told him that the killer must have been drenched in blood, yet in Foley's investigation no bloody apparel had been found. Had Constance crept into Francis's room in the middle of the night to spirit him away and kill him, she would have been dressed in nightclothes. What happened to them? Did she destroy them? Hide them? Wash them?

To follow that thread, Whicher interviewed the maid who took the family's laundry to a washerwoman in town. Had the maid, he inquired, found any unusual stains among any of the family's wash after the murder? The maid was adamant. No! Were any garments missing? Not at the time, she said, but one of Constance's nightdresses hadn't come back from the washerwoman's and was considered lost. How many nightgowns did Constance have? Three. She knew this for certain,.she replied, and if Whicher happened to be thinking that Constance did this terrible thing, well, she could dispel that outrageous notion. The very day of the murder she'd handled the nightgown that Constance had worn at the time of the murder and it was spotless.

How was it, wondered Whicher, that the maid had a particular memory of the garment? The answer was quite simple. When she came to collect clothing for the wash Constance had asked her to look in the pocket of the gown—she'd been searching for her purse and thought it might be in the pocket of the gown. Was the purse in the pocket? No.

At that point the garment was taken away to the washerwoman?

Not at the exact moment, said the maid. Before taking the gown and other garments to add them to the rest of the family's wash, Constance had asked her to go to the kitchen to fetch her a glass of water.

In his years as a detective Jonathan Whicher had mastered the art of not exhibiting any sign of what he deduced from what he'd heard from a witness, but he must have been hard-pressed to keep a straight face as the maid finished this enlightening tale. What a clever girl Constance was! With all the aplomb and skill of a London street swindler she'd carried out on the unsuspecting maid a kind of shell game. In doing so she unknowingly revealed her guilt.

Having murdered her brother, Whicher reasoned, Constance returned to her bedroom, took off the blood-spattered garment, and rinsed out the stains in the washbasin. Dried and put away, it was available to be shown to anyone who might ask to see it. When Inspector Foley did so, he was presented with three apparently spotless gowns. But were they? Obviously not. Evidently, Whicher surmised, Constance had taken a second look at the potentially incriminating garment and realized that faint traces of blood remained in the fabric. Her problem then was how to get rid of it.

Her scheme was quite ingenius. When the maid collected the wash on Monday, Constance made up the story of the missing purse. Once the maid had handled the gown—not the stained one but one of the others—the maid would be able, if asked, as she was by Whicher, to correctly state that the gown contained no stains. Then came Constance's significant request that the maid fetch her a glass of water. It was a very telling act. During the maid's absence, Constance removed the gown from the pile of wash and returned it to her bureau drawer. The gown with the bloodstains was then destroyed, leaving her with two gowns and the easy explanation that the missing one must have been lost by the washerwoman.

It was a thin reed to rest a case on, but Whicher was sure he was right. Convinced that Constance was the killer, he arrested her in the hope that in being charged the girl would be so shaken she would confess.

For the first time in his career as a detective Whicher misjudged character. Constance did not confess to him. Nor did she waver under his questioning at the hearing on the murder charge, held July 27 at the local magistrates' court. Calm and confident, she stuck to the story she'd told from the beginning. She'd been asleep in her room at the time of the murder and knew nothing of it until Elizabeth Gough told her about it in the morning.

Viewing her with an overwhelming sympathy that they'd never shown to her before, townspeople in the crowded court-room greeted Whicher's allegations with hoots of derision and shouts of utter contempt. They applauded when Constance's lawyer, a Mr. Edlin, depicted the outsider from Scotland Yard as desperately grasping at straws. He was, asserted Edlin, "a man eager in pursuit of the murderer, and anxious for the reward" of one hundred pounds that had been offered by the magistrates. With exquisite timing, Constance punctuated the allegation by crying, "I am innocent! I am innocent!"

Released by the court for lack of evidence, she walked out with a sweet smile.

Whicher departed to catcalls and jeers. These, however, were mild in comparison to the abuse heaped upon him in the nation's press. Depressed by all this, he cited "poor health" and resigned from Scotland Yard.

Presently, the unfortunate Elizabeth Gough was tried for the murder but, to the dismay of a public that was convinced of her guilt, was acquitted. Dispirited and feeling that she was doomed to be forever branded a murderess, she did her best to pick up the pieces of her life in another town, working as a seamstress.

Samuel Kent moved his tragic family to Wales, except for Constance, who left Road in 1863 to take up residence as a paying guest at St. Mary's Home in Brighton, a seaside religious retreat run by the Reverend A. D. Wagner.

With the murder of Francis Savile Kent apparently never to be solved, sensation-hungry Victorians put it out of their minds and looked for new horrors, but it was not the end of the affair. It burst into headlines again with the astonishing revelation that on April 25, 1864, in the company of Rev. Wagner, a deeply repentant Constance stood before Chief Magistrate Sir Thomas Henry and confessed that she had, indeed, with cold-hearted premeditation, killed Francis.

A few days before the deed, she said, she took a razor from her father's room and hid it in her own. On the fateful night she waited until she was certain everyone in the house was asleep. After midnight, she crept downstairs to the drawing room and opened a window, then went to the boy's room and took him, still sleeping, to a downstairs closet and slit his throat. In a letter to the *Times* two days after the confession, Doctor John Charles Bucknill, who examined Constance as to her mental condition, wrote: "She says that she thought the blood would never come, and that the child was not killed, so she thrust the razor into its left side, and put the body, with the blanket around it, into the vault" of the outhouse. She returned to the house by way of the opened window in the expectation that it would be seen as proof that an intruder had committed the crime.

Now came vindicating details that Whicher must have read with ironic satisfaction. "She went back to her bedroom, examined her dress, and found only two spots of blood on it," said the doctor. "These she washed out in the basin, and threw the water, which was but little discoloured, into the footpan in which she had washed her feet overnight. She took another of her nightdresses and got into bed. In the morning, her nightdress had become dry where it had been washed. She folded it up and put it into the drawer."

During his investigation of the murder, Inspector Foley had examined the nightdresses but found nothing. Constance, however, did a better job of it. Taking a closer look at the garment by holding it up to the light, she discovered that she could see faint traces of the blood she'd believed she'd thoroughly washed out. "She secreted the dress," continued the letter in the *Times*, "moving it from place to place, and she eventually burnt it in her own bedroom, and put the ashes into the kitchen grate."

It was while she was moving the nightdress from one hiding place to another that she'd carried out the shell game with the maid. Not until seven or eight days after the murder did she burn the stained one. In the meantime she had returned the cleansed razor to her father's room.

Why did she kill Francis? "As regards to the motive of her crime," wrote Dr, Bucknill, "it seems that, although she entertained at one time a great regard for the current Mrs. Kent, if any remark was at any time made which in her opinion was disparaging to any member of the first family, she treasured it up, and determined to revenge it."

So the perceptive but, alas, reticent Elizabeth Gough had been right on the morning after the murder—it was revenge. But it wasn't for herself, Constance insisted. In a letter to her lawyer from prison before the trial that followed her startling confession, printed along with Dr. Bucknill's letter, Constance wrote, "It has been stated that my feelings of revenge were excited in consequence of cruel treatment. This is entirely false. I have received the greatest kindness from both the persons accused of subjecting me to it. I have never had any ill-will towards either of them on account of their behavior to me which has been very kind." She'd killed not for herself but because of the second Mrs. Kent's disdainful attitude toward Constance's brother and sisters—the children of Samuel Kent's first wife.

Would she have let Elizabeth Gough hang for the murder? She told Dr. Bucknill that when Gough was accused she'd made up her mind to confess "if the nursemaid had been convicted." She also said that she was determined, if she, Constance, were convicted to commit suicide.

In view of the insanity of her mother, there was reason to question Constance's mental state. However, she was deemed fit to stand trial and was convicted of murder. But because of her age at the time of the killing, the death penalty was commuted to life in prison. She did not commit suicide. After serving twenty years, she was released from Millbank Prison in 1885, to disappear into the mists of history.

What of the bloodstained garment found in the boiler hole by Foley's man? It had nothing to do with the crime. The handprint on the windowpane, however, was a different story. It had been left there by Constance. Had it been preserved, and had Jonathan Whicher been able to examine it, he surely would have seen it for what it was—a *girl's* print. With that evidence he might have stood a better chance to prove that Constance was a killer.

Following Constance's conviction, he was offered the reward of one hundred pounds but refused to accept it.

A more enduring recognition of Sergeant Whicher's prowess as a detective was offered by the author Wilkie Collins. In his 1868 novel *The Moonstone*, which was inspired by the murder in Road Hill House, a crime is investigated by a "grizzled, elderly man, so miserably lean that he looked as if he had not got an ounce of flesh on his bones in any part of him" but whose steely light gray eyes had "a very disconcerting trick, when they encountered your eyes, of looking as if they expected something more from you than you were aware of yourself."

Stepping down from a carriage, he introduced himself: "I am Sergeant Cuff."

"A less comforting officer to look at, for a family in distress," declared the narrator, "I defy you to discover, search where you may."

If Constance Kent read *The Moonstone* in prison, she would not have been wrong in recognizing that Sergeant Cuff had been drawn from real life, from her own nemesis—Sergeant Jonathan Whicher of Scotland Yard.

FIVE

Bloody Murder

ON A SATURDAY EVENING IN JULY 1864, SEVENTY-FIVE DAYS after the newspapers blared Constance Kent's confession, a pair of bank clerks on their way to their homes in Highbury opened the door of an unoccupied first-class compartment of a North London Railway suburban train whose ultimate destination was Chalk Farm. It had departed Fenchurch Street Station at 9:50, stopped at Bow at 10:01, at Hackney Wick (Victoria Park) at 10:05, and Hackney at 10:11. After a day's work, the gentlemen were looking forward to observing the Biblical admonition to honor the Sabbath and keep it holy and to their day of rest. Delighted to see that they had the compartment to themselves, they sat opposite one other, undid the buttons of their coats, and relaxed.

Suddenly, the one facing the front of the train bolted up and gazed at his hand. "What the devil is this?" he blurted. "It looks like blood."

Urgently summoned by the horrified travelers, the station guard inspected the compartment and found blood soaked into both seats and smeared on the handle of the door. He also discovered a suitcase, a black beaver hat, and a gold-tipped walking stick that also appeared to be bloodied. Removing these items, he locked the compartment and permitted the train to proceed, then, in company with the clerks, rushed to notify the police.

A few minutes later, the engineer of a train going in the other direction from Hackney toward the Bow Street Station in London saw a large object lying between the outbound and inbound tracks. Fearing that someone had been accidentally struck, he stopped the train and got out to have a look. The object was a stout, well-dressed elderly gentleman. He was unconscious and badly hurt but breathing. Carried to a nearby pub, he was examined by a doctor, who judged that the wounds had not been the result of being hit by a train but were caused by a vicious beating with a blunt instrument after which he'd been pushed onto the tracks. Without regaining consciousness, the man died shortly after midnight.

Identified from the contents of his pockets, he was Thomas Briggs, chief clerk of the Roberts and Co. Bank of Lombard Street in London, the same firm that employed the clerks who found the blood. A resident of Clapham, he'd been a frequent user of the railway, boarding at Fenchurch Street and getting off at Victoria Park.

News of the murder stunned the public. What made this a singular homicide in the plethora of crime coverage in the press was not its brutality but that it was the first murder in history to be committed on a train. Extremely proud of their magnificent system of efficient railways, Britons were outraged. The press played up the story.

To bring the murderer to justice Scotland Yard assigned one of the original plainclothesmen of 1842. A colleague of Jonathan Whicher, Dick Tanner, had risen to the rank of Inspector. Unlike Whicher in his investigation at Road Hill House, he didn't have to delve for either the murder weapon or a motive. The weapon had been Briggs's walking stick. Based on the physical evidence, he reasoned that shortly after boarding the train Briggs had dozed off and that the killer, who'd either been in the compartment or crept into it, had attempted to steal Briggs's gold watch. Briggs awoke. The thief grabbed the walking stick and beat his victim into insensibility, then pushed him from the train. There was no doubt that Briggs had been robbed. His gold-rimmed eyeglasses were missing as was a gold pocketwatch and its gold Albert chain. Also missing was the stylish high hat that Briggs favored.

The hat that was found by the station guard was a black beaver with a low crown. Inside it, Tanner had his first clue: the name of the hat maker—Mr. J. H. Walker, 49 Crawford Street in the Marylebone area of the city. Inspecting the hat, he informed Tanner that the lining of the hat was very peculiar in character and hadn't been used by him in the lining of more than two or three hats. Briggs's own hatter, Mr. Digance, was certain that the low-crowned hat which Tanner brought around to his shop could not have belonged to Briggs. Friends of the banker who'd dined with him on the night of the murder said he'd worn a high hat. From all of this it seemed reasonable to presume that the hat found on the train belonged to the murderer and, because Mr. Briggs's hat hadn't been found, the murderer had taken it.

Acutely aware that the newspapers were devoting considerable attention to the crime and the investigation, the police gave the reporters a detailed description of Briggs's pocketwatch and its chain. The information paid off. After reading about the watch and chain in a newspaper, a jeweler with the chillingly ironic name of John Death reported to the police that he'd bought what he now believed to be Briggs's watch chain on July 11, two days after the murder. The seller, Death told Tanner, was a thin, sallow-looking man who appeared to be in his thirties.

Learning this development, newspapers blared the news and, not missing any opportunity to enliven their accounts, made note of the jeweler's peculiarly appropriate name. A week later, the name rang a bell in the memory of Jonathan Matthews, a cabman who got his news not from the papers but while waiting on cab lines and gabbing with fellow drivers. A few days earlier, Matthew told his companions and then Inspector Tanner, he'd seen a cardboard box with the jeweler Death's name on it. It had been given to his daughter by a young man named Franz Müller, who'd been engaged to Matthews's sister. Because of Müller's hot temper and his violent jealousy the engagement was broken off and Müller let it be known that he was leaving England to seek his fortune in America.

Of course, the box from Death's jewelry shop could have been a coincidence, so Inspector Tanner showed Matthews the beaver hat that had been found on the train. Matthews recognized it right away. He'd bought the hat himself, he said, in a shop on Crawford Street in Marylebone owned by Mr. Walker. The hat was a gift for Müller.

Might Matthews have a photograph of Müller? asked Tanner. Yes, indeed, replied Matthews. Shown it, John Death said there was no doubt in his mind that the man in the picture was the very one who'd sold him the gold watch chain.

Having obtained Müller's address from Matthews, Tanner lost no time in reaching the lodging house of Mr. and Mrs. Blyth at 16 Park Terrace, Bow. In the investigation of murder a detective asks three fundamental questions: Did a suspect have the means, was there a motive, and did the suspect have an opportunity to commit the crime? Tanner knew the means: the walking stick. He had motive: robbery. But what about the last? Could Müller have had the opportunity? Although Tanner's quarry was not at Park Terrace, the Blyths provided the answer.

They'd liked Müller very much, began Mrs. Blyth. "He was a quiet, well-behaved, inoffensive young man of humane and affectionate disposition." Born in the Saxe-Weimer region of Germany, he'd been an apprenticed gunsmith but had come to England seeking a better life. Unable to find employment in gunsmithing, he took a job as a tailor and had been working for a Mr. Hodgkinson. To get to and from the work he took a North London Railway train out of Fenchurch Street Station, destination Bow—the same line used by Briggs.

Might the Blyths know Müller's whereabouts? asked Tanner. He told them that he'd heard that Müller had spoken eagerly of going to America. Had he said anything about that to them? Of course he informed them of his plans, answered Mrs. Blyth. What's more, the sweet young man had written to her from Worthing. She had the letter. It began: "On the sea, July 16th, in the morning." That was enough for Tanner.

A check of recent sailings from London docks left no doubt that if Müller were on his way to America he would be aboard the sailing ship *Victoria*. She'd sailed on the 15th bound for New York and was expected to arrive there in early August.

With a warrant from Chief Magistrate Henry of Bow Street Police Station and accompanied by Sergeant Clarke, the cabbie Matthews, and the jeweler Death, Tanner dashed to Euston railway station and boarded a fast train for Liverpool.

In the office of the master of the port, he demanded, "When is the next ship to New York?"

"Four days from now," the master replied. "It's the New York and Philadelphia Company's steamship *City of Manchester*."

One can only imagine a gleeful light glinting in Tanner's eyes when he heard the magic word steamship, and the shout of delight he must have let out when he learned that the speedier *City of Manchester* was scheduled to arrive in New York harbor between two and three weeks BEFORE *Victoria*.

News of Tanner's dash across the Atlantic traveled even faster. Thanks to the transatlantic cable laid down between Ireland and Newfoundland by Cyrus West Field and a company of enterprising American entrepreneurs, word of the Scotland Yard detective's pursuit of Franz Müller was as widespread in America as it was in Britain. Fortunately for Tanner, ship-to-shore communication was years away, so during the leisurely and picturesque crossing of the *Victoria*, Müller and his traveling companions were in the dark.

Arriving in New York on August 5, Tanner discovered he was a celebrity. As sensation-seeking as the British press, New York's newspapers had devoted considerable space to the story and to the dogged detective, but—as latter-day detectives were to learn—a news story, however well intended, carries with it the possibility of thwarting the successful culmination of a case. It happened to Tanner as Victoria dropped anchor in New York harbor to await the arrival of a boat carrying the pilot, who would take the ship into port. Aboard the little boat as it plied the waters was Tanner, along with Sergeant Clarke and the two witnesses who were to identify Müller.

To Tanner's astonishment a party of excursionists sped past them to draw alongside *Victoria*, where they gleefully shouted, "How are you, Müller the murderer?"

Luckily for Tanner, Müller didn't hear them.

Summoned to the captain's cabin, Müller was arrested. He denied everything. When asked about the gold watch he had in his possession, he claimed he'd owned it for two years. His high-crowned hat, he said, had been bought a year ago. Inspector Tanner knew better. That the items would be identified as the stolen property he had no doubt.

Ordered extradited back to England, Müller was delivered by Tanner to London. "As the van passed along Bow Street," wrote Percy Fitzgerald in *Chronicles of Bow Street Police-Office*, "it was guarded by constables on foot and followed by an excited mob. The moment it stopped in front of the police-station, a fearful rush was made towards it. Some minutes elapsed before a passage could be made and kept, and Müller alighted amid a storm of groans and hisses, with a light step and almost flippant air."

Presented with Tanner's overwhelming evidence, a court convicted Müller and sentenced him to death. Appeals for clemency to the Queen by the German government were unavailing. The date for the execution on the Newgate gallows was set for November 14. Given the opportunity to make a confession on the night of the 13th, Müller refused.

"All night long the streets were blocked up with people waiting to see the painful exhibition," wrote Fitzgerald, "and it was said that 12 pounds was the price paid for a 'room with a good view.' "Led to the gallows, Müller was calm. He raised his eyes with a sort of curiosity to the beam from which he was presently to be suspended," continued Fitzgerald's account. "It was impossible, however, to feel sympathy for him; one had only to recall the scene in the railway carriage when he was battering out the brains of an old man, and then flinging him out on the railway, to be cut in pieces by the next passing train."

At the first glimpse of Müller by the expectant mob, a storm of yells rose above Newgate Prison. It continued to mount as the hood was placed over his head. A German clergyman stood at his side. "Müller, in a few moments you will be before God," he said. "I ask you again, and for the last time, are you guilty or not?"

"Not guilty."

"You are not guilty?"

"God knows what I have done."

"God knows what you have done? Does He also know that you have committed the crime?"

The trap beneath Müller's feet sprang open.

Dropping through, Müller cried, "Yes, I have done it."

Some years later, H. B. Irving, an actor and author who in 1903 brought together "connoisseurs" of crime at a dinner that became institutionalized as the Crimes Club, wrote that it was difficult at a distance of time to quite appreciate the extraordinary interest that the case aroused. "There is nothing very remarkable either in the crime or in the criminal. The trial itself is interesting as showing the conclusive weight of circumstantial evidence. That it did create extraordinary interest at the time there can be no doubt. It was the first railway murder, and the circumstances of the flight and capture of the murderer were calculated to excite the public mind."

Richard B. Altick, in writing of the Müller case in *Victorian Studies in Scarlet*, found its enduring interest lying "in its rich evocation of a social locale: particularly, in this case, the tradesmen and other occupation-types whom the accident of murder brought together in the Old Bailey courtroom."

The year after Müller swung from Newgate's gibbet in payment for his crime, Matthew Arnold, the great moralist, wrote about the railway murder in the preface to his *Essays in Criticism*. He told of conversations he conducted with a man (by coincidence he was a jeweler) who shared a railway compartment with him.

"Suppose the worst should happen; suppose even yourself to be the victim," suggested Arnold. What would happen? "We should miss you for a day or two upon the Woodford Branch; but your villa would still be rolled, dividends would still be paid at the Bank, omnibuses would still run, there would be the old crush at the corner of Fenchurch Street."

Then why had Britons become so outraged over the Müller case? He offered this answer: "Nothing could moderate, in the bosom of the great English middle class, their passionate, absorbing, almost bloodthirsty clinging to [the value of] life."

To protect the people of London against those who would snuff out life for as little gain as a man's pocketwatch there was at the time of Müller's murder of Briggs in 1864 a force of 7,113 men wearing the Metropolitan Police uniform. But they had a new look. Gone were their old-fashioned swallowtail coats and stovepipe hats, replaced by dark blue tunics and beehive hats that were to become an indelible symbol of British law and order.

But others—a handful of men like Dick Tanner—went on about their duties as before, in the plain clothes of the detective.

SIX

Detective Force

ALTHOUGH ADOPTION OF A NEW STYLE OF UNIFORM PUT THE police in step sartorially with the rest of the law-abiding population, they found themselves at a distinct disadvantage in dealing with modern criminals. Since formation of the New Police in 1829, constables had not been permitted to carry firearms. Even in face of an alarming movement toward anarchy and mobs in the streets, the English resistance to arming the police force persisted. Accordingly, the only weapons of the policeman were his wits, his truncheon, and his fists. Of course, the criminals were under no such restraints.

So it was on the night of August 1, 1876, at Whalley Range near the city of Manchester. Making rounds with another officer was Nicholas Cock. Noticing a shadowy figure lurking at the gate of a house, Cock and his partner suspected the man was up to no good. They separated to investigate. Cock followed the man onto the grounds of the house, and suddenly found himself face-to-face with his quarry and staring down the barrel of a pistol. Two shots rang out. Cock dropped to the ground. Mortally wounded, he lingered for half an hour. Asked who'd shot him, he answered that he didn't know.

Despite the dying constable's reply, the police arrested two Irish laborers, eighteen-year-old John and twenty-three-year-old William Habron. The basis for the charge was that recently Cock had given them summonses for being drunk and disorderly, and that the brothers voiced threats concerning revenge against Cock. The evidence against them was never more than circumstantial, and skimpy at that. At the trial, John was exonerated. William was convicted. But because of his age, the jury recommended mercy. The judge decided otherwise and sentenced him to death, however. After a public outcry about the flimsy evidence against Habron, the Home Secretary reviewed the case and commuted the sentence to life in prison.

Spectators had flocked to see the unfolding of the trial and it got the usual sensationalized coverage by the press. Nor did the procedings go unnoticed at Scotland Yard. Every policeman who set out to discharge his duty, whether in the new uniform or in plain clothes, was acutely aware that what had happened to Cock up in Manchester could easily happen to him in far more dangerous London. As the city exploded in population and geography during the thirty years of the old uniform, so had the criminal element. Hadn't the highly mobile James Greenacre demonstrated that the modern malefactor was fully capable of taking advantage of the opportunities provided by the rapidly evolving and increasingly complex society? If the police were to keep up with the lawless, their organization had to adapt. That required leadership.

Since 1855, Richard Mayne had been commissioner, but as David Ascoli noted in *The Queen's Peace*, he was "a strong, some say headstrong, character and an able lawyer and administrator, but he was not a policeman." Without his former co-Commissioner Rowan's special knowledge of man management, wrote Ascoli, "he was unable to establish that 'kind and conciliating' relationship with his men which had sustained the New Police through its early tribulations. Nor, despite the presence of two assistant commissioners, was he prepared to delegate his authority." Public opinion regarding the police was low. The men in their new outfits were regarded by the majority of the people as servants of the privileged classes. The press was increasingly critical, led by the barbs of *Punch*, which noted that a Bobby was "always ready to hold a gentleman's horse." Morale at Scotland Yard plummeted.

All of this couldn't have occurred at a worse time. Across the land, especially in turbulent London, there was a new wave of agitation for social change. The vanguard was the Reform League. In June of 1866 its leaders called for a demonstration to be held at Hyde Park. As soon as their intention was revealed, Home Secretary Spencer Walpole banned the meeting. To enforce the prohibition, he ordered Commissioner Mayne to deploy the police. Accordingly, Mayne assembled

3,200 men and took personal command. Thwarted at Hyde Park, the crowd headed defiantly and noisily for Trafalgar Square, itching for a fight. Their target was the police. In the brawl that broke out, twenty-eight officers were so badly injured that they were permanently disabled. Also wounded, Mayne looked upon the battle from horseback. Judging that his men alone couldn't restore order, he called for help from the army—the first time in the history of the Metropolitan Police on their own ground.

In the aftermath of the humiliation of him and his police Mayne tendered his resignation. Although Home Secretary Walpole refused to accept it, he added to Mayne's embarrassment by meeting with leaders of the Reform League to express his regrets for what everyone was now calling "Bloody Sunday."

The debacle reinforced public opinion that the Metropolitan Police as an institution had no interest in the working class and its problems. Into a situation ripe for exploitation marched a group seeking to bring an end to British rule of Ireland that had been imposed by 1801's Act of Union. Calling themselves Fenians, they took their name from third-century followers of rebellious Finn MacCool, whose motto was "Strength in our hands, truth on our lips, and cleanness in our hearts." Enthusiastic support for the Fenians came from expatriate Irishmen who'd been driven out of their homeland to the United States during the famine years of the 1840s. Forerunners of the twentieth-century's NORAID (Northern Irish Aid Committee, based in New York, which bankrolls and smuggles arms to the Irish Republican Army in its efforts to drive the English out of Ulster beginning in the 1960s), the 1867 Fenians planned an action for London in December. Unfortunately for the conspirators, two of the plotters, Burke and Casey, were arrested by Inspector Thompson of Scotland Yard and clapped into prison in the North London area of Clerkenwell. Hardly had the cell doors slammed behind them when compatriots began planning to spring them by blasting down the prison walls. A date was set: December 12.

The conspiracy leaked. An anonymous letter tipped off the commissioner. Bits and pieces of what was afoot also came to Mayne at Scotland Yard from other sources. The governor of the prison was notified. Regular police patrols around the area were increased—but only slightly.

As forecast, the plot unfolded. Two men rolled a barrel of gunpowder up to a wall, lit a fuse, and ran. Nothing happened. Mystified, the bombers scooped up the dud and fled—all of this before the eyes of a constable who *didn't bother to report it*.

The next afternoon, the bombers returned. This time, the powder ignited. Four people were killed and forty injured. Great damage was done to the surrounding buildings and the prison wall was breached. But, thanks to the prison governor, Burke and Casey had been moved to another part of the lockup where they remained in custody as four of the bombers were rounded up to join them in prison, for trials, convictions, and death by hanging—the last public executions in Britain.

Although Londoners were used to mobs, the "Irish problem" introduced them to a new dimension of violence—urban terrorism. In one form or another it would plague governments of Britain and the Metropolitan Police force for the rest of that century and periodically throughout the next. Immediate reaction to the bombing at Clerkenwell was public outrage directed toward the police. Again, as he'd done after the Bloody Sunday riot, Mayne tendered his resignation. Again, it was refused. "We told Mayne that he had made a damned fool of himself," said Under Secretary Liddell of the Home Office, "but that we weren't going to throw him over after his long public service."

What the government would not do, declining health accomplished the next year. Death removed Mayne on Boxing Day, 1868. Thirty-seven years had passed since Robert Peel enlisted him in the cause of the New Police. In that time the Metropolitan Police grew from a handful of men to a force of 8,963. No commissioner would come anywhere near to matching Mayne's record of service nor his achievements.

Taking command at Scotland Yard on February 2, 1869, was a regular officer of the Royal Engineers, Colonel Edmund Henderson. Succeeding a founding father and builder of the police force, he saw his task as solidifying what had been done and keeping in tune with the times. In the first of what would become seventeen years as commissioner, he took steps to expand the size of the force, improve the pay of officers and constables, and recognize their needs (he authorized the wearing of mustaches and beards and let off-duty officers wear civilian clothes). To modernize methods, he looked to new technologies, starting with telegraph communication between the Yard and police stations. To assist in the fight against crime he succeeded in achieving the compilation of a Register of Habitual Criminals.

High on the agenda of the new commissioner was the revamping of a struggling detective force. Mindful of historical English wariness of what the public regarded as snooping intruders into their freedom, Henderson noted, "there are many and great difficulties in the way of a Detective system; it is one viewed with the greatest suspicion and jealousy by the majority of Englishmen." Indeed, *Punch* habitually referred to it as the "Defective Force." His caveat concerning the difficulties notwithstanding, Henderson pledged that development of the detective system "will be an interesting and important duty." True to his promise, within four months of taking office he increased the number of plainclothesmen at the Yard to twenty-seven, including a chief superintendent (Frank Williamson), three chief inspectors, three first-class and seventeen second-class inspectors. In divisions around the city were 15 inspectors, 159 sergeants, 60 divisional patrols, and 20 special patrols.

Building the detective system wasn't without setbacks. Its future was jeopardized during the 1870s by a corruption scandal in which several detectives were put on trial for taking bribes. In response, the Home Secretary convened a commission to examine "the state, discipline and organization of the Detective Force of the Metropolitan Police." Its chief recommendation was establishment of a Criminal Investigation Department to be under command of an assistant commissioner to be called Director of Criminal Investigation, who would have freedom of action in his department and unimpeded access to the Home Secretary—a division of power at Scotland Yard that was destined to be a troublesome chicken coming home to roost.

To formalize this arrangement police orders were issued on April 6, 1877, creating a Criminal Investigation Department (CID). Its director was Howard Vincent. An enterprising and ambitious young lawyer, Vincent had made a study of the detective system in Paris as part of the review of Scotland Yard's embattled detectives, then applied for the top job. Under his command were 250 men. Within six years there were 800.

In very short order the new sleuths were put to the test by one of the most popular and romantic outlaws of the day. His name was Charles Peace. Born in Sheffield in 1832, Charley spent his boyhood in the show business atmosphere of Wombwell's Menagerie, where his father was a wild-animal trainer. Unfortunately, the elder Peace had less success taming his unruly son. If earning a living honestly had ever been his intention, Charley gave it up following an accident in a mill that crippled his left hand and a leg. The resulting limp combined with his short stature (five feet, four inches) and a face that he was able to contort into grotesque shapes to give him an apelike appearance that he made even more intimidating by extending his maimed arm with a false one that ended in an iron hook.

Despite a visage that demanded attention, Charley began his criminal career as a pickpocket at fairs. If harvests were slim, he billed himself as "the modern Paganini," adding to his income by entertaining in pubs with jaunty tunes on a homemade single-stringed fiddle. A naturally dark complexion was enhanced occasionally with makeup that allowed him to advertise himself as the "Great Ethiopian Musician." But musicianship was to be never more than a sideline. His real talent lay in creeping into someone else's home and taking what didn't belong to him.

Victorians called such people "portico thieves." While he was one of the first of the breed, he was not the best. Between 1854 and 1872 he was in prison more than he was out— and when he wasn't in, he was the subject of Scotland Yard "Wanted" posters.

In 1876, one of the posters attributed a new crime to him: the murder of Arthur Dyson. Charley had lived next door to Dyson and his wife in Sheffield, but the couple found him so bothersome that they went to court to seek an order against his unwanted visits. In the face of frightening threats they moved away, only to find that Charley had traced them. As soon as he laid eyes on Dyson, he carried out the threats by shooting him to death.

Although eyewitnesses provided the police with descriptions and Mrs. Dyson identified him by name, Charley appeared to have vanished from the face of the earth. Actually, he was all over the place. In Hull he burglarized a gentleman's home of silver and jewelry. In Nottingham he emptied a warehouse of silk. In London's Lambeth he was so busy that Scotland Yard attributed his burglaries to a gang. When a rash of Charley Peace thefts broke out downstream in Greenwich, another "gang" was suspected.

From Greenwich Charley moved to Peckham, got himself a grand house that he furnished with only the best purloined items, and assumed the name of Thompson. Perceived as a fine gentleman by neighbors, he shared the house with his "wife," a housemaid named Mrs. Ward, and her son. In reality, Mrs. Ward was Peace's wife, her son was Peace's stepson, and the "wife" was Peace's girlfriend. Unknowing neighbors doted on them and found great delight in being invited for musical evenings. At these cultural gatherings the highlight was performances by their host on the violin.

Presently, residents of Peckham began reporting burglaries, many of which had one thing in common: if a violin were in the house, it was stolen. Coincidentally, Thompson's collection of violins was growing. Eventually, he acquired so many superb new instruments that he asked a neighbor to allow him to store some of the overflow in her home. She did so not with suspicion but pleasure, and looked forward to being invited to Thompson's next musicale.

The invitation was for Wednesday, October 9, 1878. Thompson played, accompanied by his "wife's" singing and Mrs. Ward at the piano. A marvelous time was had by all. As usual, Mr. Thompson bade his guests a pleasant good night. For him, however, the night was just beginning. He had plans for burglarizing homes around St. James's Park in Blackheath. The venture did not go well.

Attracted by a light in a window, a pair of constables on routine patrol suspected a crime was afoot. Taking cover in the bushes, they waited for the arrival of a sergeant and then waited a while longer. Patience paid off around two in the morning. "Just a moment," shouted Constable Robinson at a hastily retreating man in the garden.

Charley Peace's answer was two shots from a pistol. "Keep back or I'll shoot you," he yelled, running as fast as his gimpy leg permitted.

As Robinson gave chase, three more shots rang out. Despite bullets nicking his head and arm, the policeman closed on the fleeing figure and wrestled him to the ground. Searching the man, who said his name was Mr. Ward, the arresting officers found the gun, a set of housebreaking tools, and a pocketknife. In the days following they also discovered Ward's true identity. With that known, Charley was charged, tried, and convicted of the two-year-old Dyson murder.

Then came a real shock. Awaiting his date with the hangman's noose, Charley astounded the police by confessing that he was the murderer of Constable Cock in Manchester. "Sometime later I saw in the papers that certain men had been taken into custody for the murder of this policeman," he said. "That interested me. I thought I should like to attend the trial."

With an impunity that enhanced his image as a daredevil, he'd done just that, sitting in the courtroom as an innocent man was convicted.

"But what man would have done otherwise in my position?" he asked. "Could I have done otherwise, knowing, as I did, that I should certainly hang for the crime?" The unfortunate William Habron was promptly set free and given 800 pounds, with apologies from the Crown.

But that wasn't Charley's only amazing revelation. To the embarrassment of the Metropolitan Police he bragged that he had visited Scotland Yard on several occasions to examine the "Wanted" posters bearing detailed descriptions of his unique physiognomy, his presence going unnoticed by the surrounding officers.

Charley stood in the prisoner's dock for the last time, his entire adult life having been spent in crime. Sentenced to hang, he sent his wife a funeral card:

In
Memory
of
CHARLES PEACE
who was executed in
Armley Prison,
Tuesday, February 25th,
1879. Aged 47.
For that I don but never intended.

"Alone among the celebrated malefactors of the Victorian era, [Peace] inspired the half-affectionate epithet of rogue," said Richard Altick in *Victorian Studies in Scarlet*. "He captured the imagination of millions . . . for he was the material of which old-fashioned ballads were made."

While Charles Peace's name and exploits have faded in the official record books of crime, they are indelible in crime fiction. "A complex mind—all great criminals have that," says Sherlock Holmes to Dr. Watson in *The Illustrious Client*. "My old friend Charlie [sic] Peace was a violin virtuoso."

The creator of Holmes must have read with some amusement of Charley's boasting of walking boldly into Scotland Yard to have a look at his "Wanted" poster. Like everyone in London, Arthur Conan Doyle read the newspapers and noted their derisive accounts of the shortcomings of the Yard's detective department. Sherlockian barbs were aimed often at the detective branch. In *A Study in Scarlet*, he referred to "some bungling villainy even a Scotland Yard official can see through." In "The Adventure of the Three Garridebs" he sees a "want of imagination" at the Yard, and in "The Adventure of the Blue Carbuncle," he thunders at Watson, "I am not retained by the police to supply their deficiencies."

Readers of Holmes stories published in *The Strand* magazine were dazzled by the fictional detective's powers of "deductive reasoning" and wondered why the detectives of Scotland Yard were lacking those skills. Punch delighted in printing lists of unsolved crimes. All of this was an unfair indictment of the police. They were having an effect on crime. In 1879 there'd been 13,128 arrests by detectives. In 1884 there were 18,343.

To assist his men in carrying out their jobs, Director Howard Vincent issued a *Police Code*. Produced in 1881, it was 454 pages of summaries of criminal statutes and preferred police procedures. Ranging from "Abandoned Children" to "Wrecking," its contents came down to two words: catch criminals. But three years after distribution of the code the capabilities of Vincent's detectives were put under the magnifying glass of public opinion in a category in which the Metropolitan Police's record of achievement was demonstrably deficient: terrorism.

The "Irish problem" was driven home again for the police at nine o'clock on the night of March 15, 1883, by the explosion of a Fenian bomb outside a government office across King Street from the A Division police headquarters in Westminster.

This audacious calling card was followed by twenty-three bombings or attempted bombings of public structures, from the Tower of London to the Houses of Parliament. Nor was Scotland Yard spared. It was rocked by an explosive device on May 30, although more damage was inflicted on the nearby Rising Sun pub than on police headquarters. By autumn of that year, the threat of further Fenian bombings forced Metropolitan Police Commissioner Henderson to station a thousand constables to guard against dynamiters all over the city.

For the head of the Criminal Investigation Department, the mere guarding of buildings did not seem to be an effective means of dealing with terrorists. In Fenian outrages Howard Vincent saw a challenge for his detectives. What was needed, he believed, was an effective intelligence-gathering system. The Clerkenwell bomb fiasco had shown that it was possible to obtain information on Fenian plottings and that, if properly followed up, to prevent them from succeeding. If the terrorists were to be defeated, he reasoned, good detective work would lead the way. Selecting his best men, he created the Special Irish Branch. Although its modern-day descendant still wrestles with the "Irish problem" in the form of the terrorist Irish Republican Army, the "Irish" was dropped from the name of the squad after it rounded up the 1883 dynamiters and put an end to IRA acts of terror, at least for a while.

The decision to continue the Special Branch was made by Vincent's successor at the top of the CID. A former inspector general of police in Bengal, India, the new chief was James Monro. Born in 1838 in Scotland, he was educated at Edinburgh High School and Edinburgh and Berlin universities. During his Bengal service, begun in 1857, he'd been a magistrate and a judge before heading the police.

On Monday, February 8, 1886, Police Commissioner Henderson's uniformed force again faced trouble in the streets. The test came on painfully familiar ground: Trafalgar Square. This time it was not Chartists protesting social conditions but the London United Workmen's Committee and the rival Social Democratic Federation. While a clash between the labor groups appeared more than likely, the response from the commissioner was unfortunately tepid. Only a small force was deployed openly with some 536 others held in nearby reserve. The immediate commander was a fifty-year veteran of the police, Robert Walker. At the age of seventy-four, he was incapable of handling the explosion that took place. Goaded by fiery orators, a mob rampaged from Trafalgar Square and swept through the streets to Pall Mall, onward to Hyde Park, and finally into Oxford Street before Inspector Cuthbert, one sergeant, and fifteen constables of the Marylebone police station charged into the mob with swinging batons and sent them scattering. In the inevitable investigation, Commissioner Henderson was held accountable for the failure of the police. Rather than suffer the ignominy of dismissal, he resigned.

Home Office watchers in the government, the press, and at Scotland Yard buzzed with the expectation that Henderson's successor would be Monro. They were wrong. Instead of the veteran policeman from Bengal, the Home Office appointed another strictly military man, General Sir Charles Warren, an engineer and administrator fresh from colonial service in Africa, where the Queen's Peace had been enforced by the army. Abrasive, opinionated, arrogant, and insistent that he get his own way, he was scornful of the civil servants of Whitehall, including Monro and his detectives. For a general of the army, the keeping of public order was, plain and simple, a matter of military force—the threat of it and, if needs be, the use of it.

Within a year of Warren's appointment, the cauldron that was London again was simmering with unrest. Social agitators of every stripe were in full bloom. Day in and day out they preached to the poor of the East End and to the hopeless and homeless who'd made a place for themselves in Trafalgar Square. In conditions similar to those of the homeless of London, New York, and other cities one hundred years later, they became squatters in the heart of the city. Around the tall pillar topped by the statue of Lord Nelson, soup kitchens flourished. Charitable groups sent in bread vans. Beggars were everywhere—interfering with passersby, smelling bad, and looking tattered and dirty. As in the case of the homeless of the 1990s, pressure mounted on the government to "do something."

It was an especially significant year. The Golden Jubilee of Her Majesty the Queen. Celebrations were being planned to mark the fifty years of Victoria's reign, yet the very heart of London had turned into what one observer called a "gypsy encampment." Another saw the square honoring the nation's greatest naval hero as a "foul camp of vagrants." The miffed merchants of the West End took the matter into their own hands by hiring armed gangs to disperse the flotsam of society.

When questions about this unseemly presence, and the possibility that the squatters might be incited to riot, were raised in Parliament, Warren announced that public meetings in the square were banned. He was answered with a call for a mass meeting for Sunday, November 13, 1887. Thus, the scene was set for another Bloody Sunday.

Warren did not disappoint. Surrounding the square with 2,000 men and a like number in reserve, and with contingents of Horse and Life Guards standing by, he had the Riot Act read, but rather than disperse, 100,000 unemployed and truly desperate people, egged on by radical oratory, descended upon the cordons of police. The fight was on. It lasted until nightfall. Warren's force prevailed.

In his annual report for 1887, Warren dealt with the event in one sentence: "During the Autumn attempts were made by unruly mobs to riot in the streets and Trafalgar Square, which proceedings were successfully coped with by the Police."

While London's second Bloody Sunday had ended in victory for Warren, it was not forgotten by the abject citizens of London nor those who saw in their plight an opportunity for fomenting their revolution. Less than a year after the melee in Trafalgar Square, they did not hesitate to whip up new frenzies as the outcasts of the city were introduced to a new terror.

SEVEN

Saucy Jack

"SORRY, POLLY," SAID THE LANDLORD OF THE LODGING HOUSE at 18 Thrawl Street, "but you know the score. If you ain't got the doss money, you don't get no bed."

She'd been sleeping there for weeks at a time—"dossing" was the word for it—but in the past few days she'd wound up spending her doss money on gin, mostly at the Frying Pan public house in Brick Lane. "I'll soon get it," answered Polly, lurching away from the door. An explanation wasn't needed. The landlord knew exactly what Polly Nichols meant. She'd raise the doss money by plying an age-old trade. Touching her new black straw hat with its black velvet trim, she gave the landlord a wink. "See?" she said. "See what a jolly bonnet I've got now."

On that Friday morning, August 31, 1888, Mary Ann "Polly" Nichols was forty-two years old and five feet, two inches in height. Her brown hair was streaked with gray. Five front teeth were missing. Her dress was threadbare and her shoes were cut-down old boots with steel-tipped toes. Her breath reeked of all the gins she'd downed all day long and through the night, paid for with more than enough doss money shoved into her hand by the men she'd sold herself to that day. Confident that she'd find a patron, she began walking.

Shortly before four o'clock on a street called Buck's Row, George Cross, a market porter on his way to work, pushed open a stable gate and found her body. He first thought that she'd been raped and was unconscious, but on closer examination he saw that she'd been slashed twice in the throat. The murder had to have taken place quite recently, Cross figured,

68

because her legs were still warm. In fact, she'd been killed within the past half-hour. This was proved by Police Constable John Neil. Buck's Row was on his beat and he'd passed by that very spot barely thirty minutes before Cross discovered her.

In all likelihood, speculated residents of the Whitechapel section of the East End, she'd been the victim of a gang that had been robbing prostitutes, two of whom had been murdered not far from the place where Polly met her death. But what really puzzled everyone in the close confines of Buck's Row was that no one had heard her scream nor any sound that might have been her killer fleeing.

The investigation was begun by Detective Inspector Frederick Abberline. A soft-spoken, portly man nearing fifty years of age, he'd joined the Metropolitan Police in 1863 and was appointed one of the first divisional inspectors of the CID in 1878.

His responsibility had been the Whitechapel and Bethnal Green area of the East End, exactly where Polly Nichols plied her trade and ran into a killer. Although he'd been transferred to headquarters at Scotland Yard in 1887, he was sent back to the old stomping grounds of Whitechapel because of his familiarity with the area.

First, he had to identify the victim. Examination of Polly's clothing turned up the mark of Lambeth Workhouse. Inquiries there produced positive identification and an account of her activities that night. "About 1:40 A.M. that morning," Abberline reported, "she was seen in the kitchen at 18 Thrawl Street when she informed the deputy of the lodging house that she had no money to pay her lodgings. She requested that her bed might be kept for her and left stating that she would soon get the money. At this time she was drunk. She was next seen at 2:30 A.M. at the corner of Osborn Street and Whitechapel Road by Ellen Holland, a lodger of the same house, who seeing she was very drunk requested her to return with her to the lodging house. She refused, remarking that she would soon be back and walked away down the Whitechapel Road in the direction of the place where the body was found." There was no doubt with regard to the hour, noted Abberline, because the Whitechapel church clock chimed at 2:30 and Holland called Polly's attention to the time. "We have been unable to find any person," said Abberline, "who saw her alive after Holland left her."

Eight days later, behind a lodging house at 29 Hanbury Street, less than half a mile from Buck's Row, short, stout, big-nosed, gap-toothed, brown-haired, blue-eyed, forty-five-year-old Annie Chapman was also prepared to engage in the "world's oldest profession" as she went down three stones steps into a backyard. Her companion, seen by a park keeper's wife on her way to early morning market, was a man around forty, dark, genteel-looking, and wearing a brown deerstalker hat. Possibly, the witness said, the man was a foreigner. She'd heard him and Annie speaking to one another. "Will you?" he asked. "Yes," Annie replied. The time was 5:30. Annie's body was found at six.

"The wretch must have then seized the deceased," reported a coroner, "perhaps with Judas-like approaches. He seized her by the chin. He pressed her throat, and while thus preventing the slightest cry, he at the same time produced insensibility and suffocation. There was no evidence of any struggle." With the woman unconscious, he lowered her onto the ground and with her lying on her back cut her throat in two places. When found, she was face up with the left arm resting on the left breast, legs drawn up, and abdomen sliced open with the small intestines and a flap of abdomen lying on the right side above the right shoulder attached by a cord with the rest of the intestines inside the body. Two pieces of skin from the lower part of the abdomen lay in a large pool of blood above the left shoulder. The cuts in her throat ran deeply in a jagged manner all the way around, left to right.

Abberline had never seen anything like it in all his years with the police. Summoned to the scene by telegraph by Inspector Joseph Chandler of the Commercial Street police station, he also found a carnivallike mood at the place where Annie had met so vicious a death. People leaned from windows of the surrounding houses to see what they could. Hanbury Street was mobbed by the curious, eager to observe. What they saw was police painstakingly combing the muddy yard for clues. One thing stood out. The killer had arranged some of the victim's possessions in what appeared to be a ritualistic display. Two rings, some pennies, and two new farthings lay neatly at her feet. A piece of muslin, a comb, and a paper case were aligned near the body, as were an envelope dated in London on August 28 and a piece of paper containing two pills. They also found a leather apron lying near a water pump.

Of the type worn by boot makers the apron drew the suspicions of East End residents and the police to a John Pizer, who was known in the area as "Leather Apron." Because a bloodthirsty public believed he was the killer, he had gone into hiding but was tracked down by detectives and arrested. Being jailed probably saved his life. Presently, he proved he had an alibi and was cleared.

Hundreds of others were questioned: butchers, doctors and surgeons, medical students, artists, pimps, sailors, merchant seamen, and the usual suspects whom police rounded up in almost any investigation. Assisting in this manhunt were detectives from H Division, including George Godley, P. S. McCarthy, Detective Sergeant Pearce, and Inspectors Reid, Moore, and Nairn, as well as Sergeant Thicke, known as Johnny Upright because of his stiff posture. Joining the detectives were scores of constables in uniform.

One was Walter Dew. On patrol around Hanbury Street, he spotted a familiar local villain named Squibby who was wanted for an assault. Squibby also spotted Dew. A footrace began. But as Dew pursued his quarry, a bystander shouted, "Jack the Ripper." Now it wasn't only Dew chasing Squibby. It was a mob shouting "Lynch him! Lynch him!" Weighing his alternatives, Squibby gave up to Dew. Barricaded together in a house, they waited for help to arrive. "All because some fool had shouted 'Jack the Ripper,' " recalled Dew in the book of memoirs which he wrote many years later after a distinguished career as a detective that included, as you will read later, a dramatic, history-making transatlantic pursuit of one of the most notorious murderers in the annals of Scotland Yard.

Observing the lack of success by the police in bringing the killer to justice, the public that could be turned into a savage mob on the basis of a shout of "Jack the Ripper" was more than willing to listen to those with political agendas who saw in the murders of common East End prostitutes an opportunity to stir up the people against the moneyed, the privileged, and the powerful who lived in the West End. If the women who were murdered had been "ladies" rather than ladies of the evening, they shouted, the police would have caught the killer.

Adding to the woes of Abberline and his associates was a series of taunting letters to him and the newspapers, whose author began with "Dear Boss" and signed himself "Jack the Ripper" and "Saucy Jack" and then provided information that appeared to prove that the writer who was "down on whores" was, indeed, the killer. Letters also poured into Abberline's office with advice on how to catch the Ripper.

On September 30 he struck again—twice. In a narrow court off Berner Street he slashed the throat of Elizabeth "Long Liz" Stride. Apparently in fear of being caught in the act, he fled without butchering her. Fifteen minutes later in Mitre Square, he encountered Catherine Eddowes and cut her to pieces. A letter to Abberline boasted of the "double event."

Terrified East Enders directed their mounting frustration and fury at Commissioner Warren, demanding his resignation. It was, said the *Star*, "War on Warren." But dismay over Warren's conduct was not limited to the public and the press. It was shared by Abberline and others within the police who felt that the police commissioner was as much a hindrance as a help, citing his interference with the investigation of the Eddowes murder when he'd ordered the obliteration of a clue. Chalked onto a wall nearby was:

> The Juwes are not
> the men that will be blamed
> for nothing.

Convinced that it was a message from the killer, the police pleaded with Warren that it be preserved until first light of day so that it could be photographed. Concerned that passersby might interpret the message as an accusation against Jews, and fearing a mob action against Jews, Warren had the words erased.

In the midst of the drumbeat for his scalp, Warren defended himself and the police, and in an article for *Murray's Magazine* criticized the organization of the Metropolitan Police in which the head of the Criminal Investigation Department was not subject to his control as commissioner. This division of authority, he argued, made efficient police work impossible. Infuriated by the article, Home Secretary Sir Charles Matthews called Warren in for a tongue-lashing. Warren offered to resign. Matthews accepted.

The next morning, they and the rest of London reeled with disgust at the discovery of the Ripper's newest victim. Her name was Mary Kelly. Another prostitute, she was spied through the window of her room by the landlord, come to collect rent. What he saw sickened him and sent him hurrying to find the police. Her death differed from the others in that she was slaughtered inside a dwelling, very near the previous killings, all of which had been committed outdoors with the possibility of the killer being seen and caught. But behind the locked door of 26 Dorset Street of Miller's Court, unworried and unhurried, Jack the Ripper labored for at least two hours in systematic destruction of Mary Kelly's body—cutting, slicing, hacking, arranging, displaying.

Although Abberline and the others could not know it at the time, it was Jack's last horror: November 17, 1888. He'd held London in terror for seventy-nine days. In that period many men were suspected of being the Ripper, among them the American actor Richard Mansfield, whose performance in a dramatization of *Dr. Jekyll and Mr. Hyde* was closed because authorities feared it might incite Saucy Jack to new horrible crimes; Robert Lees, a clairvoyant and psychic medium to Queen Victoria; Doctor Sir William Gull, the Queen's physician, and his son-in-law, also a surgeon; Dr. Montague John Druitt; Michael Ostrong, a Russian doctor and a convict; a carriage driver named John Netley; Aaron Kosminski, a Polish Jew who lived a misfit, lone-wolf, and violent existence in Whitechapel and hated women; and none other than Her Majesty's grandson and heir-presumptive to the throne, His Royal Highness the Prince Albert Victor Christian Edward, known to his friends and certain individuals in the tawdry East End as Eddy.

Suspicion turned toward the latter because of rumors he was a frequent patron of a house of prostitution in Whitechapel and because it pleased some people to bring the royal family and the monarchy into disrepute. By way of bawdy tales and whispered dark suspicions about a young man who one day might become the king of England they hoped to stoke the fires of revolution.

Had the Ripper murders continued, who can say what might have happened? The throne might have been in jeopardy. But they did stop. There was no popular uprising. Queen Victoria was not deposed. Life went on. And so did murder. Since 1888 many killers have murdered many more people than did Jack the Ripper. He had five victims. Modern serial killers number their prey in dozens, scores, and even hundreds and for a time their names are splashed across newspapers, magazines, and

TV screens. Yet none of them has evoked the lasting fascination that's been afforded Jack since he first drew a knife in Whitechapel.

Who was he? No one knows. That his identity will be proved is unlikely. But that doesn't mean we can't speculate. History's most notorious serial murderer was the topic of a television show hosted by actor Peter Ustinov on the 100th anniversary of the Ripper murders. By going over the crimes with a panel of expert criminologists, Ustinov hoped to settle upon the most likely suspect out of five men chosen by the program's producers as their leading contenders for the title of Ripper: Dr. Gull, the Prince, Montague John Druitt; Dr. R. D'Onston, a Whitechapel resident and Satanist; and the mysterious immigrant and loner Kosminski.

The presentation of these suspects in the Ripper's crimes on "The Secret Identity of Jack the Ripper" was a fascinating mixture of dramatized recreations of Jack's ghastly goings-on and bits of actual evidence from the century-old puzzler provided by the Home Office and William Waddell, the curator of the Black Museum at Scotland Yard. Among these items were a knife believed used in one of the mutilation murders, bulging files, reports and notes of the police, and some of the letters attributed to Jack. Waddell discussed recent receipt of a package of presumably lost Ripper material including the letter in which the name Jack the Ripper was first used. Analysis of it by the Home Office Forensic Science Laboratory led modern experts to conclude, "that all the letters are hoaxes and quite irrelevant to the aim of determining the identity of Jack the Ripper."

Appearing on the program to present a personality profile of the Ripper worked up just for the show were Special Agents John E. Douglas and Robert R. Hazelwood of the Behavioral Sciences Unit of the Federal Bureau of Investigation. In pioneering research on serial killers, Douglas, Hazelwood, Robert Ressler, and others at the FBI's academy in Quantico, Virginia, had devised a system for psychological analysis. The bulk of their data was collected through interviews with scores of men who had been convicted of such crimes.

On the basis of the FBI studies it seemed likely that Jack was an "organized" killer who stalked his victims and followed a well-thought-out plan. Like the patterns of serial killers a hundred years later, he escalated the violence of his acts and then had a "cooling off period" before he struck again with a frenzy. Between the double event involving Stride and Eddowes and the butchery of Mary Kelly, seven weeks went by without a Ripper murder. In light of the FBI studies, this was typical of many serial murderers. He also matched the serial-killer profile in other striking ways.

"Jack the Ripper was a white male, he was in his mid- to late-twenties, of average intelligence," stated John Douglas. Roy Hazelwood added that Jack was single, had never been married, and probably had not socialized with women at all, and had great difficulty interacting with people and women in particular. He explained that the times when the crimes were being committed, between midnight and 6 A.M., indicated that Jack had not been accountable to anyone and, therefore, was not married.

The FBI also deduced that Jack "lived very close to where the crimes were committed because these types of individuals generally start killing within very close proximity to their homes." If Jack was employed it would have been in a menial type of job requiring little or no contact with the public. "He would not be employed in a profession," declared Hazelwood. So much for Gull, D'Onston, and all other suspected doctors, in the FBI view. "As far as his criminal history goes," continued Hazelwood, "as a child Jack would have set fires or abused animals. As an adult Jack would have been engaged in some erratic behavior, causing neighbors to call the police."

Regarding the Ripper's mental health, Douglas proposed that he would have been the product of a broken home. "He was raised by a dominant female figure in his household who in all probability physically if not sexually abused him as a child." He'd be disheveled in his appearance and people would notice that he was nocturnal, preferring to go out in the evening hours under the cloak of darkness, stalking, walking many blocks, trolling for victims.

"Jack hated and feared women at the same time," Hazelwood said, continuing with the profile. "He also was very intimidated by women. I'm sure everyone noted how quickly Jack subdued and killed his victims. This is very important in understanding Jack because it tells us that taking of life was not of primary importance to him. It was secondary to the mutilation itself. That is actually the key to understanding Jack. The mutilations were sexually motivated. By displacing the victims' organs, he in fact neutered or desexed them and therefore they were no longer anything to be feared."

With a pixieish Ustinovian look of astonishment, the host of the show quipped, "It's perhaps British understatement to suggest that he killed five women because he felt *uncomfortable* in their company."

The opinion of Hazelwood, Douglas, Waddell, and others on the panel was that Jack the Ripper had been the only man on the list of "suspects" who fit the FBI profile: the mystery man Kosminski.

Indeed, he had been high on the list of likelies in the offices of Scotland Yard, and appeared to be the highest one in the mind of Sir Robert Anderson, who took over from James Monro as head of the CID in August 1888 and became embroiled in the tug of war over the independence of the detective force that had led to Warren's resignation. In his memoirs, *The Lighter Side of My Official Life*, Anderson did not name Kosminski outright. "I will merely add," he wrote, "that the one person who ever had a good view of the murderer unhesitatingly identified the suspect the instant he was confronted with him. In saying that he was a Polish Jew I am merely stating a definitely ascertained fact."

Kosminski certainly fit the FBI's latter-day profile of a serial killer.

"This man became insane owing to many years of indulgence in solitary vices," wrote Ripperologist and City of London police officer Donald Rumbelow in his *Complete Jack the Ripper*. "He had a great hatred of women, especially of the prostitute class and had strong homicidal tendencies: he was removed to a lunatic asylum about March 1889. There were many circumstances connected with this man which made him a strong suspect." While no one can say with certainty who was the Ripper, it's deemed significant that after Kosminski was taken off the streets, the killings stopped.

However, another "Ripper Centenary" TV drama dealing with the murders, starring Michael Caine in a convincing portrayal of Inspector Frederick Abberline, did not select Kosminski as the culprit. This mini-series construed the Queen's physician (Dr. Gull) to be the Ripper, as had the 1979 film *Murder by Decree*, in which Christopher Plummer played Sherlock Holmes. This movie, based on a novel of the same title, gave the doctor a fictitious name but Gull was the real-life inspiration. Its scenario rested on a proposition that a conspiracy had been hatched to save the monarchy by covering up a scandal involving Victoria's grandson, Prince Albert Victor, who was said to have married and fathered a child with a commoner—Annie Crook—who was also Catholic. The plotters then set out to find Annie and the baby. In doing so they had to kill Annie's friends. So, they invented Jack the Ripper. Further impetus for this theory and details of the scheme were provided by Stephen Knight in *Jack the Ripper: the Final Solution*, published in 1986.

Why the Ustinov program and other theorists listed Prince Albert Victor as directly involved in the murders is a puzzle. That Eddy couldn't have done any killing himself was proved by Abberline's investigation. The Prince was far from London when some of the murders were being committed, as one of the show's panelists, Ann Mallalieu, a barrister, Queen's Counsel, and former judge, pointed out.

Unless startling new evidence surfaces to point a conclusive finger at one of the traditional suspects or a new one, it seems likely that the debate over the Ripper's identity will continue. Lacking any such discovery, it seems reasonable to conclude that, because the killings stopped with the confinement of Kosminski and bolstered by Anderson's memoirs, Kosminski was the culprit.

Alas, Abberline wrote no memoirs and recorded no private thoughts as to Jack's identity. But in all that has been written in the more than a century that has passed since the murders no writer has summed up more succinctly the Jack the Ripper story than did Abberline in his report after the murder of poor Polly Nichols. "Inquiries were made in every conceivable quarter with a view to trace the murderer," he wrote, "but not the slightest clue can at present be obtained."

Although Prince Albert Victor Christian Edward was cleared in the Ripper murders, Eddy was involved in a sensational scandal the next year involving crimes in a notorious house on Cleveland Street.

Scotland Yard's man on the case was Frederick Abberline.

EIGHT

Naughty Boys

ON JULY 4, 1889, ON THE OCCASION OF THE 113TH ANNIVERSAry of the Declaration of Independence, as America's ambassador was receiving felicitations on behalf of the government of the Queen of England, whose ancestor had lost the thirteen colonies, Police Constable Luke Hanks was looking into the theft of money from the Receiver General's Department in the Central Telegraph Office in St. Martin's-Le-Grand in the City of London. Standing before P. C. Hanks was fifteen-year old messenger boy Charles Thomas Swinscow. Because he was found to have more money in his pocket than one might have expected for a youth of his station in life, he was suspected of the theft of eighteen shillings. "I didn't have as much as that," said the boy. "I had fourteen shillings."

Even that was a lot. "Where did you get it?" asked Hanks.

"I got it for doing some private work away from the office," said Swinscow.

"For whom?"

"For a gentleman named Hammond."

"Where does he live?"

"Number 19 Cleveland Street."

Constable Hanks was familiar with Cleveland Street. Everyone in London was. Running diagonally northward from Goodge Street to Marylebone Road, it was a West End colony fancied by artists and those in society who found *la vie Bohème* exciting. The Montmartre of London, the little stretch of studios and quaint shops was unconventional, daring, even revolutionary. Among its many luminaries were the English poet, artist, and decorator William Morris; feisty

Irish-socialist-playwright George Bernard Shaw; and another witty and outrageous six-foot-three-inch Irishman who seemed to be always accompanied by a coterie of vivacious and handsome young men—Oscar Wilde.

That a youth of such low status as Charles Thomas Swinscow had anything to do in Cleveland Street beyond delivering telegrams struck Constable Hanks as odd. What did Swinscow do for this man Hammond? he asked.

Swinscow hesitated.

"C'mon, boy," insisted Hanks. "Out with it."

Fidgeting, Swinscow refused to answer.

"All right," growled the constable, "I'll have to charge you with theft."

Swinscow's reticence crumbled. "I will tell you the truth," he muttered. "I got the money for going to bed with gentlemen at Hammond's house."

Questioned further, he told of behaving "indecently" with a clerk of the General Post Office in a basement lavatory. His name was Henry Newlove. It was he who had introduced him to Hammond, where he'd got into bed with a gentleman in the back parlor. For this, he continued, he was paid a half-sovereign of which he was permitted to keep four shillings. The balance was handed over to Hammond.

Two other telegraph boys had also been recruited by Newlove, volunteered Swinscow. "And what are their names?" demanded Hanks. Swinscow replied, "George Wright and Charles Thickbroom."

Seventeen-year-old Wright told a similar story. He'd had a sexual encounter with Newlove and been introduced to Mr. George Hammond, who introduced him to gentlemen who had sex with him at the house. Asked by Newlove if he knew of "another nice little boy" who was younger and shorter than himself, Wright said he did. His name was Charles Ernest Thickbroom.

Confirming Wright's account, Thickbroom, also seventeen, told Constable Hanks that he went to Cleveland Street and was introduced by Hammond to a gentleman, whereupon they got into bed "quite naked" and "played with each other." He was paid four shillings. He went to the house a second time, he said, and engaged in similar activity. On both occasions he'd gone there in his uniform.

Confronted with the statements by the three boys, Newlove

admitted everything. The four were immediately suspended from their jobs and told to go home. However, Newlove got word to a fourth youth, Frank Hewitt, who'd introduced him to Hammond two years before. Hewitt warned Hammond and a man who lived with him at the Cleveland Street house. Known as the Reverend G. D. Veck, though the clerical collar was fraudulent, Veck moved into a Howland Street boarding house under the name Barber. Hammond beat a hasty retreat to his brother's home in Gravesend and from there to Paris.

Thunderstruck at hearing what some of his employees had been doing in their off hours, Postmaster General C. H. Raikes turned to the commissioner of the Metropolitan Police and demanded an investigation.

In the months between the end of the Ripper investigation and the discovery of the male brothel on Cleveland Street, Home Secretary Henry Matthews had taken a step at Scotland Yard that he hoped would patch things up after the power struggle that had culminated in the resignations of Sir Charles Warren and the head of the CID, James Monro. To take over for Warren as commissioner he recalled Monro. Among the men at Scotland Yard, it was a popular decision. Unlike Warren, Monro was a professional policeman who understood, as did the founders of the Metropolitan Police, Rowan and Mayne, that the police were not the representatives, in Monro's words, of "an arbitrary and despotic power" but "a disciplined body of men engaged in protecting the 'masses' as well as 'classes' from any infringements on the part of those who are not law-abiding."

Whereas Warren had resorted to brute force in attempting to deal with large street demonstrations, Monro had met the public protests by the unemployed and a strike on the London docks with restraint. There were no more Bloody Sundays. Nor was there any shrinking from pursuit of those in the privileged classes accused of violating the law, as the investigation of the doings at the house on Cleveland Street were about to prove. To take charge of the case, Monro turned to the same detective who had led the Ripper investigation.

Since promoted to chief inspector, Frederick Abberline was instructed on July 5, 1889, to obtain warrants for the arrest of Hammond and Newlove. The next day he applied to the magistrate at Great Marlborough Street Police Court, charging that "they did unlawfully, wickedly and corruptly conspire, combine, confederate and agree to incite and procure George Alma Wright and divers other persons to commit the abominable crime of buggery against the peace of Her Majesty the Queen."

A capital offense since the reign of Henry VIII, buggery—or sodomy—had been revised in the criminal code in 1861 to a crime for which the penalty was life imprisonment. Other acts of a homosexual nature short of buggery could be prosecuted only by charging that they were inherently a conspiracy to commit the more serious act. But in 1886, while considering revisions in the Criminal Law Bill in the hope of suppressing the brothels that thrived everywhere and employed very young girls, Henry Du Pre Labouchere, editor of *Truth* and one of the most powerful Radicals in the House of Commons, introduced an amendment to the bill to make *all* homosexual acts criminal offenses. He proposed that "any male person, who in public or private, commits, or is a party to the commission of, any act of gross indecency with another male person, shall be guilty of misdemeanor, and being convicted thereof, shall be liable, at the discretion of the court, to be imprisoned for any term not exceeding one year with or without hard labor."

The measure became law on January 1, 1886.

Under it, Abberline obtained warrants to arrest Hammond and Newlove, and headed to Cleveland Street but found the house was locked up and empty. He had better luck at the Camden Town home of Newlove's mother. The youth was there.

Taken into custody, Newlove turned to Abberline. "I think it is hard that I should get into trouble," he said bitterly, "while men in high positions are allowed to walk about free."

Astonished, Abberline asked what he meant.

"Why, Lord Arthur Somerset goes regularly to the house on Cleveland Street," answered Newlove, "and so does the Earl of Euston and Colonel Jervois."

While Newlove was jailed, Abberline quickly determined that Colonel Jervois was posted at the army barracks in Winchester, and from a stake-out of Cleveland Street by Police Constable Richard Sladden he was able to report to Monro that "a number of men of superior bearing and apparently of good position have been seen to call there accompanied by boys in some instances, and on two occasions by a soldier."

Where was Hammond and why hadn't he been arrested?

"I have received information—confidentially—that Hammond is now in Paris," reported Abberline. "I beg to ask that the French authorities be communicated with to ensure if possible his arrest." In reply to the request, the Foreign Office noted that in the treaty on extradition between England and France the offense of buggery was insufficient grounds for demanding that Hammond be arrested and handed over.

Stymied regarding Hammond, Abberline had better results in following up on Newlove's accusation regarding Lord Somerset. In pursuit of this lead Constable Sladden arranged to meet Swinscow and Thickbroom in the vicinity of Somerset's club in Piccadilly to see if the boys could identify him as the man who'd been with them at Cleveland Street. Both did so. Somerset was then followed to the Hyde Park Barracks, Knightsbridge, where Sladden learned that Somerset was a major in the Royal Horse Guards known as The Blues.

Petty theft of post office money had mushroomed into a scandal involving one of the great families of the empire. The third son of the eighth Duke of Beaufort, Henry Arthur George Somerset had served with distinction in campaigns in Egypt, was wounded and decorated, had stood for Parliament, and was the superintendent of stables for the Prince of Wales.

Against this vaunted reputation stood the word of three male prostitutes. Would anyone believe them? Constable Sladden did. So did Abberline. And so did Monro. As did the director of public prosecutions, Sir Augustus Stephenson. And the solicitor general, Sir Edward Clark. They recommended that Somerset be summoned to answer a charge under section 11 of the Criminal Law Amendment Act—Labouchere's new homosexuality statute. But an even higher authority had to sign off on such an order—Attorney General Sir Richard Webster. He expressed doubts about the reliability of the testimony of the three young men and asked for more convincing testimony.

That would be Hammond's, but he was in France.

Might the French police help? To find out, Abberline went to Paris. The Sûreté couldn't be budged. "Unless great weight is brought to bear upon the French Police," he reported, "they are not likely to put themselves to much trouble in the matter."

Meanwhile, Lord Somerset was under discreet surveillance. On two occasions he was interviewed at Hyde Park Barracks

but denied any knowledge of the house on Cleveland Street
and of boys named Swinscow and Thickbroom. He could not
deny that he knew a third boy named Algernon Allies. A handsome, curly-haired twenty-year-old who'd been employed at
Somerset's club, Allies had attracted Somerset's attention and
loyalty. After he'd been arrested for stealing money from the
club, Allies told the police, Somerset sent him to Hammond
with a request that he be looked after "as a friend of Mr.
Brown."

In tracking down the bogus clergyman George Daniel Veck,
the police found that he had letters on him addressed to "Mr.
Brown" from Allies asking for money. They also found a letter
from the elusive Hammond that said: "Let me know when it
is safe to come back."

Allies insisted that Brown was Hammond. The attorney
general had doubts and directed that "no proceedings be taken
against him."

Had prosecution of Somerset been authorized, it would have
been difficult if not impossible. He'd fled from England to the
amenable climate of Homburg, Germany, never to return. But
from his exile he wrote letters that raised disturbing questions
about the involvement of an even grander name than his in
the scandal of Cleveland Street. The insinuation was that he'd
absconded so as to protect Prince Albert Victor, the Queen's
grandson, the son of His Royal Highness the Prince of Wales,
and heir presumptive to the throne.

There was no doubt that Prince Eddy, also known as "Col-
lars and Cuffs," was often in Cleveland Street. He was seen
frequently in the company of the artists and literary lights
who lived and partied there. Had he ever been inside the
notorious number 19? "I am told that Newton has boasted
that if we go on, a very distinguished person will be involved
(PAV)," wrote Assistant Public Prosecutor Hamilton Cuffe to
his boss on September 16, knowing that "PAV" stood for
Prince Albert Victor. "I don't mean to say that I for one instant
credit it (Newlove's assertion) but in such circumstances as
this one never knows what may be said, be concocted or
be true."

Did Eddy dally with boys in the notorious house? The noted
historian of the affair, H. Montgomery Hyde (*The Cleveland
Street Scandal*) wrote in another book about the Victorian era
(*Their Good Names*) that Eddy had been a frequent caller at

the house. And in his biography of the Prince (*Clarence*) he described Prince Albert Victor as a bisexual.

In spelling out what he believed was an elaborate Palace-based plot to invent Jack the Ripper so as to extricate Eddy from his embarrassing marriage to the Catholic commoner Annie Crook, whom Eddie purportedly met in a shop in Cleveland Street across from the male brothel, Stephen Night, in *Jack the Ripper: The Final Solution*, wrote that the Prince fell in love easily and often with women, men and boys. "It is no surprise, then," he added, "that Eddy should have allowed himself to be drawn into the brothel, not because he was desperately homosexual but because he allowed himself *to fall in love* (Mr. Night's italics) with his closest friends, be they male or female."

The rumors about Eddy remained just that—rumors—while indictments were returned against Hammond, Veck, and Newlove on thirteen counts of procuring six boys "to commit divers acts of gross indecency with another person" as well as conspiracy to commit the same acts. Although Somerset was not named, it was impossible to keep secret the fact that someone of high station had been involved in the scandal and for suspicions to be raised that the Conservative government of Prime Minister Lord Salisbury was doing its best to conceal the name. Taking the lead in calling attention to the cover-up was the author of the homosexuality law. "What is this case," thundered Labouchere in Parliament, "but a criminal conspiracy by the very guardians of morality and law, with the Prime Minister at their head, to defeat the ends of justice?"

As a result of a conspiracy or not, Lord Somerset neither in person nor by name figured in the trials. Eventually he made his way to the French Riviera and remained an exile until his death in 1926. Perhaps in that time he ran into another ex-patriot who six years after the disclosures of the naughtiness of the boys of Cleveland Street felt the sting of England's sodomy laws, for in 1895, Oscar Wilde was arrested by Scotland Yard detectives to answer a charge of sexual misconduct with Lord Alfred Douglas, known to Oscar as "Bosie."

In the trial, Wilde was asked to explain a phrase he'd used in a letter to Bosie: "the love that dare not speak its name." He answered:

The love that dare not speak its name in this century is
such a great affection of an elder for a younger man as
there was between David and Jonathan, such as Plato
made the very basis of his philosophy, such as you find
in the sonnets of Michelangelo and Shakespeare. It is
that deep spiritual affection that is as pure as it is perfect. It dictates and pervades great works of art like
those of Shakespeare and Michelangelo and those two
letters of mine, such as they are. It is in this century misunderstood; so much misunderstood that it may
be described as the love that dare not speak its name.
And on account of it I am placed where I am now. It
is beautiful. It is fine. It is the noblest form of affection. There is nothing unnatural about it. It is intellectual and it repeatedly exists between a younger and an
elder man where the elder has intellect and the younger
all the hope and joy and glamor of life before him.
But that this should be so the world does not under-
stand. The world mocks it and sometimes puts one in
a pillory.

The understanding that Wilde hoped for from the succeeding century still had not been realized in the 1940s, when
Quentin Crisp was stopped by Metropolitan Police detectives
on the streets of London and falsely charged with soliciting
sex from men. Crisp then delivered a speech to the judge
that has become almost as famous a plea for understanding
homosexuality as Wilde's in a country that required its police
to pursue and arrest violators of the sodomy laws.

The speech got Crisp acquitted, allowing him to remain free
and go on to achieve fame in his own country and in the United States with a television production of his reminiscences,
The Naked Civil Servant of what it was like to be "queer,"
as he unashamedly put it, in England in the middle of the
twentieth century. But just as Wilde's speech didn't change
the law, neither did Crisp's.

In a daring and controversial film produced in Britain in
1962, *Victim*, Dirk Bogarde portrayed a homosexual lawyer
caught in a blackmail scheme. The point the film attempted to
make was that the law encouraged the victimization of homosexuals. Ironically, exactly that outcome had been predicted at

the time Parliament adopted Labouchere's amendment. Opponents of the measure called it the "Blackmailer's Charter."

A century after Cleveland Street and the subsequent trial of Oscar Wilde, gay community leaders presented the Home Secretary, Kenneth Baker, with an analysis, based on Home Office statistics for 1989, to show how gay and bisexual men were being punished for consensual acts that society tolerated among heterosexuals.

It claimed that consenting homosexual relations between men age sixteen and over resulted in 3,500 prosecutions, 2,700 convictions, 380 cautions, and at least 40 prison sentences. "We are particularly alarmed to learn that the number of convictions for the consensual offence of indecency between males was nearly four times greater in 1989 than in 1966, the year before the ostensible decriminalization of male homosexuality in England and Wales," said Peter Tatchell, co-organizer of a gay group called Outrage.

The Home Office and the police denied that homosexuals were singled out and that gay men were deliberately entrapped.

Animosity toward homosexuals in England had also splashed onto the front pages of newspapers and onto TV news programs in 1969. On September 29, 1969, a dozen teenagers set out to "hunt queers." Armed with sticks and swinging fists, they descended on Wimbledon Common, a known gathering place for homosexual men, to attack and beat a man to death. The police arrested the leader of the mob, an eighteen-year-old choirboy who had been awarded the Duke of Edinburgh Bronze Medal for life-saving as a member of St. John's Ambulance and Royal Marine Cadets. Ironically, his name was Hammond.

In the final disposition of the Cleveland Street scandal the Hammond who had run the brothel was never prosecuted. From his sanctuary in Europe, he fled to America, settled in Seattle, and faded into obscurity. Swinscow and Thickbroom lost their jobs (punishment enough in the hard times of 1889 London). Allies, who was not prosecuted in return for his testimony, made a futile appeal to Somerset's father for help because he was "destitute" and also vanished into the mists of history. Newlove received a sentence of four months at hard labor. Veck got nine months.

Prince Eddy, whose life remains a controversial part of two great Victorian sensations, Jack the Ripper and Cleveland

Street, died of pneumonia (some say madness) at the age of twenty-eight, in 1892.

That same year, at age fifty-two, Frederick Abberline gave up being a policeman and retired. He lived until 1916.

After losing a fight to improve the pension rights of the men who served under him, Commissioner Monro resigned from the Metropolitan Police in disgust in 1890, to return to Bengal where he founded and ran a medical mission. Had he remained at his post he would have found himself at work in grand new surroundings.

NINE

New Scotland Yard

COMMISSIONER JAMES MONRO'S RESIGNATION WAS SUBMIT-
ted to home secretary Henry Matthews on June 12, 1890,
to become effective on June 21. Within forty-eight hours
Matthews named a successor. He was to be Colonel Sir Edward
Bradford. A cavalry officer, veteran of the Indian Mutiny, and
most recently the head of the political and secret departments of
the India Office in London, Bradford enjoyed a reputation for
decisiveness. Certainly no one questioned his courage. When
his left arm was mangled during an encounter with a tiger he
had endured its amputation without benefit of anesthesia.

Within hours after Bradford arrived at Whitehall Place on
June 23, he was faced with a crisis over unhappiness in the
ranks about pay and pensions, the issue which had caused
Monro to quit. A group of delegates representing the disgrun-
tled officers from seven police divisions staged a noisy demonstration at the Bow Street police station. Bradford's response
was an order banning all such exhibitions. Five days later the
rank-and-file presented him with a petition pointing out a 15
percent gap between the weekly pay of a police officer and the
wage standards for the general labor market. "Besides being
underpaid as compared with ordinary workmen," it asserted,
"our conditions of living and abode are different and more
expensive than those of workmen." Bradford replied to the
petition on July 1, promising to give it sympathetic consideration. But on July 5, after transferring a militant leader of
the wage protest, he refused to meet with a delegation on the
grounds that the members did not have authority to represent
anyone.

At the Bow Street police station that very evening 130 men refused to go on duty. Summoning them to appear before him at Scotland Yard the next day, Bradford fired the nine men whom he considered the ringleaders, telling them that they were unfit to wear their uniforms. The other ninety-one were ordered transferred. A general strike was threatened but did not take place, although political agitators tried to take advantage of the situation by gathering in Bow Street. Met by mounted police with the support of two troops of Life Guards, they were soon dispersed.

All of this blew over in mid-August, with the passage of a new Police Act that granted a modest pay raise to put police on a par with the labor market and make improvements in the pension system. With tempers damped, the new commissioner turned attention to restoring morale and confidence by visiting every station in the police district and meeting with the rank-and-file. "It was something that not even Charles Rowan had done," noted police historian David Ascoli, "and it was yet another indication of slowly changing attitudes both towards and within the service."

An ear to the problems of the men was not the only change introduced by Bradford. To ease workload, beats were altered. Lightweight summer uniforms were authorized. Conditions within station houses were improved and several new police stations were built, although they were modest compared to what was going up on a tract of former swampland within the shadow of Parliament and lying beside a new roadway between Westminster Bridge and Blackfriars, along the Victoria Embankment of the Thames.

A plan to occupy the land with a suitable building was put forward in 1875 by Colonel J. H. Mapleson. It proposed a grand opera house. Enthusiastically embraced by government and public, the project got under way in December, with the Duke of Edinburgh officiating at the laying of the foundation stone. Unfortunately, the project was underfunded and ran out of money. Rather than becoming the Grand National Opera House, the project appeared to be a white elephant until Home Secretary Matthews turned to the distinguished architect Norman Shaw to come up with a plan for a new home for the Metropolitan Police.

Although Shaw had designed imposing neo-Gothic churches and country homes, and had created several elegant private buildings and business structures along the Embankment, he'd never done a government project. Believing that an architect must be guided by his artistic intuition, he quickly discovered that he had to deal with government committees, public opinion, criticism from the press, and the barbs of Commissioner Sir Charles Warren, who said that Shaw was building a monument to the past rather than the future. Frustrated but undaunted, Shaw insisted on having his way and ultimately prevailed. Work began. And promptly ceased.

Hardly had the excavations started when diggers unearthed the dismembered body of a young girl. From the overcrowded Whitehall Place headquarters that the new building was intended to replace rushed detectives of the CID, but with no clues and no way of identifying the victim, they were stymied. The murder was never solved. Construction work resumed.

A quintessentially Victorian edifice, it was faced on the lower floors with granite quarried by inmates of Dartmoor Prison. Unlike modern-day executives whose status is measured by the grandeur of offices on the uppermost floors of skyscrapers, the top brass of the Metropolitan Police moved into lower stories' commodious offices with the commissioner ensconced in a second-floor turret with windows overlooking the Thames. Climbing stairs to the brickface upper reaches was left to the lower echelons. Of course, these sweaty climbers also had the benefits of even more spectacular views of the river than their commissioner and, in an era without air-conditioning, cooling summer breezes wafting off the water.

Entered from the south through gates facing the Embankment and by way of Derby Gate, a short sloping street from Whitehall, the building has been described as part medieval fortress and part French chateau. From the third floor to the Mansard roof, it was a tangled maze of stairwells, corridors, offices, and rooms of all sizes and shapes and, at the very top, attics that defied anyone to enter wearing a beehive policeman's helmet.

Completed in December 1890, the building immediately filled up, requiring two departments to remain at Whitehall Place—the Public Carriage Office (the traffic department) and the Lost Property Office, crammed with no less than 14,212 umbrellas.

Because the unofficial name for the Metropolitan Police office had enjoyed such widespread acceptance, Shaw's new structure was named New Scotland Yard.

For the next seventy-seven years it would become one of the most photographed and romantic structures in London, thanks to preparers of travel brochures, makers of mystery movies seeking picturesque London settings, and authors of detective novels—not the least significant of whom was a thirty-two-year-old physician-turned-writer who made his dramatic literary debut in *Beeton's Christmas Annual* two years before Commissioner Bradford moved into Shaw's grand police palace.

TEN

Sherlock Doyle

HE IS THE MOST FAMOUS DETECTIVE EVER TO WALK THE corridors of Scotland Yard, yet he existed only in the fertile imagination of a writer. He was Inspector Lestrade. We do not know his first name, only his initial: G. Although he appears thirteen times in the immortal adventures of Sherlock Holmes, nothing is known of the life outside the Yard of the detective whom Dr. Watson described unflatteringly as sallow, ratfaced, and dark-eyed and whom Holmes saw as quick and energetic but wholly conventional, lacking in imagination, and normally out of his depth—the best of a bad lot who'd reached the top in the CID by bulldog tenacity.

The creator of Lestrade as a foil and occasional help to the sleuth of Baker Street was Arthur Conan Doyle. Born on May 22, 1859, at 11 Picardy Place, Edinburgh, Scotland, he was of an old aristocratic but artistic Irish family. His grandfather John Doyle was a gifted caricaturist. His father Charles was a sketch artist. Grand-uncle and godfather Michael Edward Conan was an artist-war correspondent and music and literary critic for the London *Morning Herald* and Paris correspondent of the *Art Journal*. And Uncle Richard Doyle was an excellent, if moody, violinist.

It was Richard who took Arthur to London for the first time in December of 1874, an especially murderous season. That month ninety-six bodies were dragged from the Thames, most of them with slit throats. Garrotings, abductions, armed robberies, and other crimes filled the columns of the newspapers. At Scotland Yard the registry of known criminals exceeded 36,000. Arrests were tallied at 60,000 a year. Property losses attributed to portico thieves and others were put at a million pounds a year. Early that month, at Marylebone Police Court, a deranged man with a long criminal record had to be subdued when he screamed "This is my witness!" and drew a knife on the judge. Breaking loose, he tried to hurl himself out a window. His name, noted the *Times*, was Moriarty.

As if the crime that surrounded young Conan Doyle were not sufficient, he visited Madame Tussaud's exhibition at Portman Square on Baker Street, where his interest in history drew him first to the likenesses in the Hall of Kings and the Napoleon Room. But the greatest delight, he told his mother in a letter, was the Chamber of Horrors, where among the representations of gory murders he gazed at a waxen image of James Greenacre holding the very knife he'd used to cut off the head of the hapless Hannah Brown.

Everywhere he went in the muddy, clogged, and roiling streets of a city of 4 million people Conan Doyle found beggars huddling in rags. Seeing these wretches pleading for a few coins from the elegantly dressed gentlemen on their way to their offices and banks or to one of the newspapers of Fleet Street, Conan Doyle's first glimmerings of a story might have appeared in his mind—the tantalizing question of what might happen if one of those dandy gentlemen discovered that he could earn more money as a beggar, as Neville St. Claire was to do in "The Man with the Twisted Lip." In the pitiful homeless boys whom Londoners dismissed as "street Arabs" did he spy the face of the future Wiggins, leader of "the unofficial police force" that posterity would come to know as the Baker Street Irregulars?

"Art in the blood is liable to take the strangest forms," says Holmes to Watson in "The Greek Interpreter." It's as fitting a biography of Conan Doyle as any. The talent for writing fiction that was to make him rich and famous manifested itself while he was a medical student at the University of Edinburgh with "The Mystery of the Sasassa Valley" which he sold to *Chambers' Journal* in 1879. Always in need of money, he continued as an author of short stories and novels without much success until, in 1877, he filled up the time in his medical consulting room to which few patients came by writing A *Study in Scarlet*. To his amazement and delight it was bought by *Beeton's Christmas Annual*, one of many "shilling shockers" that murder-minded Victorian readers gleefully devoured. Brought out in book form in 1888, when London was agog with the doings of Jack the Ripper and dismayed with what people perceived as ineptitude at Scotland Yard, *A Study in Scarlet* introduced an extremely clever private consulting detective who employed the "Science of Deduction" to solve a murder at 3 Lauriston Gardens that had stumped "the smartest of the Scotland Yarders," Inspector Tobias Gregson, and his associate Lestrade. "They are as jealous as a pair of professional beauties," said Holmes to his friend Dr. John H. Watson. "There will be some fun over this case if they are both put upon the scent."

Holmes's debut was a sensation. "The failure of the police to solve the puzzle of the Ripper murders only accentuated a psychological need for a Holmesian hero," wrote Charles Higham in a 1976 biography of Conan Doyle. "If the public could not find him in life, they would find him in books, and find him they did." From 1887 to the Roaring Twenties, the detective who resided at 221B Baker Street and his "biographer" Dr. Watson tackled cases of mystery and murder in fifty-six short stories and four novels by Conan Doyle and even more in pastiches, on the stage and in hundreds of movies and television shows written by others but based on his creation. In the Conan Doyle "canon," as Sherlockians reverently call the body of work, Holmes encounters a score of "official" policemen and one policewoman but none more often than "friend Lestrade."

The prevailing attitude at Scotland Yard toward Mr. Sherlock Holmes and his creator was anything but friendly. Depictions of "the Yarders" as inept bunglers with a chronic need for the help of a consulting detective smarted. In Conan Doyle's sleuth they saw a snobbish and condescending individual who had the luxury of *choosing* cases for which he was frequently rewarded with large sums, while they had to take crime as it came at them and had had to fight to obtain wages equivalent to that of ditchdiggers. Did Holmes have to wade into the midst of street brawls or a knife fight in a public house? Was there a Home Office looking over his shoulder? When did Holmes ever have to sit down and write a report to a superior officer? The solving of murders and mysteries by "deductive reasoning" was easy in stories. Finding out who chopped up a woman and scattered her remains all over the city in real life was quite another matter. Little wonder then that in the first issue of

Police Review and Parade Gossip The Organ of the British Constabulary that came out on January 2, 1893, its founder John Kempster gave the back of his hand to Arthur Conan Doyle in particular and critics of the police in general. "The policeman is not to be regarded as a mere chattel or machine," he wrote. "He is a man and a citizen."

Scotland Yard's disdain notwithstanding, the popularity of Holmes among the people continued undiminished, so much so that when Conan Doyle grew weary of his creation and killed him off in a titanic struggle with Professor James Moriarty ("the Napoleon of Crime") at the Reichenbach Falls, public opinion—and Conan Doyle's mother—demanded that the author bring him back to life. He did so in 1902. But the tale that slaked the public's thirst took the form of a case that had occurred years earlier than the deadly struggle in Switzerland. Titled "The Hound of the Baskervilles," it "teamed" Holmes with an old friend summoned from London to the dreary moors of Dartmoor by an urgent telegram.

"Wire received. Coming down with unsigned warrant," said the reply from Scotland Yard. "Arrive five-forty.—Lestrade." The "best of a bad lot" also figured importantly in the story that brought Holmes back to life and explained how he'd staged his death at the Reichenbach Falls, "The Adventure of the Empty House." From that moment on, Conan Doyle produced Sherlockian adventures until shortly before his own death in 1930, leaving Holmes to a posterity that refused to accept that the detective and his trusty companion Watson ever died. "Shall they not always live at Baker Street?" asked Sherlockian scholar Vincent Starret. "Are they not there this moment as one writes? Outside, the hansoms rattle through the rain, and Moriarty plans his latest devilry. Within, the sea coal flames upon the hearth and Holmes and Watson take their well-won ease. So they will live for all that love them well: in a romantic chamber of the heart, in a nostalgic country of the mind, where it is always 1895."

Inevitably and perhaps to the further vexation of the real detectives at New Scotland Yard, Holmes's adventures came to life on stage. The production was *Sherlock Holmes* and it premiered in London at Henry Irving's Lyceum Theatre on January 30, 1902. The play was written by and starred William Gillette, who would go on to make a career of the title role and, incidentally, create the indelible image of Holmes as a pipe-smoking figure wearing an Inverness cloak and deer-stalker cap. Portraying a page boy named Billy in his theatrical debut was a lad by the name of Charles Chaplin, for whom Fate held future stardom as the "Little Tramp" in silent films. (A century later another Billy in a revival of the Gillette play went on to movie stardom: Christian Slater.) At its opening in London, Gillette's play got a prolonged standing ovation from an audience, including King Edward VII and Queen Alexandra and a panoply of Edwardian nobility, that would not go home until both Gillette and Conan Doyle made speeches.

Among those applauding was the Marquess of Anglesey, whose famous collection of jewelry valued at 150,000 pounds was at that moment being stolen. In desperation the Marquess turned to Conan Doyle for help. Employing deductive techniques with which he'd endowed his literary creation, Conan Doyle suggested that the culprit was the Marquess's valet, John Gault. Investigation by Scotland Yard proved it. Meanwhile, Gault, who'd taken the gems in association with his prostitute girlfriend, had fled to Paris where in due course he was arrested and sent to prison. Released in 1911, he committed a murder and was executed by guillotine. In the meantime Conan Doyle was helpful in tracing the whereabouts of some of the loot, determining that Gault's accomplice had fenced her share. The gems were recovered but in a city of prostitutes the girl was never found.

"It was inevitable that the author of Sherlock Holmes stories should often be called upon to enact the role of his imaginary detective," wrote Starret in *The Private Life of Sherlock Holmes*. One of these cases involved the disappearance from London's Langham Hotel of a country squire whose family feared had been robbed and murdered. Looking into the circumstances at the hotel and by checking railway schedules, Conan Doyle deduced that he had disappeared willingly and then wired the family that they would find him in a city other than London where he could lose himself in a crowd. The man was located in Edinburgh. In a similar case a prospective groom dropped out of sight on the eve of the wedding. Conan Doyle deduced where he was and also showed the bride that the man was unworthy of her affections.

On several occasions in the Sherlock Holmes canon the great detective directed his powers to proving that police had arrested the wrong person. Conan Doyle undertook the same mission twice. In 1906 he learned of the imprisonment of a young law student for maiming horses in Staffordshire. The crimes had been committed in 1903, so George Edalji had been in jail for three years by the time the case came to Conan Doyle's attention. Investigating the youth's background, he found that Edalji was of mixed race; his mother was English and his clergyman-father was Parsi. In this appearance of a colored clergyman with a half-caste son in a rude and unrefined parish, Conan Doyle reasoned, there was bound to be "some regrettable situation."

What he discovered in his investigation was a case in which the police were "all pulling together and twisting all things to their end." As he read the official records, the "unmistakable accent of truth forced itself" upon him. "I realized that I was in the presence of an appalling tragedy," he wrote, "and that I was called upon to do what I could to set it right."

Among the strange events of the case were the facts that at the time when the animals were being mutilated Edalji was asleep in the same room as his father, that the Reverend Edalji always locked the door of the room upon retiring, and that he was a light sleeper and would have been awakened if his son had crept out of the room. "This may not constitute an absolute alibi in the eye of the law," Conan Doyle wrote in the *Daily Telegraph*, "but it is difficult to imagine anything nearer to one unless a sentinel had been placed outside the door all night." He then noted that when the father's testimony didn't fit the scenario the police had changed the time of the mutilations from night to morning.

Edalji had also been accused of—but not tried for—sending a series of threatening letters. Conan Doyle showed that they'd been in at least two handwritings, neither of which was Edalji's.

But the most exculpating discovery of all was that Edalji was so visually impaired that he was unable to recognize anyone at the distance of six yards. Yet the police maintained that to commit the crime he had to cross the right of way of the London and North Western Railway, a complex of rails, ties, fences, and hedges.

Faced with Conan Doyle's reasoning, authorities reopened the case and exonerated Edalji of the mutilations. But in a bizarre twist the committee that reviewed the case found that Edalji had contributed to the miscarriage of justice by sending the letters and so was not entitled to any compensation for his having spent three years in prison for a crime he didn't commit. Conan Doyle denounced the outcome as a blot upon English justice.

Conan Doyle's undoing of the injustice done to Oscar Slater would take longer. Accused of the murder of an elderly woman and theft of her jewelry, Slater was convicted in Glasgow in May 1909 on very flimsy evidence. Approached by Slater sympathizers who were impressed by his efforts on behalf of Edalji, Conan Doyle went into the matter reluctantly. But when he glanced at the facts he concluded that "this unhappy man had in all probability no more to do with the murder for which he had been condemned than I had." After reviewing the facts, he published a pamphlet, "The Case for Oscar Slater." Point by point, he demolished the evidence and the witnesses and demonstrated how Slater could not have been the killer. He then declared: "The trouble, however, with all police prosecutions is that, having once got what they imagine to be their man, they are not very open to any line of investigation which might lead to other conclusions. Everything which will not fit into the official theory is liable to be excluded." The words might have been those of Sherlock Holmes to Dr. Watson on the shortcomings of Scotland Yard.

Reversal of fortune for Slater was not as swift as in the Edalji case. Although there was an official inquiry as a result of Conan Doyle's efforts, nothing came of it and Slater remained in prison until a new trial freed him in 1927. Although Slater was awarded six thousand pounds in compensation for all he'd been put through, and knowing that in his unceasing efforts on behalf of freeing him Conan Doyle had spent hundreds of pounds of his own money, and even though he'd promised Conan Doyle reimbursement, Slater gave the champion of his cause nothing. "It was," wrote Conan Doyle, "a painful and sordid aftermath to such a story."

Recognition of Arthur Conan Doyle's extraordinary achievements had by that time been made by a more exalted personality than the ungrateful Slater. On August 9, 1902, Conan Doyle was knighted by King Edward VII. A devoted reader of Sherlock Holmes who claimed that the detective's adventures were the only works of fiction he could ever finish, the King arranged for an additional honor for Sir Arthur. He was created Deputy Lieutenant of Surrey.

Official recognition of Scotland Yard's unique relationship to Conan Doyle and his immortal literary creation required a bit more time. It came in January 1974 at the yearly gathering of the Sherlock Holmes Society of London. The guest of honor was Sir Robert Mark, the commissioner of the Metropolitan Police.

> It is a cause for particular pleasure that I, a representative of that Force which Holmes always regarded with such tolerant derision should a mere eighty-six years after his first detective feat be entrusted with the task of honouring his memory. He was really the first person to make the investigation of crime respectable. And in the public mind to give that process the shape of the ancient morality play—right against wrong, good against evil. Time and changing social conditions have enabled us, the police, to assume that role and to inherit the public approval that he won for what had been regarded as menial if not a worse activity. For this we shall always be in his debt though he would no doubt be horrified to know it.

Despite Commissioner Mark's nod of appreciation to Sherlock Holmes, some Scotland Yarders still deeply resent the Sleuth of Baker Street. Among them in 1991 was the curator of the Black Museum. In an interview in connection with this book, William Waddell bridled at the mere mention of Sir Arthur Conan Doyle and his timeless literary legacy. "Sherlock Holmes," he declared, "is a fraud. The idea that one may deduce facts about a criminal from the depth of footprints in the earth is preposterous. I can also assure you that it is impossible to tell anything from the ash of a cigar or cigarette. Doyle knew nothing about solving crimes! As for Holmes, what was he, really, but a drug addict?"

Ironically, at the moment when Waddell was denouncing Holmes and standing guard over Scotland Yard's private "by invitation and with escort only" museum, not far away from Waddell's office tourists at 221B Baker Street were flocking to pay admission to enter and explore a museum to a fictional character who remains, in the public's mind, England's most famous and enduring detective.

ELEVEN

Poisonous Cream

AS A PHYSICIAN AND A WRITER ABOUT CRIME CONAN DOYLE made note that fellow doctors periodically exhibited a facility for taking human lives as well as saving them. "When a doctor does go wrong he is the first of criminals," says Sherlock Holmes in "The Adventure of the Speckled Band." "He has nerve and he has knowledge. Palmer and Pritchard were among the heads of their profession."

Two years before Conan Doyle's birth Dr. William Palmer had stood in the dock of the Old Bailey, accused of murder. A rascal as a child, a rogue and rake as a youth, a poor medical student, gambler, womanizer, and father of at least fourteen illegitimate children in the five years when he was apprenticed physician in Cheshire, Palmer was convicted and hanged for poisoning another gambler. But that was only the latest of his homicides. He'd administered strychnine to his wife, one of his children, mother-in-law, brother, a bookmaker to whom he owed 800 pounds, and the husband of a woman he had been romancing. "His career supplied one of the proofs of a fact which many kind-hearted people seem to doubt," wrote Sir James Stephens in *The History of the Criminal Law*, "namely the fact that such a thing as atrocious wickedness is consistent with good education [and] perfect sanity."

The next doctor to appear before an Old Bailey jury charged with murder was Thomas Smethurst. The victim was Isabella Bankes, who had entered into a bigamous marriage with Smethurst in apparent belief that he loved her. But what Smethurst lusted for was the several thousand pounds the young woman possessed. To obtain it he poisoned Isabella just enough to make her ill, coaxed her into making out a will with him as beneficiary, and then finished her off. Although he was found guilty, questions were raised about some of the evidence at the trial. As a result of a review by the Home Office the verdict was overturned. Released from prison, Smethurst was arrested on the charge of bigamy. He confessed, served a year, promptly applied for probate of Isabella's will, and collected on it!

For money, Palmer and Smethurst had turned their backs on their oaths as physicians. The next villainous doctor to shock the sensibilities of Victorian England was vain, flamboyant, thirty-five-year-old Edward William Pritchard, who poisoned his wife with aconite and antimony simply because he was certain he could get away with it. When he feared that his mother-in-law suspected him, he poisoned her. Still supremely self-confident even as he ascended to the gallows on July 28, 1865, in Glasgow, he said to a clergyman, "I shall see you in Heaven." The cleric replied: "Sir, we shall meet at the Judgment seat." Gathered before the scaffold as Pritchard "dropped" in the last public execution in Scotland were 100,000 spectators.

It's unlikely that the heinous crimes of these doctors were known to prostitute Matilda Clover a quarter of a century later as she discussed business arrangements in Lambeth Road with a tall gentleman wearing a large caped coat and high silk hat. He had a large mustache, a pronounced squint, and an American accent. With terms settled, Matilda escorted him out of the crisp October air and into her squalid room. A few hours later, neighbors who were accustomed to noise were awakened by her agonized screams. Alone in the room, Matilda was racked by convulsions that were diagnosed by a doctor's assistant as effects of years of alcohol abuse.

Her death the next morning passed unnoticed by the police until a peculiar letter was received on November 28 by the prominent London physician William H. Broadbent. Signed "M. Malone," it accused Dr. Broadbent of having poisoned Matilda and demanded 2,500 pounds in return for which the good doctor would be given "the evidence." Broadbent took the letter over to Scotland Yard.

Inspector Tunbridge suggested that Broadbent put a notice in the agony column of the *Daily Chronicle* accepting the terms of the letter. The doctor's house was then put under watch. When no one appeared Tunbridge judged that the letter had come from a lunatic. What Tunbridge did *not* do was ask the police of the L Division, which encompassed Lambeth, to investigate the circumstances of Matilda Clover's death.

Had they been called in they surely would have recalled the death of another South Bank prostitute just a week before Matilda died. The cause of death in the case of Ellen Donworth had never been in doubt. She'd been poisoned with strychnine. Futhermore, within a few days of her death the local coroner had received a letter offering information on the murder for a price. Two weeks after that a partner in a bookselling firm received a letter from "H. Bayne" claiming to have letters that incriminated the partner in Donworth's murder. "If you employ me at once to act for you in this matter," said the writer, "I will save you from all exposure and shame in the matter." Scotland Yard's response was to advise the bookseller to post a sign in a window accepting Bayne's offer so that detectives could watch for Bayne to show himself. He did not. The case was closed.

Six months later the deaths of prostitutes Alice Marsh and Emma Shrivell by poisoning stirred memories. The Donworth case was reopened. But aside from strychnine, did the deaths of Marsh and Shrivell have any connection to Donworth?

The answer was not long in coming. The connection was more letters. One was received by a respected physician in Barnstable. Unless Dr. Joseph Harper paid 1,500 pounds, warned "W. H. Murray," the doctor's son, a medical student at St. Thomas's Hospital, would be named as the murderer of Marsh and Shrivell. A similar letter was sent to the foreman of the coroner's jury that investigated the deaths.

Vivid in the memories of the detectives of Scotland Yard was another slayer of prostitutes: Jack the Ripper. Was Jack back? Had he surfaced four years later with poison as his weapon? Was a new terror about to grip London? With these unsettling questions in mind the detective force set to work. Besides the same cause of death and the letters, the only other lead they had was a vague description by a constable of a man he'd seen coming out of Donworth's house around the time of her murder.

The next event was the appearance at Scotland Yard of a man who lived in the same lodging house as the son of Dr. Harper. He told Inspector M'Intyre that another lodger had told him that he knew for a fact that young Harper had murdered a woman named Loo Harvey. "I shadowed them one night and I saw him give her two pills," he said. "She collapsed immediately and was found dead in the street. I imagine she was buried as an unknown."

This was obviously a joke, replied M'Intyre. No one named Loo Harvey had been found dead. But for the record, he asked, what was the name of this jokester?

The man replied, "Doctor Neill Cream."

"I'll remember it," promised M'Intyre.

Not long after the macabre conversation Loo Harvey showed up alive. But the story she related in a letter to Scotland Yard indicated that she'd had a close call. A night or two after Matilda Clover's tortured death, Louisa said, she'd been at the Alhambra and St. James music halls where she met a man who spent the night with her at a hotel in Berwick Street. Telling her that he had noticed a few spots on her forehead, he promised to bring her some pills to "eradicate" them. That night she met him again opposite Charing Cross Station and then walked with him along the Embankment. He gave her two pink capsules. Not liking the look of them, she pretended to swallow them but kept them in her hand. When her solicitous benefactor was looking away she threw the pills into the Thames. Watching all of this from a distance, she added, was her lover Charles Harvey.

What was going on here? First, a man named Neill Cream told a fellow lodger that he'd watched a woman named Loo Harvey drop dead after being given two pills by a medical student but Cream hadn't informed the police—indicating Cream was perpetrating a boarding house prank. Now the very woman whom Cream had named comes forward with a story of being given pills, exactly as Cream described except that she was very much alive.

Who was this Doctor Cream?

M'Intyre soon found out, not through an investigation but from a most unexpected source. In a state of agitation a well-dressed, almost gaunt, stoop-shouldered, broad-browed, mustached and squinting figure presented himself to M'Intyre at the Yard. "It's a scandal that in a great city like this," the man whined, "that I should be subjected to such an insult. My name, sir, is Neill Cream. I was born in Glasgow, but brought up in Canada. For the last few days my foot-steps have been dogged by villainous-looking persons. I believe they will try to murder me. I want you to send a detective to protect me from them."

"I'm sorry that you should be worried," answered M'Intyre calmly. "I will do what I can to help you. In fact, I'll protect you myself."

The next afternoon M'Intyre met Cream at his lodging house and walked with him along Waterloo Road. It wasn't a route chosen at random. Along the way, as M'Intyre had planned, they passed one constable—the same who'd seen a man leaving the scene of Ellen Donworth's murder. Later at his office in Scotland Yard, M'Intyre asked the constable if Cream had been that man. "He's very like him," said the constable, "but I wouldn't like to swear to it."

As Cream's protector, and by now a trusted friend, M'Intyre had no trouble getting a sample of Cream's handwriting. Unfortunately, it did not match the writing in the blackmail letter that had been sent to Dr. Harper. Undaunted and convinced that Cream was his man, M'Intyre nonchalantly acquired a sheet of Cream's writing paper. Examining the watermark, he found that it matched the paper on which the letter to Harper was written. Of course, the Fairfield-Superfine mark could have been a common type.

A paper manufacturer told M'Intyre: "It's not British made."

"Perhaps it's American," suggested M'Intyre.

"If I were you," said the expert, "I'd inquire in Canada."

A cable from M'Intyre to Canadian police was answered with confirmation that the paper had been manufactured in the very town where Neill Cream had lived for years.

By now the doctor suspected something was amiss. Since he'd asked for protection against the "threatening gang," Cream had had M'Intyre as an almost constant companion and had come to suspect that the Scotland Yarder wasn't watching out for strange men but was keeping an eye on him. On several occasions he asked the detective if he was about to be arrested. The inspector assured him that he wasn't, but as the fidgety Cream continued to fret M'Intyre reversed himself and arrested him on a charge of sending threatening letters.

With the doctor safely in custody a search could be made for persons who might be able to connect Cream to the murdered women. When the investigation led M'Intyre to the mysterious death of Matilda Clover, he requested that the body he exhumed. The autopsy disclosed strychnine poisoning.

Investigation of Cream's lodgings turned up the small pill-box in which Cream carried his deadly capsules.

Finally, there was Louisa Harvey. "I know the prisoner," she declared at Bow Street Court as Cream gazed at her incredulously, "for he once gave me two long pills."

Next came a string of witnesses who had seen Cream with the other murdered women immediately before they died.

Who was this more subtle Jack the Ripper? In the light of research carried out a century later by the Behavioral Sciences Unit of the Federal Bureau of Investigation, he was typical of the "organized" serial killer. Cunning and arrogantly convinced that he would never be caught, he delighted in the sensations that his crimes created and relished taunting the police with letters and by brazenly calling attention to himself with the lie about being afraid for his life. Before most serial killers set out on the hunt for victims, the FBI study of the 1970s learned, they engage in other criminal acts and often have been convicted; in Cream's case it was arson, just as in the Son of Sam case. The object of the biggest manhunt in the history of the New York City police, David Berkowitz had also started as an arsonist. Others had a record of torturing and killing animals. Frequently games played as children were rehearsals for their adult crimes, as in the case of Edmund Kemper, who twisted heads of dolls as a boy and beheaded his victims as a man. A common trait of such killers is hatred of women; prostitutes are easy prey. Jack the Ripper had been such a man. So was Doctor Cream.

In the wake of his arrest for murder the full story of his life became known. Born in 1851 in Glasgow, Cream had emigrated with his family to Canada. After earning a medical degree from McGill University, he spent most of his career as an abortionist. As a result of a botched operation in Chicago he was convicted of murder in 1880 and served ten years in Illinois's Joliet Prison. Stripped of his license to practice medicine, he left prison and turned up in London and promptly set out on a mission to kill prostitutes.

Indicted for "willful murder of Alice Marsh, Ellen Donworth, Emma Shrivell, and Matilda Clover; also for sending to Joseph Harper a letter demanding money with menaces, without any reasonable or probable cause; for sending a similar letter to William Henry Broadbent; and for attempting to administer to Louisa Harris (Harvey) a large quantity of strychnine with attempt to murder her," he was tried only in the more-easily proved case of Matilda Clover.

The jury took ten minutes to convict.

A year and a day after killing Matilda he met the hangman. Manipulative to the end, as the trapdoor sprang open under him, he shouted, "I am Jack the. . . ."

On the basis of those last words some lists of suspects in the Jack the Ripper puzzle include Cream. But if he'd been in Joliet prison in 1888, how could he have slaughtered prostitutes in Whitechapel?

The obvious answer, say "Cream-Ripper" enthusiasts, is that he had a double. They went by the same name and provided alibis for one another.

When Cream paid for his crimes on November 15, 1892, it had been twenty-four years since Palmer's poisonings shocked Britain, twenty-one since Smethurst followed him to the dock at the Old Bailey, and seventeen since Pritchard had murdered his wife and mother-in-law.

Palmer killed for insurance money. Smethurst murdered for inheritance. Pritchard seems to have poisoned simply to prove that he could get away with it. And Cream poisoned prostitutes apparently for the fun of it.

Eighteen years would go by before another doctor killed, but this time it was for the love of a woman.

TWELVE

The Unsinkable
Inspector Dew

WHEN VICTORIA REGINA DIED ON JANUARY 22, 1901, THE sprawling Metropolis of London that decked itself in mourning crepe was the center of an empire on which the sun never set and had doubled in size since she ascended to the throne in 1837.

The city itself had grown. The population was now 1,635,270. The muddy streets of Victoria's coronation year were now paved and bustling with the commerce of a world in which Britain ruled the waves. Protecting the city from the splendid headquarters of New Scotland Yard were the descendants of the Bow Street Runners and the brave handful of Peelers—now nearly 16,000 strong. Since 1829 the Metropolitan Police had had successes and failures under six commissioners.

At the helm during Victoria's funeral and the coronation of her son Edward VII was Colonel Sir Edward Bradford. Appointed in 1890, he had presided as commissioner over a period of relative tranquillity within the police and in the body politic. In charge of the 800 men of the Criminal Investigation Department was Robert Anderson. But in this, his eleventh year, he announced that the time had come for "a more restful life."

His successor was Edward Henry. A professional policeman, Henry had served in South Africa and before that had been with the legendary police force of Bengal, India. The son of a London physician, Henry had gone to "the jewel in the crown" of the Empress Victoria at the age of twenty-three to enter the civil service. In 1891, at age forty-one, he was named inspector general of the Bengal police. Described as charming, intelligent, cultivated, and imaginative, he'd shown a talent for organization and a fascination with anything new in the area of criminology. Of special interest to him from the moment he took over was finding a dependable system of positive identification of criminals.

Pioneering work in that field had been done in France by Alphonse Bertillon of the Préfecture of Police. Commonly called the Sûreté, it was the first detective force in the world, dating back to Napoleon when it was used primarily for spying—precisely the sort of detective force that freedom-conscious English people had dreaded might be introduced in Britain. Revamped in 1810, the Sûreté had become a genuine police force. Its inspiration was the venerated Eugene François Vidocq, and his legacy was a vast archive of French criminality. Working as a clerk amidst those bulging dossiers, Bertillon had become obsessed with how to flawlessly identify criminals. He thought the answer was to classify an individual's unique physical traits by taking his anatomical measurements—ears, nose, head, hands, and other features. By combining these data with photographs of criminals, he believed, it was possible to create files that would make identification and apprehension of suspects easier. The forerunner of modern "Wanted" posters, mug shots, and other processes, the system was called anthropometry. French newspapers termed it *Bertillonage* and trumpeted its successes.

The acclaim attracted the attention of Edmund R. Spearman, who was associated with Britain's Home Office. Dissatisfied with Scotland Yard's system of keeping criminal records (primarily a list of names), he visited Paris to inspect Bertillon's system.

Another Englishman to call upon Bertillon with an interest in his process was Francis Galton, a geneticist and cousin of Charles Darwin, author of the sensational book on evolution, *The Origin of the Species*. While also working on anthropometry, Galton became intrigued by the work of an official in India by the name of William Herschel, who had noted that no two human handprints were the same and that the swirling lines on the tips of fingers could be used for infallible identification. It was called dactyloscopy.

Galton's contribution to the science of fingerprinting was historic. Through systematic study of individual patterns he saw that the odds against two people having the same prints were one in 64,000 *million*. He also proved that the patterns of a person's fingerprints remained unchanged from birth to death.

Spearman and Galton urged that both Bertillon's anthropometry and Galton's dactyloscopy be adopted and developed at Scotland Yard. But it took the advent of Henry as head of the CID to give the latter impetus. In landmark research of his own in India he'd provided the one thing Herschel and Galton had not come up with—a means of fingerprint classification. The findings were published in the book *Classification and Uses of Fingerprints*. Once installed at Scotland Yard he lost no time creating the Central Finger Print Bureau and personally trained the staff. Its first success with fingerprint evidence was in the conviction in 1902 of Harry Jackson, a burglar who left a perfect handprint in wet paint at the scene of the crime.

Hardly adjusted to running the detective branch, Henry found himself in the top job at New Scotland Yard. On March 4, 1903, less than two years after Commissioner Bradford appointed him to succeed Anderson, Bradford handed in his own retirement papers. The Home Secretary promptly shifted Henry to the commissioner's second-floor turret office, where one of his first steps was the merger of the old Register of Habitual Criminals and the new Finger Print Bureau to create the Criminal Records Office. From that moment on, fingerprinting was Scotland Yard's primary means of identifying criminals.

Within two years the value of fingerprints was demonstrated in two sensational cases. One was at the same time a triumph and a tragedy. The case was that of Adolph Beck, convicted of robbery in 1894 after more than a score of victims pointed him out as the thief. It was a case of mistaken identity. Unlike the Dr. Cream case, in which there'd been speculation that Cream had a double, there really was a man who was the spitting image of Beck. But it was twenty years before the look-alike was found and convicted of the crimes for which Beck had been sent to prison. Fingerprinting would have cleared him, but in 1894 it had not been used. Freed, Beck was given 5,000 pounds in compensation. As a result of the miscarriage of justice, for the first time in the legal history of Great Britain a court of appeals was created.

The second case to show the importance of fingerprinting as corroborative evidence occurred less than a year after Adolph

Beck was released. The crime was murder. The place was Deptford, a drab borough of southeastern London. The victims were a frail old woman who'd been found with her head bashed in and her husband, discovered beaten to death in his small, ransacked paint shop below his wife's bedroom. The motive was robbery.

Scotland Yard's first detective on the scene was Detective Chief Inspector Fox. He immediately summoned the new head of the CID, Melville Macnaghten. Short and fastidious and with a gentlemanly bearing, he was one of the old-timers at the Yard and had been in on the Ripper case, in which fingerprinting, had it been available, would have left no lingering doubts as to Saucy Jack's identity. A policeman with foresight, he had been an early enthusiast of Henry's fingerprint bureau. When Fox exclaimed that he had found an opened moneybox he and Macnaghten grasped the possibilities.

Determining that none of his men had touched the box, Macnaghten wrapped it in a cloth and sent it to the fingerprinting bureau. A clear thumbprint of a man was found.

Meanwhile, by dogged legwork and with a little eaves-dropping on local gossip, Fox settled on a pair of suspects. Locals with a reputation as good-for-nothings but who had never been arrested, they were Alfred and Albert Stratton. Soon, Fox unearthed reports of the brothers' activities on the night of the murders that lent credence to the likelihood of their guilt. Macnaghten had them brought in for fingerprinting. Comparison of the prints with the one on the box proved that it belonged to Alfred.

At the trial at the Old Bailey neither the judge nor the jury had ever heard of dactyloscopy but that didn't prevent them from accepting the evidence. The Strattons were convicted and sentenced to hang.

The lot of British criminals would never be the same. In the meantime, Henry's classification system swept the world, although by an odd twist of history and some image making on his own behalf, it was Alphonse Bertillon who garnered the lion's share of credit for introducing fingerprinting.

Another old-timer in Commissioner Henry's stable of sleuths was Walter Dew, famous at the Yard for his footrace with a thief whom residents of Whitechapel mistook to be Jack the Ripper and whom Dew wound up rescuing from certain lynching. Born at Far Cotton, Northampton, he was one of eleven children. A disinterested student who had left school at the age of thirteen, he remained at loose ends until he joined the Metropolitan Police at nineteen.

Assigned to the Paddington Green police station, he volunteered to track down a gang of sheep stealers in the Harrow and Sudbury areas, armed, as he recalled, "with small wooden truncheons as against the sharp butchers' knives which the raiders carried."

Courageous, diligent, and patient, Dew worked his way up the ranks and got his detective's badge, getting the nickname "Blue Serge" from his dapper style of dressing. Physically, he had exactly what a good plainclothesman required. Broad-shouldered, beetle-browed and with a shock of white hair, he had the looks of a quite ordinary man of middling years.

Coinciding with Dew's rise to detective ranks was the organization of a distinct squad to deal with murders. Formed in 1907 and empowered to investigate homicides throughout England and Wales, the unit was unofficially called the "Murder Squad." Its first chief was Superintendent Frank Froest. A keen-eyed detective, he had a reputation for tenacity and had won acclaim for his dogged pursuit of an infamous swindler, Jabez Balfour, arresting him in Argentina.

Among the first to be selected by Froest to serve with the squad, Dew was sent to Salisbury, Wiltshire, where a twelve-year-old, onelegged boy had been found dead in bed, his throat cut ear to ear. According to the local police, the motive for the murder appeared to be robbery. Half of the eight pounds that the boy managed to save in the hope of buying an artificial limb had been taken from the bedroom where the boy had been slain. The boy's mother, Mrs. Flora Haskell, reported having heard a noise and had been nearly knocked down by a man as he fled from the bedroom.

With the same dismay experienced by Jonathan Whicher when he learned that vital evidence had been destroyed in the Constance Kent case, Dew discovered upon his arrival at the scene of the crime that Mrs. Haskell had been allowed by the local chief constable to wipe away all traces of blood and to clean the house. The only remaining evidence was the murder weapon, a recently sharpened knife from Mrs. Haskell's kitchen.

Unable to locate witnesses who might have seen a man running from the house and perplexed as to why a murderer would take only half of the boy's money, Dew concluded that there was no intruder and that Mrs. Haskell had murdered her son.

Although a coroner's inquest returned a verdict of willful murder, allowing Dew to arrest the mother, some jurors at her trial were persuaded by her attorney, Rayner Goddard (later to become Lord Chief Justice of England), that the evidence was not conclusive beyond a reasonable doubt. Because of the deadlock, a second trial was held, ending in the woman's acquittal.

When Jack the Ripper had been out looking for whores Dew had been twenty-five years old. In 1910 he was forty-seven. Despite his elevation to the rank of chief inspector under the command of Melville Macnaghten, head of the CID, and Frank Froest of the Murder Squad, Dew remained at heart a beat man. The paperwork bored him. Being tied for hours on end to a desk at the Yard nettled. But it was there on March 31, 1910, that he was given the first thread in the case of a missing woman that became what Dew described in his memoirs as "the biggest murder mystery of the century."

The woman who stood before him was Mrs. Louise Smythson. She was, she said, a member of the Music Hall Ladies' Guild. Formed by women who'd enjoyed or were engaged in careers on the musical stage or were married to music hall performers, the guild took pride in looking after its own. Worry over a popular member of the guild had prompted Smythson to call upon Chief Inspector Dew. The woman she'd come to talk about was Belle Elmore, whose married name was Crippen.

Just what was there about Belle that had the ladies of the guild worried? asked Dew.

A report had been received that Belle had died somewhere in America, said Mrs. Smythson, but neither she nor other ladies of the guild who felt affection for Belle believed the story. They suspected foul play. Expressionless, Dew asked the detective's timeless question: why? The woman's answer was a bewildering list of circumstances. First, Belle had dropped out of sight without so much as a "fare thee well" to her friends of the guild. Her husband explained the sudden disappearance with a story of his wife going to America. Then

came the news that Belle had died but her husband's accounts
of the circumstances to various friends of his wife had been
filled with inconsistencies. To some he'd said that his wife
had died at sea. Others had been told that she had passed
away in California. Even more puzzling was the fact—and
it *was* a fact; someone had checked!—there was *no record*
of Belle having taken any ship from England to America.
And there was the relationship between Dr. Crippen and a
young woman by the name of Ethel LeNeve. Furthermore,
Dr. Crippen had attended the Criterion Ball with the LeNeve
woman *who was wearing Belle's jewelry.* "Am I overstepping
the law by conveying these suspicions to you?" asked Mrs.
Smythson.

"No," said Dew. But, he went on with a nod in the direction
of a stolid row of steel cabinets; the files were chock-full of
cases of "missing persons" that turned out to be nothing more
than the gossip of busybodies. Wives were known to leave
their husbands because they couldn't get divorces. Husbands
were known to associate with women who weren't their wives.
Some went so far as to give their girlfriends gifts. Such behavior was deplorable but it wasn't illegal, he said.

As for Dr. Crippen's accounts of his wife's death, wasn't
it possible that he was so stricken with grief that he was
confused?

Or, said Dew, "Maybe he doesn't believe in telling his
business to the world." Unless Smythson were prepared to
file a *charge*, there was nothing Scotland Yard could do.

Unwilling to take such a drastic step, Smythson left Dew's
office disappointed and embittered. She told friends: "I was
under the impression that Scotland Yard kept their eyes on
all suspicious persons!" But for the friends of Belle that was
not the end of it. On June 30, John and Lil Nash called at
the CID to describe their own concerns to a social friend,
Superintendent Froest.

With attentive blue eyes and stroking an elegantly waxed
mustache, he listened to their story. They had called on Dr.
Crippen to convey their condolences, they said, and had been
surprised to discover that he was vague about Belle's death in
California and could not produce the certificate of death that
he claimed to have. After they'd spelled out their suspicions,
Froest called in Inspector Dew and asked them to repeat their
story. Whether Dew recalled his meeting with Mrs. Smythson

isn't known; he didn't record it in his memoirs. Whether he remembered or not is immaterial. His boss wrote out an order: "Have the doctor seen and shaken up."

On July 8, accompanied by Detective Sergeant Arthur Mitchell, Dew went to Crippen's home at 39 Hilldrop Crescent, a tree-lined curving street in Holloway, North London. A modest middle-class dwelling, it had on the first floor a master bedroom, a smaller one which Belle used for storage of costumes, a bathroom and a lavatory. On the top floor were three small bedrooms. In the basement were the kitchen, a breakfast room, and a coal cellar. Above, on the ground floor were two parlors. The door of the front one was approached by ten steps, but as was the custom of the time visitors rarely entered through the front door. This parlor was reserved for "receiving." Casual guests and friends were admitted to the second parlor by the side door. As Dew and his companion knocked on it they could see that behind the house was a well-tended yard with a flower garden, a small greenhouse, and a freshwater aquarium, bounded by a low brick wall. After knocking on the door several times, Dew concluded that Crippen was not at home. He found him at his office in Albion House.

The first impression of Dr. Hawley Harvey Crippen was of a "little man." He wore gold-colored wire-rim eyeglasses. The gray eyes peering through them were strongly magnified, giving them a bulgy look. Light brown hair was brushed over a bald spot. His mustache was a straggly, sand-colored bow above a receding chin. In demeanor he appeared so calm that Dew suspected that Crippen expected sooner or later that a policeman would say, as Dew did on that Friday, "We have called to have a word with you about the death of your wife."

"I suppose I had better tell you the truth," said Crippen.

"That would be the best course," said Dew.

"The stories I have told about my wife's death are untrue. As far as I know she is still alive." To the best of his knowledge, he said, she'd gone to Chicago to live with her lover, an ex-prizefighter named Bruce Miller. All the stories about her going to America, dying at sea, dying in California—all of it had been lies intended to cover up the embarrassment and abject humiliation of a blind, foolish cuckolded husband. Worse, he said, his lies to Miss LeNeve had put her in the position of living with him as a wife.

Convinced, and so sympathetic to Crippen that he joined him in a hearty lunch at a nearby restaurant, Dew had him and LeNeve sign statements and then returned with them to Hilldrop Crescent, where he and the sergeant made a cursory inspection of the house from attic to cellar. He then assisted Crippen in drafting an advertisement to be published in a Chicago newspaper:

Will Belle Elmore communicate with H.H.C. or authorities at once. Serious trouble through your absence.
Twenty-five dollars reward to anyone communicating
her whereabouts to Box No.——.

"Of course I shall have to find Mrs. Crippen to clear this matter up," said Dew as he left the house.

"Yes, I will do everything I can," said Crippen. The words were another lie. The next day, Saturday, July 9, he was gone.

Again in the company of Detective Sergeant Mitchell, Dew returned to Hilldrop Crescent but this time they were joined by others—burly men with grim expressions on their faces and picks and shovels in their hands. "There was one place in the house which had a peculiar fascination for me," Dew recalled. "This was the coal cellar."

On Wednesday, July 13, he knelt in its black dust and began poking around the bricks of the floor. When one of them shifted he toiled away hopefully, all sense of fatigue vanishing in the excitement of hope. The brick came out. Others followed. Dashing out to the garden where others were digging, Sergeant Mitchell commandeered a shovel. The work was not easy. The ceiling was low. The light was dim. And beneath the bricks was a layer of hard clay. Five inches down, the shovel reached what Dew called the "nauseatingly unmis-takable" evidence.

Driven outside by the stench of rotting flesh, they gulped fresh air. "When we had sufficiently recovered," Dew recalled, "we resumed our task." Repeatedly overcome in the putrefied closeness of the cellar and needing fortifying sips of brandy, they continued digging, turning up a human torso wrapped in a man's pajama top. In an attempt to obscure the sex of the corpse the genitals had been obliterated. They found neither limbs nor a head. Most shocking of all, they discovered that the body had been skillfully stripped of bones.

Despite the genital mutilations, there was no question that the corpse was female. Buried along with the remains was a lime-encrusted woman's cotton undervest and a metal hair curler that provided important evidence that the woman in the makeshift grave was Mrs. Crippen. A stage performer, she was known to bleach her naturally dark tresses. Clinging to the curler was a tuft of straw-blonde hair with dark brown roots.

The cause of death was determined in an autopsy to have been poisoning by hyoscine hydrobromide. As nearly as could be determined, she'd been murdered around the time in early February when her neighbors and friends were informed by Dr. Crippen that his wife had gone for a visit to America and would be returning in a few months.

Presently, Chief Inspector Walter Dew was able to report to Froest and Macnaghten with certainty that she had met her death on Monday night, January 31. He based this deduction on the singular change in the habits of the Crippens. For as long as anyone could remember, they had played whist on Sunday nights with Belle's friends, the famed mime artist Paul Martinelli and his wife Clara and another theatrical couple, Mr. and Mrs. John Nash. She was Lil Hawthorne of the Hawthorne Sisters and he was her manager. These get-togethers were held on Sunday evenings because that was the only night on which most entertainers didn't have to work. For a reason never explained Crippen had insisted that they come for cards and dinner not on Sunday, January 30, but the next night. It was the last time Belle's friends and neighbors saw her.

Further indication that she had been disposed of on the 31st was Crippen's dropping in on a newsagent a day or two later to cancel her standing order for the theatrical publications, *The Stage* and Era.

What was Crippen's motive for killing his wife? asked Dew's boss. Brushing his wedgelike black mustache, Dew smiled. "Ah yes," said Macnaghten. "The other woman. Ethel Clara LeNeve."

By now, Dew had learned all about Crippen. It was an old and familiar tale—middle-aged married man falls for vivacious young woman. But in many other ways the saga of "the little man" Dr. Hawley Harvey Crippen was unique. Born in Michigan in 1862, he based his claim to the appellation "Doctor" on an 1883 diploma as an eye and ear specialist at the Ophthalmic Hospital in New York City. For the next fifteen years he never practiced for more than two years in any one place. In 1887 he married and had a son but the wife died a few years later. The period of mourning was brief. In 1893 he married seventeen-year-old Cora Mackamotzky, who preferred to call herself by the simpler name of Cora Turner. A buxom girl of moderate beauty, she had a theatrical bent and, presently, was calling herself Belle Elmore.

When her husband's medical business, which by now could be rightly called quackery, took them to London, Belle planned on taking West End theaters by storm but in her only appearance she was hissed off the stage. Thereafter, her only connection to the glamor of show business was vicarious: membership in the Music Hall Ladies Guild.

At 39 Hilldrop Crescent, Belle was, by all accounts of her neighbors, a shrew. She was also an adulteress who struck up a romance with a former prizefighter, the same one whom Crippen had claimed she'd run off to join in Chicago. Given such a cold home life, it was not surprising that Crippen sought solace elsewhere. Enter Miss LeNeve, a typist in Dr. Crippen's Albion House office.

Then it was a short step to murder by hyoscine hydrobromide and a shallow grave for Belle in the coal cellar.

"If his nerves had remained unshaken," mused Macnaghten, "and he had had the courage to take a long lease on the house which held his guilty secret. . . ."

"Yes," said Dew, "he might have gotten away with the perfect murder."

But he didn't. He panicked. The question now was: where was he? All of Britain demanded an answer.

While Dew conferred with Macnaghten and Froest, all the resources of New Scotland Yard were directed to finding the fugitive. Thousands of circulars and "Wanted" posters papered King Edward VII's realm. At every railway station constables carried descriptions of Crippen and LeNeve. Newspapers blared the gory details of the "North London Cellar Murder" along with portraits of the wanted man and his paramour. Police departments on the continent and in America were alerted. Samples of the handwriting of Crippen and LeNeve were provided to hotels, banks, and post offices. Descriptions of Belle's missing jewelry were widely distributed. The seaports were placed under close watch from Bristol to Liverpool.

But even as all this was going on Inspector Dew was painfully aware that between his talk with Crippen on July 8 and the unearthing of Belle's body five days later his quarry had had plenty of time to make good his escape. Was he not a consummate liar? Was he not the sort of nondescript "little man" to whom no one would give a second look? And . . . hadn't he pulled the wool over the eyes of one of Scotland Yard's best detectives?

Ruminating on the case in his office, Dew peered through a window at summertime London. Mid-July. Everywhere, those who had the luxury of time and the liberating jingle of money in their pocket were seeking escape—not from brutal murder but from the stifling heat—by flocking to seaside resorts. Holiday season!

In the midst of such happy crowds a "little man" could be lost, and that is what had happened to Crippen. Hurriedly leaving London the day after his unsettling conversation with Dew, he traveled north with vacationers to Harwich and across the Channel to Belgium. At the moment he was not a wanted man. But for how long? A day? A week? At what moment would Inspector Dew decide that it was time for another chat with Dr. Crippen and thereby discover that he'd gone? How soon would Dew find Belle in the basement? When might Hawley Harvey Crippen pick up a newspaper and see his name in the headlines? *And* his face?

The eyeglasses had to go, of course. And the mustache. So must Ethel's luxurious hair. Furthermore, he reasoned, if police might soon be searching for a middle-aged man in the company of a woman who was young enough to be his daughter, did it not make sense for Ethel to disappear? But how could he leave her? He loved her! He'd *killed* for her! No. They would make a run for it together, but not as wife-killing lover and paramour. They would make their escape to an enveloping anonymity in Canada. And they would do so posing as . . . father and son!

A gallant girl (or was she a trapped one?), Ethel endured his hacking off her hair without a murmur and then sat still for the trimming-up of Crippen's ragged handiwork by a professional barber in Antwerp. Regarding the result, they stared blankly at one another for a moment, then broke into laughter. Neither did she demur at having to wear tight, uncomfortable, and unflattering boys' clothing that he acquired for her. He also came up with an identity for them—John Philo Robinson and his sixteen-year-old son. Mr. Robinson was a merchant. Master Robinson was a sickly lad who suffered from deafness and never spoke.

The masquerade did not fool the Brussels proprietor of the Hotel des Ardennes for a minute. The worldly Monsieur DeLisse took one look at the son's feminine walk and knew a homosexual when he saw one! Madame DeLisse envisioned a different story. The "boy" was a convent girl who'd fallen in love with her professor and now they were eloping to Canada. It had to be Canada, she thought, because the gentleman never stopped talking about the delights of Old Quebec.

To reach his dream destination Crippen booked passage on a Red Star liner scheduled to sail for Montreal on July 31. That meant they would have to wait in Brussels for three weeks. For Ethel, the city was idyllic. She delighted in sightseeing and especially enjoyed viewing the famous statue Mannikin Pis and was amused by her companion's description of how during "rag week" the city's children dressed up the famous urinating urchin like a Garde Civique and paraded him around. They picnicked in the Bois de Cambre where bands played. To her it all seemed very beautiful and peaceful.

Suddenly, this Garden of Eden took on ominous overtones. On July 15, Crippen picked up a copy of the newspaper *L'lndependence Belge* and stared at the headline: "Actrice Assassine." Had not the news been so alarming, Crippen might have found the newspaper's generous depiction of Belle as an actress amusing. But the cat was out of the bag. He was wanted for murder. Travel plans would have to be changed immediately. Luckily, the Canadian Pacific Line's passenger-carrying cargo ship *Montrose* was sailing on July 20 from Antwerp, its destination Quebec, its scheduled date of arrival July 31. It was an inferior ship but considering the urgency of the circumstances he had no choice but to arrange two passages. He gave the travelers' names as Mr. Robinson and son.

Refitted by converting cold-storage holds into dormitories for the purpose of transporting troops to South Africa during the Boer War, the 5400-ton *Montrose* was transformed again after the war into a "steerage" ship to convey emigres to the promises of the New World. As she departed Antwerp there was room for 280 such dreamers and 20 voyagers in second-class cabins. To Dr. Crippen's dismay, there were no first-class accommodations.

The skipper was a remarkable old salt who'd gone to sea as a boy. Since then Henry Kendall had seen much of the world and all kinds of passengers, and he considered himself to be a shrewd judge of character. Before being given the helm of *Montrose* he'd been chief officer of the *Empress of India*, a passenger ship that was a favorite hunting ground for cardsharps. With an unerring eye he'd spotted the "bounders," as he termed them, at a rate of at least one per voyage. An avid reader of detective novels and a follower of crime in newspapers, he knew of the North London Cellar Murder and had brought along several newspapers containing accounts of the horrible crime.

Among the second-class passengers coming aboard at Antwerp, two stood out. The first thing to strike the captain as odd was their luggage. They had only one small valise between them. Then there was their clothing. The father came aboard wearing a gray frock coat and trousers and a white hat, hardly the attire for a crossing. As to the boy, his outfit was ill fitting, he had no overcoat, and his hat didn't look right, either. And what about their faces? The captain put great store in what a person's face revealed. Seated with the Robinsons for lunch, he studied them and found Mr. Robinson's interesting on two points: He was in the process of growing a beard, which struck Kendall as peculiar for a man of Robinson's maturity, and there was an indentation on each side of the bridge of his nose that indicated he'd worn glasses for many years. But even more unusual was Master Robinson's face. It was decidedly feminine. Lunch with them was notable for two other peculiarities: The father hardly stopped talking; when the son spoke, which wasn't often, the voice was high pitched.

By now, Captain Kendall's appetite for a bit of detective work was far greater than his desire for lunch. Excusing himself, he left the dining salon to have a look at the Robinsons' cabin. Because the pair had only the one piece of luggage, there wasn't much to examine. However, their hats were there. Both seemed to be new. Mr. Robinson's had the name of a Brussels hatter stamped on the inner band. The boy's band was stuffed with tissue paper.

Retiring to his quarters, Kendall assembled his newspapers and dug out the July 14 edition of London's *Daily Mirror*. The paper had had a scoop that day. One of its photographers, name of Parker, realizing that a woman who lived upstairs from him was a cousin of Ethel LeNeve, had purloined a photo of Ethel from the cousin's apartment.

Bending over the portraits of the suspects in the London Cellar Murder, Captain Kendall discerned in Crippen's picture a likeness to passenger J. P. Robinson. Of course, Crippen had a mustache and eyeglasses. Fishing in his desk drawer, the captain found a chunk of white chalk and, with the deftness of a Sherlock Holmes, applied the chalk to Crippen's glasses, then to his mustache. It was Robinson!

With mounting excitement Kendall turned to the photo of LeNeve. Laying aside the chalk, he took up a pair of calipers and measured the woman's face. After transferring the data to a piece of cardboard and cutting around the lines, he fitted the cutout over the photo of LeNeve. The features were those of Robinson's "son."

As a "student" of crime and a lifelong sailor, Kendall was keenly aware of the Müller railway murder case in 1864 and the ensuing dramatic transatlantic pursuit of the killer by Detective Dick Tanner. In the intervening four decades the slow-going sailing ships of a past age had given way to fast steamers and, more important, wireless telegraphy had arrived. The lack of ship-to-shore radio had been a plus for Müller; Tanner had no way of informing the captain of Müller's ship that he had a murderer aboard. In Dew's manhunt for Crippen, radio was about to become an advantage. Over *Montrose's* wireless Kendall sent the following to his shipping firm's office in Liverpool:

HAVE STRONG SUSPICIONS THAT CRIPPEN LON-DON CELLAR MURDERER AND ACCOMPLICE ARE AMONG SALOON PASSENGERS. MOUSTACHE TAKEN OFF, GROWING BEARD. ACCOMPLICE DRESSED A BOY. VOICE MANNER AND BUILD UNDOUBTEDLY A GIRL. BOTH TRAVELLING AS MR AND MASTER ROBINSON. [Signed] KENDALL.

Since Dick Tanner's day there'd been another invention: the telephone. Melville Macnaghten's rang as he dressed for dinner on Friday, July 22. On the line from Scotland Yard was an apologetic Inspector Dew. Speaking calmly and deliberately, he expressed regret at having disturbed his boss at home and then informed him that he'd just received a Marconigram from the Liverpool police concerning Crippen.

"Read it to me," said Macnaghten. Dew did so. "Better come over for a chat," said the head of the CID.

Upon Dew's arrival with the message from Captain Kendall via the shipping line via the Liverpool police, Macnaghten greeted Dew with a worried expression and questions. Suppose Kendall were wrong? Remember Adolph Beck? What if this were another case of mistaken identity? "If so, this case will be hopelessly messed up," he said. "I don't care to dwell on the eventualities."

"I feel confident it's them," answered Dew.

Macnaghten read the wire again. "So do I," he said. "What do you suggest?"

Before leaving the Yard, Dew had done some fast checking. "The White Star liner *Laurentic* sails from Liverpool tomorrow. I believe it is possible for her to overtake the *Montrose* and reach Canada first."

With a smile Macnaghten sat at his desk and began writing. "Here's your authority," he said, handing Dew a sheet of paper. "I wish you all the luck in the world."

The *Laurentic*'s running time was seven days. Kendall's ship would need eleven. But *Montrose* had a three-day headstart. With the luck Macnaghten had wished Dew would set foot in Quebec with one day to spare. On the 27th, *Laurentic* passed *Montrose* in mid-ocean. Dew radio'd Kendall: "Will board you Father Point. Please keep any information till I arrive there strictly confidential."

Kendall shot back: "What the devil do you think I have been doing?"

It was true that Kendall had given Crippen not a clue that he'd been spotted, but he and the other passengers were the only people in the world who didn't know. Kendall's wireless updates on the doings aboard his ship, picked up by newspapers on both sides of the Atlantic, were vivid reading. J. B. Priestly described it: "The people, who have a sure instinct in these matters, knew they had seats in a gallery five hundred miles long for a new, exciting, entirely original drama: *Trapped by Wireless!*"

The end of the drama was written by Dew. He boarded *Montrose* early on the morning of Sunday, July 31. Suitably nautical in a blue pea jacket and accompanied by similarly disguised Canadian police, he was directed by Captain Kendall to a little man in a gray coat with a fresh beard and bulgy eyes. Quietly, Dew said, "Good morning, Dr. Crippen."

THIRTEEN

Crime Doctor

THE CREATOR OF PHILIP MARLOWE, ONE OF CRIME FIC-
tion's most popular private detectives, was puzzled by
Dr. Crippen's crime. "Here was a man who apparently had
the means and opportunity and even the temperament for
the perfect crime, and he made all sorts of mistakes," he
said in *Raymond Chandler Speaking*, published in 1962. "I
cannot see why a man who would go to the enormous labor
of de-boning and de-sexing and de-heading an entire corpse
would not take the rather slight extra labor of disposing of
the flesh the same way, rather than bury it at all."

Raymond Chandler was right. It *was* a terrible blunder,
for a tiny portion of the remains of Belle Elmore which
Inspector Dew dug from the clay beneath the brick floor at
39 Hilldrop Crescent became the central piece of evidence
in Crippen's trial. A patch of horseshoe-shaped skin from
her abdomen, it was lifted with a pair of pincers from a
jar of formalin and passed to the jury on a soup plate by
prosecution witness Dr. Augustus J. Pepper. If it could be
shown that it had come from Belle's corpse the Crown's
case against Crippen was secure.

Like the establishment of a truly professional police force
in Britain, forensic pathology had had a long and bumpy
road to acceptance, but by the turn of the twentieth century
the Home Office had recognized that in the investigation
of murders Scotland Yard detectives needed to call upon
surgeons who were skillful in the autopsies of people who'd
met sudden, violent deaths. In 1908 when Augustus Pepper
was named Home Office Pathologist he handed over his

post as Senior Pathologist at St. Mary's Hospital to his best student, Bernard Spilsbury.

If nothing else had occurred in the Crippen case, had there been no theatrical overtones, no first-time use of wireless radio in a murder investigation, no Captain Kendall, no transvestite Ethel LeNeve, no meek and mild-looking suspected wife killer, the Crippen trial would have become a landmark on the geography of crime solely because it was Dr. Spilsbury's first appearance in a murder case.

An earnest-looking thirty-three-year-old who'd spent many years in the pathology lab of St. Mary's to become knowledgeable on scar tissue, he testified that the scarred skin found in the cellar of Crippen's house was consistent with the hysterectomy which Belle was known to have had. Confidently and with gentle patience and the use of slides and a microscope, he gave jurors, the judge, and courtroom spectators that included Sir Arthur Conan Doyle, the actress Phyliss Dare, and actor-managers Sir Herbert Beerbohm Tree and Sir John Hare and W. S. Gilbert of Gilbert and Sullivan a crash course in forensic science in general and the recognition of scar tissue in particular.

The case went to the jury on October 22. They were out less than half an hour. Their verdict: guilty.

Insisting to the end that Ethel had had nothing to do with the murder, the "little man" Hawley Harvey Crippen went to the gallows on November 23. "Dr. Crippen's love for the girl, for whom he had risked so much, was the biggest thing in his life," wrote Dew in his book about the case. "He never seemed to care so much what happened to himself, so long as her innocence was established."

Tried as an accessory after the fact, LeNeve was acquitted and released. She boarded the liner *Majestic* for New York on the day that Crippen was hanged.

Eighteen days before Crippen met the hangman at Pentonville Prison, forty-seven-year-old Inspector Dew took early retirement with a comfortable pension from Scotland Yard to write a memoir of "the biggest murder mystery of the century" and then settled down to tending his garden at his home in Worthing, where he died on December 16, 1947, at the age of eighty-four.

Captain Kendall collected a reward of 250 pounds. Four years later, at the exact spot where Dew boarded the

Montrose to arrest Crippen off the Canadian coast, he was skipper of another ocean liner that sank, taking more than a thousand passengers to the bottom. Rescued, the sleuthing skipper lived another fifty years, dying in 1965 in a London nursing home at the age of ninety-one.

Stage fame that had eluded Mrs. Crippen as Belle Elmore came to her in death. There was a play, *Trapped by Wireless*; a 1944 movie, *The Suspect*, starring Charles Laughton as Crippen; and in 1961 at the Strand Theatre in London a musical with tunes by Wolf Mankowitz and lyrics by Monty Norman called *Belle or the Ballad of Doctor Crippen*, which proclaimed:

> You can't beat a British crime,
> The hunt and the trial,
> And the hanging all in style
> Is better than a pantomime.

The case also inspired Alfred Hitchcock to produce a film about a Crippen-like wife killer, *Rear Window*, in which Hitchcock dealt with the recurring dilemma of the murderer who dismembers the corpse: what to do about the head? Belle's was never found. Recalling that about a week after the murder Dr. Crippen took the night boat across the Channel to Dieppe, Sir Melville Macnaghten wondered, "Did he drop a dirty clothes bag (or something of the sort) over the side?"

Having Belle's head would have made prosecution of Crippen easier, of course, but Dr. Spilsbury demonstrated that there are other ways to identify a headless and fingerless body. And in so doing he raised the curtain on a new act in the drama of British crime, in which Scotland Yard detectives would have to share the billing with the forensic pathologist. For the better part of the next three decades that co-star was to be Bernard Spilsbury.

Although he was the son of a chemist, he'd shown no real passion for science and seemed to drift into studying medicine. But in taking A. J. Pepper's classes in pathology he discovered his calling. Diligent, observant, and tenacious in the lonely and grim work of the autopsy rooms at St. Mary's Hospital, he became just the expert who was required in the Crippen case, but he brought into the Old Bailey courtroom a quality that went far beyond his command of his subject. Described by crime historian Jürgen Thorwald in *The Century of the Detective* as good-looking, carefully dressed, a carnation in his buttonhole, his voice clear and resonant, he was "a man who combined great talent as a pathologist with a high degree of expressiveness and the appearance and poise of a gentleman."

None of those qualities were evident in the central figure of the next sensational murder case to challenge Scotland Yard and the Home Office's brilliant forensic pathologist. In 1911 Frederick Henry Seddon was forty years old, small in stature, almost bald, and an all-around cold fish. For twenty years he'd been a district inspector for the London & Manchester Industrial Insurance Company. On an annual salary of 400 pounds he supported himself, a wife, and five children in a house which he owned at 63 Tollington Park.

Into the third floor of the dwelling in the summer of 1910 moved forty-eight-year-old Eliza Barrow, a heavyset widow with considerable wealth consisting of a large bank account, lots of jewelry, securities, and a house that was occupied by her cousins, the Vonderahes. Suspecting them of having designs on her wealth, Eliza, accompanied by a nine-year-old nephew, chose to board with the Seddons. She did so in apparent contentment until August of the next year, when she suffered what a physician diagnosed as "epidemic diarrhea." Intrinsically tight with her money, she refused to be admitted to a hospital. Twelve days later she was dead. Without examining the deceased, the doctor certified his previous diagnosis as the cause of death.

Learning of the demise of their rich cousin, the Vonderahe family promptly inquired into what they expected to be a handsome inheritance. Calling at the Seddon residence, Mr. Vonderahe was informed by the neighbors that the family had gone to the seashore on holiday. When he called again on October 9, he was stunned to learn there was no inheritance. But what about Eliza's property? Bank accounts? The securities? Jewels? Seddon's explanation was even more startling. He produced documents signed by Eliza which had turned over everything to him in return for his guaranteeing a weekly payment to her for the rest of her life. He then showed Vonderahe a record of having carried

out his part of the deal. Finally, he gave Vonderahe a bill
for one pound. As Eliza had had only ten pounds at the
time of her death, he explained, and as Seddon had spent
eleven pounds in caring for her young nephew, Vonderahe
actually owed *him*!

The next day the irate and suspicious Vonderahe stormed
into Scotland Yard demanding an investigation. Assigned to
look into the matter was Chief Inspector Alfred Ward and
two detective sergeants, Cooper and Hayman. Delving into
the most likely suspect, Seddon, they picked up unsettling
facts about the insurance man. Chief among them was his
reputation for avarice. But was this unpleasant, greedy little
man a murderer? To answer that question it first had to
be determined that Eliza Barrow met an untimely and
unnatural death.

Authorized by the Home Office to exhume the body,
Spilsbury went to work. His verdict was unequivocal. The
woman had not died from epidemic diarrhea. Nor from any
other natural cause. She'd been poisoned, probably with
arsenic. Self-admittedly not expert in poisons, he turned to
someone who was a recognized authority, Dr. William Henry
Willcox, who had been deeply involved in the Crippen case
by identifying the fatal dose of hyoscine in Mrs. Crippen's
organs. After conducting hundreds of tests on the remains
of Eliza Barrow and a series of complex calculations of
the weight of the remains, he became convinced that her
body contained sufficient quantities of arsenic to warrant
a charge of murder by arsenic poisoning.

On December 4, 1911, Chief Inspector Ward greeted
Seddon in front of his home and charged him with murder
and his wife with complicity. The case came to trial at the
Old Bailey three months later. In what has been described
as one of the fiercest battles over forensic toxicology ever to
have been fought in a London courtroom, Willcox engaged
in a three-day match of expertise and scientific wits with
Seddon's attorney, Edward Marshall Hall, himself an expert
on arsenic.

The crux of their duel was the arsenic content of Eliza's
hair. Willcox contended that she'd been given a huge dose
of the poison two weeks before her death. But Hall forced
him to admit that because of the known absorption rate
of arsenic, such an amount had to have been taken into

the body over a year's time for it to have penetrated to the very tips of her hair, as Willcox claimed. Hall also elicited the fact that it was routine procedure to wash the hair of a suspected arsenic victim to be sure that the poison had not been picked up from outside, from cemetery soil, for instance. Had Willcox washed Eliza's hair? Willcox admitted he had. Where did the arsenic come from? Clearly, not from any that was administered only two weeks before her death?

Staggered by Hall's point, Willcox struggled for an explanation. He'd found the hair laced with arsenic. Of that there was no question. But if it hadn't been absorbed by the natural body processes, where did it come from? Searching his mind for an answer as he stood in the witness box, he went back over all that had happened: the exhumation, Spilsbury's autopsy determining that death hadn't been natural, his own autopsy searching for arsenic. Vaguely, a possible answer took shape in his mind. "There is one point which I have not mentioned, which I ought to mention here, which rather affects these results," he said to Hall, "and that is that when I took the hair for analysis it was at the *second* examination, and the hair had been lying in the coffin, and it was more or less soaked in the juice of the body."

The implication was that if the hair had absorbed arsenic from an outside source, namely the body fluids in the coffin, there had to have been arsenic in the body's tissues.

With Hall's dismissal of his answer as unconvincing and an excuse made up after the fact ringing in his ears, Willcox rushed back to his laboratory. Taking a strand of hair from a corpse he knew to be uncontaminated with arsenic, he placed it in a pool of body fluids from Eliza's coffin. Checking it four days later, he found that it had absorbed a great deal of the poison. Recalled to the stand by the prosecution, he reported on the experiment.

Two days later the jury found Seddon guilty of murdering Eliza but acquitted his wife. He was hanged on April 18, 1912, at Pentonville Prison, but not before being informed that Eliza's properties had been disposed of for a small fraction of what he had thought they were worth. "Well," he cried, "that finishes it!"

In a catalog of motives for murder the homicides which had catapulted Bernard Spilsbury's macabre profession into the limelight—Seddon's lust for riches and Crippen's love for a younger woman—were hardly original. Greed and sex were passions as old as mankind, as were all the other reasons for killing, and they continued to be. Such deeds might be unforgivable. But they were understandable. The brutal death that brought the body of little Willie Starchfield into Spilsbury's mortuary on January 8, 1914, was not.

The curly-haired boy was, he judged, about five years old. He'd been strangled somewhere between two and three o'clock that afternoon. After examining the contents of the boy's stomach, Spilsbury could say with certainty that around that same time he'd eaten a piece of currant cake. Beyond this scant information Spilsbury could give Chief Inspector William Gough no leads.

The boy's body had been discovered on a North London railway train when it stopped at Mildmay Park on route from Chalk Farm and Camden Town stations. A sixteen-year-old cabinet maker's apprentice named George Tillman had seated himself in an empty compartment and was bending down to tie his boot lace when he saw something under the opposite seat. Getting down to have a look as the train pulled out, he discovered a child's body. Tillman noted the time: 4:32 P.M. Spilsbury's assessment of the time of death as two to two-and-a-half hours before that was a good beginning. It permitted Gough to do some arithmetic and time-table checking, and conclude that the child had been killed on the train around the hour when it began its journey into the reaches of North London and that the body had been carried back and forth between the stations until it was found.

Reports in the newspapers of the shocking murder of a child, Gough hoped, would result in an identification. The fulfillment of that hope wasn't long in coming. Red-eyed and shaking with dread, Mrs. Agnes Starchfield of 191 Hampstead Road, Camden, reported that her son Willie was missing. An out-of-work tailoress, she'd left the child in the care of her landlady, Mrs. Emily Longstaff, while she went out job hunting. Around half-past twelve, she told Gough, Mrs. Longstaff sent Willie on an errand to the stationer's shop just down the road. He hadn't been seen since. They'd both gone out looking for him around three o'clock and had searched all over for him. Even before she positively identified the body, Gough was certain that the boy in Shoreditch morgue was Willie.

Because the train on which he'd been found stopped at Camden Town Station, Gough hoped that someone along the route might have seen the boy and whoever was with him either boarding the train or on it. Perhaps someone who worked for the North London Railway had noticed him. Luckily, that's just what had occurred. At about 2:07 when the train passed the St. Pancras signal box, recalled signalman George Robert Jackson, he'd observed a man with a dark mustache and a dark coat bending over someone who had fair, curly hair. "I thought it was a girl," he said.

There was more. Another signalman, Joseph Rodgers, had found a length of cord along the tracks near Broad Street Station. Was it of a type that could have strangled Willie? Spilsbury said it could be.

Another witness was located. A commercial traveler, Richard White had been at Camden Town Station just before two o'clock on the day of the murder and had seen an "Italian looking" man in the company of a small boy in the ticketing office.

Meanwhile, newspaper stories of the murder of a child—and the description of the tragic lad—struck into Mrs. Clara Wood's kind and maternal heart like a knife. She had seen just such a winning child on the very day that the poor little boy had been murdered. She'd been doing a bit of shopping in the Kentish Town Road when she'd seen such an adorable sight that she'd exclaimed, "Oh, bless it!" Near the corner of Angler's Lane, she volunteered to the police, she'd watched a young boy munching cake that a man had bought for him. Would it help if the police were to have the very kind of treat she'd seen the lad enjoying? If so, she had an entire cake just like it. She'd bought it, she said, in the event the police might find it helpful. It was currant cake and, yes, said Dr. Spilsbury, it could be of the kind Willie had eaten.

What about this man she'd seen with the boy? Could Mrs. Wood describe him? Of course! He was swarthy,

Italian looking. Thick, brown, curly hair. If she saw him again, could she identify him? Oh, yes. Absolutely!

"Perhaps you will have the opportunity," said Gough.

It was not idle speculation. He knew such a man—the boy's father. Separated from his wife, he'd been in prison twice for not supporting her and their child from his earnings as a newspaper hawker on the corner of Oxford Street and Tottenham Court Road. To ensure the wife's support a court had ordered direct payment to her of an award of one pound a week that John Starchfield had been given in recognition of his capture of a gunman who'd run amok in the bar of the Horseshoe Hotel in 1912. In bringing down the gunman Starchfield had been nearly killed by a bullet to his stomach.

Gough had questioned Starchfield at midnight on the day of his son's death and he'd seemed shockingly unmoved. But he said he had not been anywhere near Camden Town that day. He said he'd been asleep all day in his lodging house and that another lodger could attest to it.

Gough didn't believe a word of it then, and was confirmed in that view by the accounts of the man seen with Willie that had been given to him by Mrs. Wood, the signalman, and Richard White. They fit Starchfield to a T.

The clincher came at the coroner's inquest. With Starchfield present, Mrs. Wood was asked if she'd again seen the man she'd noticed buying cake for a young boy. "Yes," he said, pointing out Starchfield. "There!"

Asked if he could identify the man he'd seen in the railway station, Richard White pointed to Starchfield and declared, "That is the man."

"It's a damned lie," roared Starchfield.

Gough's victory proved short-lived. At Starchfield's trial, held on March 31, the judge decreed that without corroborating evidence there was insufficient evidence to convict Starchfield. Furthermore, ruled the judge, the coroner who handled the case had so thoroughly botched the process of gathering statements from witnesses that they were useless as reliable testimony. Starchfield was released.

Gough was sure of his case and of what had happened on that train. It didn't start out to be a murder, he believed. The boy's father intended only to abduct his son as a way of getting back at his wife. As Gough saw the events that followed: "They enter the train at Chalk Farm at 1:59 and then Starchfield makes the suggestion that the child should leave his mother and come to live with him. The child refuses and holds out against all his father's pleadings. Losing his temper, Starchfield strikes the child and then, becoming alarmed at his cries, puts the piece of cord he used to tie up his newspapers around the boy's throat to try to quieten him. The child struggles, the cord tightens."

It was reasonable to assume, Gough explained, "that the man threw the cord out of the window, hid the body under the seat, and left the train at the earliest possible moment."

Starchfield insisted that Willie had been taken and killed by vindictive friends of the man he'd so heroically captured.

To the cheers of sympathetic supporters who refused to accept the idea that a certified hero murdered his own son, Starchfield walked out of the court a free man. But his victory was also to be brief. He died two years later from the effects of the old gunshot wound.

The route of the railway on which Willie Starchfield came to his death had contributed to a transformation of the geography north of London from pastoral getaways of eighteenth-century city dwellers to a sooty, crowded district of working-class homes for those who toiled in the interests of commerce that moved upon the railways, the Regent's Canal and the roadways named for their destinations: Camden Town, Caledonian, Barnsbury, Highbury, Islington, and the thoroughfare where Mrs. Wood was charmed by a little boy munching currant cake, the Kentish Town Road.

While Chief Inspector Gough was investigating Willie's death, Detective Inspector Arthur Fowler Neil leafed through the latest bulletins forwarded to all police districts from headquarters at Scotland Yard. Stationed in Kentish Town, Neil was an unsmiling man whose roundshouldered, slouching posture had earned him the nickname "Drooper Neil."

Among the notices sent by Superintendent John McCarthy was a file labeled "Suspicious Deaths." A batch of newspaper clippings, the file related to a bride of one day who had been found dead in her bathtub that past December. The victim was listed as Margaret Elizabeth Lloyd of Highgate, part of Neil's district.

It was a tragedy, of course, but why, Neil wondered, was a death the local coroner had attributed to accidental drowning brought on by a case of pneumonia, which combined with the shock of a hot bath to cause "an attack of syncope," listed as "suspicious?"

The next news item in the file provided Neil an intriguing answer. Dated a year and a day earlier, the clipping reported: "Bride's sudden death. Drowned After Seizure in Hot Bath. Mrs. George Smith, of 80 Kimberley Road, Portsmouth, who was married only six weeks ago, died suddenly in a Blackpool boarding house." The coroner's verdict was that the heat of Mrs. Smith's bathwater had shocked the woman's enlarged heart, causing either a fit or a faint and then drowning. This event, which was remarkably similar to the death of Mrs. Lloyd, had occurred in a hotel in the Irish sea city of Blackpool, well beyond Inspector Neil's jurisdiction. But the coincidence was so striking to Mrs. Smith's death that he left for nearby Highgate the next day.

The landlady of the boarding house at 14 Bismarck Road was Mrs. Blatch. Understandably puzzled why a detective from Scotland Yard had come about an obvious accident, the lady was nonetheless cooperative in recalling the incident. A bedroom and bath, with living room privileges, was booked by Mr. Lloyd on the seventeenth of December, she said. He was medium-sized, athletic-looking, and had keen eyes. He was a very particular man, she recalled, who insisted on inspecting the room *and* the bath before he signed the register. That evening he inquired about a doctor, explaining that his wife was not feeling well. The next day Mrs. Lloyd felt much better, continued Mrs. Blatch, and before going for a walk with her husband, had asked Mrs. Blatch to draw a hot bath for her while they were out. Mr. Lloyd went out again later to buy some tomatoes for supper but forgot his key and had to ring to be let in. At that time he'd asked if his wife had come down. Told that she hadn't, he dashed upstairs and found that she'd drowned in the bathtub.

Did Mrs. Blatch know where Mr. Lloyd could be reached? No. He'd stayed to arrange the funeral, she said, and then moved out without leaving a forwarding address.

"May I see the bathtub?" asked Neil. Made of iron, it was fifty inches long at the bottom. The top rim was sixty-six. How a woman could drown in it was hard to grasp. Yet the doctor who'd conducted the autopsy told Neil he'd found no signs of violence and every sign of drowning. In fact, said the doctor, there were only two points in the entire affair that had seemed odd: the widower had exhibited no grief and he had bought a cheap coffin.

As Neil left the doctor's office he was hailed by a local detective. "My name's Dennison," he said "I heard that you were looking into the death of Mrs. Lloyd. There's something you ought to know about what happened at another boarding house. The woman who runs it told me that Mr. Lloyd inquired about renting a room from her. But when he asked about a room with a bathroom with a tub that someone could lie down in, she felt uncomfortable about the situation and turned him away."

Returning to Kentish Town, Neil cast a wide net. The next day it produced his first clue as to a motive for murder. On file in the probate court was Mrs. Lloyd's will. Made out on the day of her death, it named her husband as sole heir. The will had been presented soon after her death to a lawyer on Uxbridge Road by Mr. Lloyd. Next to come to Neil's attention was a life insurance policy for 700 pounds with Lloyd as the beneficiary, applied for *before* Margaret Elizabeth Lofty became a bride.

Then came another thunderbolt. Having sent a summary of his Highgate investigation along with the newspaper account of the 1913 bathtub death of Mrs. George Smith to the police in Blackpool, he received a startling response. It was an account of the circumstances of Smith's drowning that exactly matched those in Mrs. Lloyd's death—a man who insisted on a room with a bathtub, the wife's "illness," calling a local doctor to treat her, an improvement in her condition, an evening walk, the wife's bath, the husband locking himself out while fetching food (in this case it was eggs for breakfast rather than tomatoes), and discovery of the wife's accidental drowning. But there was more: 500 pounds in insurance taken out by the woman the day before her wedding and a will made out in her new husband's favor just two days before they left on a belated honeymoon.

Authorized by Sir Charles Mathews of the Office for
Public Prosecution to arrest Lloyd/Smith, Neil set a trap.
Because the payment of the proceeds of the insurance
policy of the late Mrs. Lloyd had not yet been made (at
Neil's request), Neil had the office of the lawyer who'd
drawn up Mrs. Lloyd's will put under surveillance in the
hope that Lloyd/Smith would eventually show up to collect
the insurance money.

On February 1, 1915, a man matching Lloyd's description appeared at the law office. Walking up to him, Neil
wondered what women could see in a man of this type.
Sallow in complexion, bad features, a big sensual mouth—
the sort of fellow a decent man would shun as unlikable.
Introducing himself, Neil asked, "Are you John Lloyd?"

"Yes, I am."

"The same John Lloyd whose wife was drowned in a
bath on the night of December 18th last, at Bismarck
Road, Highgate?"

"Yes, that's me."

"From my investigations, I have reason to believe you
are identical with George Smith," Neil continued, adding
what he knew of the marriage and Blackpool death of
"your last bride."

"Yes, that is so," said Lloyd, "but that does not prove
that my name is Smith! I don't know the name of Smith.
My name's not Smith."

"Very well," said Neil, "I am going to detain you for
making a false attestation on oath to a registrar."

Lloyd/Smith relaxed. So it wasn't a charge of murder!
"Oh, if that's what you're making all this fuss over," he
said, "I may as well tell you, I am Smith."

Expecting a quick and relatively painless disposition of
the fraudulent oath charge, Lloyd/Smith had no way of
knowing that his fate was about to be placed in the
hands of a man from whom Death kept few secrets—
Bernard Spilsbury.

When Neil applied for permission to investigate the
brides' deaths, Public Prosecutor Sir Charles Mathews
had shaken his head and said, "It is incredible to me
that a man could murder two women by drowning them
in a bath. I have never heard of such a thing during the
whole of my lifelong experience." Neither had Spilsbury.

At age thirty-seven he was now the principal pathologist at the Home Office, consultant to London's coroners and by virtue of his showing up at the scenes of crimes along with the detectives from Scotland Yard, practically a member of the Metropolitan Police.

What he would be looking for in autopsies of what the newspapers headlined as "The Brides in the Bath" was proof that the two women hadn't drowned as the result of being stricken by fits or fainting spells *and* evidence of violence. Determining that so long after drowning deaths, when science hadn't yet provided the infallible techniques of later generations, was a difficult task. But Spilsbury's examination of the exhumed body of Margaret Lloyd left him convinced that neither illness nor heart attack caused her to slip beneath the drowning water of her bath.

Neither did he find any signs of violence of the kind he would expect if she were struck a blow or had resisted being held under water. Perhaps the autopsy of the woman in Blackpool, he said to Neil, would show otherwise.

As they were about to leave for the city on the Irish Sea where Mrs. Alice Smith died in a zinc bathtub, Neil received two stunning communications. The first was from the chief of police in Herne Bay, a resort on the North Sea coast of Kent fifty-three miles east of London. There, on July 13, 1912, a woman by the name of Bessie Williams had been found drowned in the bathtub that had been bought, only four days previously, by her husband for their rented house. In response to this remarkable coincidence Neil sent photos of Lloyd/Smith to the Herne Bay police. The second letter to Neil was from none other than Sir Arthur Conan Doyle. He'd heard of the strange death of Mrs. Williams, said the author of the Sherlock Holmes stories, and had done some investigating. The man named Williams, he reported to Neil, had changed his name to John Lloyd and disappeared!

Temporarily leaving the Herne Bay case in the hands of two detectives whom he sent from London, Neil accompanied Spilsbury to faraway Blackpool. Although Alice Smith's body was greatly deteriorated, Spilsbury came to the same conclusions he'd drawn in Lloyd's death. Arriving in Herne Bay, Neil and Spilsbury found the circumstances of the death of Mrs. Bessie Williams virtually identical to the other. Furthermore, the pictures of Lloyd/Smith had been positively identified as Williams.

As persuasive as all this was to Neil and Spilsbury, what they had was circumstantial and not enough to be certain that a jury would convict the suspect. Just who that man of many wives and many names was, Neil now knew. Investigation by Neil's men had determined that he was George Joseph Smith. Born in 1872, the son of an insurance agent and a ne'er-do-well from the age of nine, he'd been in and out of reformatories, jails, and prisons all his life, primarily for fraud, swindling, and theft involving lonely women.

Was he a killer? If so, how did he do it? Spilsbury had a theory. It went this way: the newlywed husband is in a playful mood as his bride bathes; he clutches the unsuspecting woman by the feet and wrenches them upward and over the rim of the tub; her head is instantly submerged; water rushes into her nose and causes shock and sudden loss of consciousness; she drowns; there are no marks of violence on the body. Prior to this, of course, Smith had concocted his wife's "illness" and called in a doctor—the same one who would certify the death as an accidental drowning caused by the "illness."

Was it possible to do what Spilsbury theorized? Could a man force a woman's head under water in a bathtub by jerking her legs upward? Neil decided to find out. Using the tub in which Alice Smith drowned and hiring several women swimmers of the same size and weight as the brides in the bath, he experimented with ways to push them under the water without leaving telltale marks of a struggle. He learned that it was impossible. He then tried Spilsbury's method.

Seizing one of the young swimmers by the feet and pulling her sharply upward, he watched her head slide beneath the water precisely as Spilsbury theorized. She went under so quickly that she had no chance of grabbing hold of the sides of the tub. Then, to Neil's horror, the young woman passed out. Working frantically to revive her with the help of a servant and a hastily summoned doctor, Neil envisioned newspaper headlines: "Detective Arrested for Drowning Woman in Bathtub!"

Presently, the swimmer revived to inform Neil, and later Spilsbury, that at the very second the water rushed into her nose, she'd passed out—just as Spilsbury theorized—despite the fact that she, unlike the brides, had been expecting the dunking!

When Smith stood trial at the Old Bailey in June 1915, Neil's relating of the nearly tragic outcome of the bathtub experiments sent shudders through the jury. With grim faces they listened to the testimony of 112 of the 150 persons from whom Neil had taken statements. Fascinated, the jurors heard that Smith had married seven times since 1898, and had used the names John Lloyd, Henry Williams, Oliver James, and, ironically, Oliver Love.

Although testimony and evidence in the case spanned seven days, the jury's deliberations took twenty minutes. Smith was condemned to hang.

It was a triumph for Inspector Neil's traditional detective work and Spilsbury's dramatic new approach to forensic pathology, in which the policeman and the scientist are partners from the beginning, at the scene of the crime.

Spilsbury's achievements were acknowledged in 1920 with a knighthood bestowed by King Edward VII. Meanwhile he'd conducted 5,000 more autopsies. By the time he relinquished the post of Home Office Pathologist, he'd done tens of thousands, but when he died in 1947, it was his earliest work that was dug out of the files of Fleet Street newspapers for their obituaries: the scar in the Crippen case, Willie Starchfield's final treat, and the brides in the bath. There was no mystery to be unraveled as to Spilsbury's own death: He'd committed suicide.

When sentence was pronounced by the judge in the Smith trial, to Neil's consternation and bewilderment, it was greeted with shrieks and moans of hundreds of women who'd flocked to the Old Bailey for the trial and who, it must be supposed, had they met Joseph Smith as he'd met others like them, would have happily married the man whom Neil had found so repulsive.

Why did women find Smith so fascinating? Four years before Joseph Smith came to justice, Sir Arthur Conan Doyle offered an insight into such women. "One of the most dangerous classes in the world is the drifting and friendless woman," says Sherlock Holmes in "The Disappearance of Lady Frances Carfax." "She is the most harmless, and often the most useful of mortals, but she is the inevitable inciter of crime in others. She is helpless. She is migratory. She has sufficient means to take her from country to country and from hotel to hotel. She is lost, as often as not, in a maze of *pensions* and boarding houses. She is a stray chicken in a world of foxes."

When Sir Arthur Conan Doyle and Detective Inspector Arthur Fowler Neil arrived at Herne Bay in 1915 to look into the curious death of Bessie Williams, they'd found the seaside town ringed by barbed wire and bristling with fortifications. In Conan Doyle's words, there was "an east wind coming . . . such a wind as ever blew on England yet."

It was the howling wind of world war.

The present New Scotland Yard on Broadway off Victoria Street reflects none of the romance that has been attached to the name "Scotland Yard" for 163 years.

The original site of Scotland Yard, near Trafalgar Square and known as Great Scotland Yard, remains an active police facility.

When the 1692 Parliamentary Reward System offered boun-
ties for capturing thieves, professional criminal Jonathan
Wild made a fortune turning in his associates. But after he
swindled a blind woman, officials decided he had gone too far.
A special law put him out of business by hanging him, to the
cheers of onlookers. It would be almost two hundred years
before London had a thoroughly professional police force.

Before the creation of the Bow Street Runners and the later
Metropolitan Police, law and order depended on a system of
nightwatchmen. Usually elderly men (no one else wanted the
job), they were called "Old Charlies" and had little effect on
preventing crime.

Sir Robert Peel's efforts to create a professional police force in London succeeded in 1829 with the formation of the Metropolitan Police. Londoners called the "new police" Bobbies.

Because London's first police station was in Bow Street, its officers were called "Bow Street Runners." They continued to act as "thief takers" for several years after the organization of the first professional law enforcement agency at Scotland Yard, known as the Metropolitan Police.

When the Metropolitan Police Office opened in 1829 in an area known as "Scotland Yard," the name became synonymous with the city's police. It remains so today.

In the Victorian era, the London Bobby donned the beehive helmet that remains the symbol of the modern Metropolitan Police. This Victorian-period drawing shows that homelessness is not a new police challenge.

Uniforms of the first Metropolitan Police officers were designed to give them the appearance of ordinary citizens. Organized by Sir Robert Peel, they were called "Peelers" and "Bobbies." The style of uniforms has changed but those who wear them are still called Bobbies.

In attempting to prove that teenager Constance Kent had murdered her three-year-old stepbrother, Scotland Yard's top detective, Jonathan Whicher, ran into the scorn of townspeople and jealousy on the part of local police in the rural county of Kent. Vindication of Whicher's brilliant deductions in the case came years later with Constance's confession.

THE BOY WITNESSES.

WESTEND SCANDAL CASE, SKETCHES IN COURT.

Victorian newspapers and magazines gleefully played up "the Cleveland Street scandal" involving several notable gentlemen, a group of postal messengers, and naughty goings-on in a male brothel. Investigation of the case was assigned to Inspector Frederick Abberline, who had investigated the murders of Jack the Ripper.

A GUY FOR NOVEMBER.
RESPECTFULLY DEDICATED TO COL. HENDERSON AND THE METROPOLITAN POLICE

Accusations of police brutality and other excesses have plagued the Metropolitan Police since its founding in 1829. This cartoon was aimed at Commissioner Edmund Henderson and his force following police suppression of a workers' protest in 1866.

Dr. Hawley Harvey Crippen, who murdered his wife out of love for Ethel le Neve, is in a permanent display at Madame Tussaud's Chamber of Horrors. Scotland Yard Inspector Walter Dew found a faster ship to pursue them across the Atlantic and arrested them as they landed in Canada.

Among the celebrated male-factors of the Victorian era, ugly, deformed murderer and robber Charley Peace eluded capture for years and inspired the half-affectionate epithet of rogue. Among his charms was a talent as a violinist.

Bobbies waded into squatters at Trafalgar Square on June 6, 1897, to clear the area on the occasion of the Diamond Jubilee of Queen Victoria. The square has been a frequent scene of clashes between police and social and political protestors.

George Joseph Smith found a unique way to get rid of his wives. Drowning them, he collected on their insurance policies until Inspector Arthur Fowler Neil and pathologist Dr. Bernard Spilsbury discovered the secret of "the brides in the bath" and sent Smith to the gallows.

A piece of currant cake proved to be a crucial clue for Chief Inspector William Gough in solving the 1914 murder of five-year-old Willie Starchfield aboard a London train. Unfortunately, the jury refused to accept the evidence that the killer was the child's father.

When George Joseph Smith was sentenced to death in 1915, shrieks and moans of protest were heard from hundreds of sympathetic women who had flocked to his trial at the Old Bailey despite the fact that he had murdered three of his six wives.

The Metropolitan Police pass in review on the occasion of the appointment of Gen. the Rt. Hon. the Viscount Byng of Vimy as Commissioner, 1928.

The style of police uniforms has changed over the years but walking a beat has always meant checking the locks of doors, as this constable demonstrated for a newspaper photographer in 1936.

Cornwall Constabulary police historian Ken Searle wearing the tunic and winter helmet of 1910–1936 and holding (*l. to r.*) the summer issue helmet of 1910–1936, tin helmet of WWII, and the headgear worn at the Coronation of Queen Elizabeth II.

FOURTEEN

The Case of the Winking Head

IT COULD BE ARGUED THAT THE FIRST WORLD WAR WAS A family spat that got out of hand. Many of the nations involved were ruled by relatives either by blood or marriage of the late Queen Victoria. When it was over European monarchy was pretty much finished. Britain's King George V was an exception. So was King Albert I of Belgium, whose country's neutrality had been ignored by soldiers of Victoria's German nephew Kaiser Wilhelm, forcing thousands of Albert's subjects into exile across the Channel.

Some found refuge in the Devonshire village of Tor, where they stuck in the mind of twenty-six-year-old Agatha Christie who at the time was working at a military hospital at Torquay and considering trying her hand at writing a mystery novel. "Who could I have as a detective?" she asked herself. Might he be one like Sherlock Holmes? "I should never be able to emulate *him*," she thought. Should Edgar Allan Poe's Arsene Lupin be a model? "Not my kind," she decided. Someone like young French journalist Joseph Rouletabille in Gaston Leroux's *The Mystery of the Yellow Room*? He was the *sort* of person: foreign. Remembering the colony of Belgians at Tor she asked: Why not make him a *Belge*? A refugee Belgian police officer! A retired detective. Not too young a one.

She named him Hercule Poirot, gave him a sidekick called Captain Arthur Hastings, and in the tried-and-true tradition of Sherlock Holmes's Inspector Lestrade, a Scotland Yard detective as foil and occasional resource—Inspector Jimmy Japp. In due course as Christie's career soared Poirot met

141

Japp's boss at Scotland Yard, Superintendent Battle (no. first name given, no initial). "What is your style, Superintendent?" asked Poirot. "A straightforward, honest, zealous officer doing his duty in the most laborious manner—that's my style," said Battle. "No frills. No fancy work. Just honest perspiration." Real Scotland Yarders must have liked that when they read it.

Battle's specialty was crime among aristocrats and he had a harsh opinion of them. "You see, the majority of the people are always wondering what the neighbors will think," he explained to Poirot in *The Secret of the Chimneys*. "But tramps and aristocrats don't—they just do the first thing that comes into their heads, and they don't bother to think what anyone thinks of them." As Battle indicates, the Great War which upset established societies in Europe caused no such cataclysm in England. The class system that was in effect before the war was still in place after 1918. The only noticeable difference between the Edwardian era and the postwar period was the absence of the young men who'd gone off to war with cocky assurance of quick victory and happy homecomings and instead died in countless trenches.

Losses were no less noticeable in the ranks of the Metropolitan Police. Of the more than 4,000 men who served in the armed forces, 864 were killed or wounded in action and two constables were killed during one of thirty-two air raids on London. Not so readily calculated was the effect that the war was having on those who remained at home to secure domestic peace. The effect on them was one of morale. With the cost of living going up at an estimated 133 percent and their wages basically unchanged, members of the force felt economically squeezed. Many saw their only hope for relief in joining the ranks of the illegal Police Union.

The issue had come to a head on August 25, 1917, with the dismissal of a constable in Hammersmith for union activity. For the second time in the history of the police there was a mutiny. But this time it ended in total victory for the union. Meeting with the leaders of the strike, Prime Minister David Lloyd George promised immediate substantial pay improvements, reinstatement of the dismissed constable, and recognition of the union when the war was over. Critics accused him of buying off the strikers. Moreover, the deal with the union had undercut Commissioner Edward Henry, who felt he had no choice but to offer his resignation. It was promptly accepted. For a dedicated public servant who'd guided the Metropolitan Police through a long, difficult period of growth and development since his appointment in 1903, it was a "shabby reward," wrote historian David Ascoli in *The Queen's Peace*. He was undoubtedly the most distinguished Commissioner since Mayne and had won, to a degree that Mayne had not, the admiration and respect of his men.

Named as his successor was General the Right Honorable Sir Nevil Macready, whose main tasks would be implementation of the Prime Minister's deal with the union and the requirements of a new Police Act then working its way through Parliament, restoring morale within the police and rebuilding public confidence. All of this was jeopardized on July 31, 1919, with the calling of a national police strike by the union leaders who felt that their deal with the Prime Minister had been scuttled. Macready reacted swiftly, firing the ring leaders and those who'd followed them—about 1,000 men out of a force of 1,900. As a result, the union was crushed and Macready turned his attention fully to postwar rebuilding.

To appreciate the most significant change that had overtaken the Metropolis, Macready had only to look out his window where the age-old traveling companion of the human race—the horse—was on its way into memory, replaced by the "horseless carriage." If the automobile was everywhere, could its use by criminals lag behind? Clearly, the police would have to keep up.

Accordingly, in 1920 Macready acquired two vans. Because they had been built during the war by the Crossley Aircraft Manufacturing Company, a newspaperman came up with a name for the police who patrolled in them: the "Flying Squad." But the public whose ancestors had coined the terms "Runners," "Peelers," and "Bobbies" came up with a different monicker. In the colorful logic of cockney rhyming slang, "Flying Squad" brought to mind the demon barber of Fleet Street. Hence, the popular name for the Flying Squad became "Sweeney Todd," and, presently, the even shorter "Sweeney."

The main objective of the squad was to thwart gangs of crooks who had perfected their skills of smashing the windows of retail establishments (primarily jewelry stores) and grabbing all that their pockets could hold, then making a run for it. The technique added to the lexicon of English crime a term that remained in use for the balance of the "century of the automobile." They called it "smash-and-grab."

Effective from the start at dealing with the fleet-footed robbers, the Flying Squad was made even more successful in 1922 when its patrol cars were equipped with radios to receive messages from headquarters relayed by the London transmitter of the brand-new British Broadcasting Company (BBC).

Macready's command of Scotland Yard was brief: 1918-1920. Upon his retirement, another military man took charge. Moving up from assistant commissioner was Brigadier General Sir William Horwood, whose previous police experience was as provost-marshal of British forces in France and running the police force of the North Eastern Railway. Described by a contemporary as an unattractive man who never smiled or returned a courtesy and mistook arrogance for leadership, he was known as the "Chocolate Soldier."

Service in the army had *not* been a shaping experience in the life of thirty-four-year-old Patrick H. Mahon, who came to the notice of Scotland Yard in April 1924 at the midpoint in General Horwood's eight years as police commissioner. Although Mahon had made an impassioned plea to be allowed to join the army rather than be sentenced to prison for the 1916 burglary of the National Provincial Bank of Sunningdale, which was highlighted by a brutal hammer attack on a charwoman, in a scornful denunciation of him as a thorough-paced hypocrite that the army could do without, the judge sentenced him to five years' penal servitude.

It was not Mahon's first criminal act. In 1910 he'd forged a check for 123 pounds in order to finance a love tryst on the Isle of Man with a woman who wasn't his wife. Brought back to face the music, he charmed the victim (his employer) and his adoring wife into forgiving him, and got a suspended sentence from an equally considerate court. Latter-day psychiatrists and criminologists who are familiar with similar personalities, such as the charming and vain serial murderer of young women Theodore (Ted) Bundy, might describe the womanizing, larcenous Patrick Mahon as a typical manipulative personality. Born in 1889 in Liverpool, he grew up to be a handsome, athletic youth who was as attractive to women as they were to him. The one who got him to the altar was a pretty dark-haired girl with whom he fell in love at school. They married the year before he ran off to the Isle of Man with the other woman and then had his narrow escape from prison.

To get away from the resultant scandal the Mahons moved to Wiltshire, where he got a job at a dairy farm, earned a reputation as a sportsman for his prowess on the local football field, and fathered a daughter. Soon after, he was arrested for embezzling sixty pounds from his employer. But this time he was sentenced to a year in prison. Released to his wife's ever-forgiving arms, he settled in another Wiltshire town where, presently, there was a rash of burglaries in the midst of which the Mahons decamped to Sunningdale and his conviction for bank burglary and assault.

Exuding the old charm and brimming with promises of reform, he again returned to his faithful wife, settled in Kew, and took a job with his wife's employer, Consols Automatic Aerators, Ltd. He did so well that when the firm went broke the bankruptcy administrator asked him to be sales manager. At the same time the receiver hired a typist at another firm, thirty-seven-year-old Miss Emily Bealby Kaye. When she met Mahon in the course of business, the competent, experienced, and not unattractive Emily fell for him immediately and obsessively.

The affair was unlike any of Mahon's previous philanderings. Emily was not to be easily discarded. She demanded marriage. When Mahon told her he would never leave his wife, she suggested that they take a holiday and go away together and spend a week or two in a spot where they could be alone. There, she would convince him of her love and he'd learn that he could be perfectly happy with her. The retreat she had in mind was a bungalow on a stretch of lonely beach between Eastbourne and Pevensey Bay. It would be, she said, a "love experiment."

Mahon had something quite the contrary in mind. Packed into his bag as they traveled by train to the secluded hideaway was a knife that he'd bought at a shop in Victoria Street.

On the train an argument broke out. As it continued at the cottage, her shrill demands took on aspects of an ultimatum, insisting that Patrick abandon his wife, child, job, and promising future to run off with her to South Africa. She may have told him that she knew about his criminal record, hoping that if their love experiment failed to persuade him, blackmail would. It also seems likely that she informed him that she was "in a family way."

When he still refused to throw over everything for her, Mahon said later, she grabbed a small axe used for breaking up large lumps of coal and hurled it at him. When it glanced harmlessly off his shoulder he lunged at him with clawing fingers. As they struggled, they fell to the floor. Her head hit a coal scuttle.

As she lay unconscious, Mahon turned to his bag. Opening it, he stared at it contents. He knew what he had to do. He'd planned for it by buying the knife. But faced with the reality of the next awful task that confronted him, he could not bring himself to cut up the corpse. Carrying it into the bedroom, he covered it with a fur coat.

After spending the night at a hotel in Eastbourne, he went back to London and dined that evening with a woman named Duncan whom he'd met a few days earlier, telling her that his name was Waller. For reasons known only to him (he said later that he was desperately in need of human company), he invited Miss Duncan to the cottage at Eastbourne. She agreed to join him on Friday (Good Friday, actually).

Returning to the cottage, Mahon at last summoned the courage to dismember Emily's body, but because there was no time to get rid of it before the arrival of Miss Duncan, he concealed it in Emily's wardrobe trunk and left it in a locked room.

Upon her arrival, Duncan accepted his explanation that the room was locked because it contained valuable books. A remarkably unsuspicious individual, she didn't question why he left her on her own in Eastbourne the next day while he went to the Plumpton Races. Nor did it seem odd to her that he abruptly ended their stay at the cottage on Easter Monday and whisked her back to London.

That night he stayed with his wife at Kew but early the next morning he headed back to Eastbourne to dispose of

Emily Kaye's sundered corpse. A cold wind whipped up the dark waters of the choppy Channel and howled at the corners of the cottage. Rain slashed against the windows. Glowering black clouds rumbled with thunder. Lightning flashed. The blaze in the hearth cast ghostly shadows.

Fetching Emily's head, he set it upon the coals. Hunkered down, he watched the dark hair burst into foul-smelling flames. With morbid fascination he stared as the fire licked at the flesh.

What happened then was worthy of a Victorian novel of gothic horror: A bolt of lightning rent the sky and thunder shook the cottage.

Mahon shrank back from the fire in terror.

Emily's eyes had opened and were staring at him.

Shaking with fright, he raced out into the tempest. Hours went by before he could force himself to go back and resume his gruesome work. The hour was late. He didn't have enough time to complete the destruction. He had to return to London because his absence from home and work might stir up questions.

He spent the rest of the week at his job and returned to Eastbourne the next weekend in hopes of finishing the disposal. But still there wasn't sufficient time. Increasingly uneasy in what he now considered a haunted house, he made up his mind to get rid of the remaining bits of body parts by tossing them from the train on his way back to London. Believing that nothing about the cottage could be traced to him, and confident that he'd got away with murder, he filled a Gladstone bag and carried out his plan, save for the knife, two pieces of silk, a towel, a scarf, Emily's underwear, and a brown racquet case—all stained with blood and liberally sprinkled with a disinfectant. Intending to dispose of these potentially damning items around London, he arrived at Waterloo Station and checked the locked bag.

In the timeless tradition of wives who suffer the slings and arrows of deceitful spouses, when Mrs. Mahon found the receipt in her husband's pocket she was curious. Her immediate fear was not that he was seeing another woman—she was used to that. She was afraid that he was caught up in his second vice: gambling. Accompanied by a friend who'd been a police officer, she took the receipt to Waterloo Station and claimed the bag. Although the friend was unable to open it, he did manage to pry the top wide enough to see that its contents were spattered with blood. Telling Mrs. Mahon that nothing could be done at that moment, he sent her home with instructions to replace the check and say nothing to her husband. He then rushed to report what he'd found to an old friend at Scotland Yard.

Chief Inspector Percy Savage knew just what to do. He had the bag watched. The next evening, it was claimed. "Pardon me, sir," said Constable Mark Thompson politely, tapping Mahon on the shoulder. "I'd like to see what's in the bag."

Mahon answered that he'd lost the key.

"In that case, sir," said Thompson, "I must ask you to come with me to Kennington Road Police Station, where the bag will be opened."

Savage was waiting for them. Emptying the bag, he found a sliver of flesh. "What's this?" he demanded.

Despite Mahon's best efforts on the train from Eastbourne, he had not disposed of all the remains. "I must have carried meat for my pet," he said. "I'm fond of dogs. I suppose I've carried home meat for dogs in it."

"You don't usually wrap dog's meat in silk. Think up something better than that. I believe these stains are human blood."

With a smirk, Mahon replied, "You seem to know all about it."

They fell silent for a quarter of an hour.

"I wonder," said Savage at last, "if you can realize how terrible it is for one's body to be active and one's mind fail to act. You did something terrible. Now it's time to talk about it."

Mahon pondered the words for a long moment. "Since you seem to know everything," he said morosely, "I might as well tell you the truth."

The confession was lengthy and vivid—but it was not the confession of a murderer. It was self-defense, he said. "She came at me like a tigress, clawing my face and neck," he continued. "I was in fear of my life. It was in sheer desperation that I closed with her. She was amazingly strong. Suddenly I felt us falling. I was on the floor, stunned.

Emily lay there, too. She didn't get up. Her head had struck a coal scuttle with terrible violence."

At the trial Sir Bernard Spilsbury would not commit himself to an opinion on the precise manner of death, but he did allow that it could not have been caused by Emily's head striking the coal scuttle. He did state with certainty that at the moment of her death Emily was pregnant.

Testimony from Chief Inspector Savage concerned what the investigation by Scotland Yard and the East Sussex Constabulary had turned up at the cottage: a dismembered body and evidence of attempts to get rid of it by burning. They had also recovered various items: a woman's comb and brush, a woman's gold watch, a woman's hats and garments, saucepans that had been used to boil human flesh, a bloodstained saw, a biscuit tin containing the heart and other organs.

The head was not found. Neither was the uterus. Did that make Mahon a murderer? What evidence was there to link him to the woman *after* her murder? It was known, said Savage, that Emily had withdrawn 500 pounds in savings from her bank in 100-pound notes. Three of those notes were changed after the murder by Mahon using false names.

Questioned by his lawyer, Mahon was asked, "Did you desire the death of Miss Kaye?"

Mahon answered: "Never at any time."

At that moment Nature provided a dramatic flourish that the brashest creator of fiction would not have dared to write. The courtroom was shaken by a crash of thunder and lit by a flash of lightning. Perhaps recalling the dark and stormy night when he gazed in horror as Emily's dead eyes opened accusingly, Mahon shrank into the corner of the witness box, cowering in terror.

On his way to the gallows at Wandsworth Prison on the third of September 1924, Mahon finally admitted his crime. He told his jailors that he killed Emily because she had become "a nuisance."

FIFTEEN

The Girl with the Pretty Feet

SHORT, NATTILY DRESSED CHIEF INSPECTOR ROBERT DONALD-son was not exactly an ideal model for a Metropolitan Police recruiting poster. But the looks were deceiving. He enjoyed the reputation among colleagues at Scotland Yard of a two-fisted copper who never shrank from wading into the roughest situations to subdue the most violent of criminals, some of whom packed pistols. As a member of the Murder Squad he had had his share of homicide cases and had closed the book on all of them. That made him the right detective to be called upon to take charge of the investigation of a murder in the popular seaside resort of Brighton.

Put on the map in 1784 when the Prince of Wales (later King George IV) went there for bracing sea air, Brighton had been the summer retreat of Queen Victoria and had attracted the cream of London society ever since. But it also had a seamy side. A visitor saw all the gaudy trappings of a holiday town for the common folk: red-blue-and-predominately-white seafood stalls assailing the nostrils with scents of vinegar and brine, fortune tellers, a waxworks à la Madame Tussaud's, arcades with penny-in-the-slot peep shows and pin tables, greasy-spoon cafes, souvenir stands, pubs, dance halls, and naughty postcards. The current phrase for an outing was: "A dirty weekend in Brighton."

To Chief Inspector Donaldson there were better places to take his family. Scotland, for instance. But in mid-June 1934 a telephone call to the commissioner of the Metropolitan Police from Brighton's police had Donaldson packing his bags for a fifty-one-mile trip to the seaside at the behest of Chief Constable Captain W. H. Hutchinson. He had a trunk murder on his hands.

It was not Brighton's first. In 1831, twenty-six-year-old laborer John Holloway had killed his wife Celia, taken apart the body with a penknife, and stuffed her chopped-up remains into a very large trunk that more than accommodated the five-foot three-inch victim. Because it was Britain's first trunk murder, it provoked more than the usual interest, so much so that after Holloway was hanged 23,000 people filed through the town hall in the space of six hours to gaze at his corpse.

Three-quarters of a century passed before English history recorded its second trunk horror, though not in Brighton. In 1905 a tin box with a homemade airtight cover had been employed by Arthur Devereux after the chemist's assistant poisoned his wife and two-year-old twin sons with morphine. He stored the corpses in a London warehouse and thought he'd gotten away with it until they were discovered three months later by his inquiring mother-in-law. Arrested in Coventry, Devereux pleaded insanity at the trial. To no avail. He was hanged at Pentonville Prison.

Aficionados of trunk murders had to wait twenty-two years for the next. On Tuesday, May 10, 1927, an apparently abandoned trunk was opened in the cloakroom of Charing Cross Station. Inside were the chopped-up parts of a young woman.

Summoned to the scene from Scotland Yard, chief detective inspector George Cornish and Frederick Porter Wensley, chief constable, Criminal Investigation Department, were not without clues. Markings on the trunk appeared to be initials, and there was a shipping tag bearing the name "F. Austin" of St. Leonard's. That F. Austin had committed a murder and left his calling card seemed unlikely and, indeed, he had not. The trunk had belonged to him but had been sold quite some time ago.

While detectives were sent out to make inquiries at second-hand luggage stores, others were scouring London's laundries in hope of identifying the laundry marks on articles of the victim's clothing. Within twenty-four hours they had a name: Holt. And an address: Chelsea. They also had a break: Mrs. Holt had given some of her old clothing to her cook, since dismissed. The cook's name had been Roles. Would Mrs. Holt be willing to have a look at the dead woman? It was an unpleasant task but Mrs. Holt believed in doing her duty as a citizen. She had no trouble confirming that the dead woman and her former cook were the same.

Night-long legwork by Wensley and others in search of people named Roles turned up a man of that name who'd lived for a time with the woman in question. She had called herself his wife and had used his name, but they had split up and he had not seen her for quite a spell. Perhaps some of her women friends could assist them, he suggested to the police.

One did. The dead woman's real name, she said, was Minnie Bonati. She had been married to an Italian waiter, she said, but they were separated. Locating the husband, Wensley brought him in. His identification of his ex-wife's remains was quick, based on a crooked index finger. During questioning, he provided an iron-clad alibi for the hour when the trunk was checked at Charing Cross.

Fixing the date and time when the trunk was left had been a matter of pure luck. A shoeshine boy with a laudable curiosity had found the cloakroom voucher that had been issued for it. With the call slip in hand, Wensley was able to match its number with those of the vouchers of items left at the station just before and after the trunk was deposited. Again, Lady Luck smiled on the police. A woman who'd left an item before the trunk was checked recalled seeing the trunk being unloaded from a taxi. Next, the porter who had assisted with the trunk remembered that he'd had a devil of a time helping the trunk's owner get it out of the taxi. Now it was simply a matter of locating the taxi driver.

The driver recalled the passenger with the trunk very well. He'd picked him up immediately after dropping off two gentlemen, probably lawyers, at the Westminster Police Court in Rochester Row. The man who hailed him, the driver continued, had asked him to help bring the trunk from a block of offices. "What have you got in here?" the cabbie had asked with a groan. "Money?"

"No," was the man's answer. "They're books."

Did the cabbie remember the man's looks? That might be difficult, he said, as the man had turned down the brim of his hat and pulled up his coat collar, obscuring his face.

If Minnie Bonati had been killed at the location where the cabbie picked up the trunk, said Wensley to Chief Inspector Cornish, it was a damned cheeky act—right across the street from a police station!

From the beginning of the case attention had been focused on the trunk. A photo of it had been distributed to newspapers and circulated among used-trunk dealers. Presently, it was seen and recognized by a Brixton Road shopowner, but as to describing its purchaser and when it had been sold, he was vague. However, a bus driver who also saw the photo was quite clear about a man he had seen with the same trunk as he boarded the bus in the Brixton Road. The man had left the bus between Vauxhall Road and Victoria Station near Rochester Row. Might the driver remember what the man looked like? He was not sure. The man wore his hat low over his face and had a turned-up coat collar.

Wensley did not miss the significance. The bus driver saw a man with an empty trunk and the cabbie had helped a man bring a very heavy one from the Rochester Row office block. Every available person engaged in the offices was interviewed. Sure enough, a black trunk had been noticed standing for some little time in one of the corridors. The impression was that it belonged to the office of Edwards & Co., Estate and Business Transfer Agents. But the firm had gone bankrupt and the offices vacated as of May 9, the day before the trunk was left at Charing Cross. The name of the party who'd rented the offices and sent the landlord a letter concerning the failure of the firm was a Mr. John Robinson.

Who was Robinson and where was he? A trace of the check he made out to the landlord led Wensley to a bank. Its records led to Robinson's lodgings in Camberwell. But Robinson had also left that address, apparently for Lancashire but leaving no forwarding address. Quite possibly at a deadend, Wensley asked to have a look at Robinson's rooms. Again, luck was on his side. Slipped beneath the door was a telegram Robinson had sent to a friend but which, for some reason, couldn't be delivered and so was returned to the sender. The address to which the telegram

was addressed was immediately put under surveillance, as
was the man who lived there.

On May 19, ten days after Minnie Bonati's body was
found in the trunk at Charing Cross, the man who was
being watched stopped near the Elephant and Castle pub
and met an individual who bore a striking resemblance
to Robinson. Asked by two police officers to accompany
them to Scotland Yard, Robinson readily agreed.

Originally a Blackpool tram driver, he'd served in the
army until 1923 and then held a variety of jobs. Most of
the time he'd been a barman, he said. Lately, he tried
his hand as an estate agent, unsuccessfully. He had no
recollection of a trunk in a corridor in the Rochester Row
offices. "So far as I know," he said, "I have never seen
Mrs. Bonati or any of her associates."

"I wonder if you would mind accompanying me on a
call upon two men whom we believe can identify Mrs.
Bonati's murderer," said Wensley. It was a bit of bluff.
He knew that neither the cabbie nor the used-goods dealer
had had a good look at the face of the mystery man
with a trunk. But if Robinson balked it would be a most
incriminating act. "I have nothing to be afraid of," said
Robinson, cheerfully lighting a cigarette. "I'll be happy
to go with you." As expected, neither the cabbie nor the
merchant could identify him.

If Robinson were to be linked to the murder of Bonati,
other evidence would have to be found. If it existed, reasoned
Wensley, it would be at the scene of the murder. Convinced
that the woman had been killed by Robinson in his office,
he ordered two of the Yard's best detective sergeants—
Clarke and Burt—to give it a going over. There'd been
one search already. But this time, said Wensley, he wanted
it done with a fine-tooth comb. No matter how trifling an
object might be, he told them, look at it. Then look at
it again.

They found slim pickings. If Robinson had committed
a murder in the offices he'd done a scrupulous job of
cleaning up. There were two rooms sparsely furnished
with the basic requirements of a business office—desks,
chairs, cabinets, typewriter, wastebaskets, and an ashtray.
Obviously for the use of the recent cigarette-smoking
tenant, it lay on the largest of the desks. Noting that

it was spotless, Sergeant Clarke again ruminated upon the meticulous manner in which Thompson had cleaned up before moving out, even emptying the ashtray. Indeed, the only clue that the rooms had been recently occupied was the wastebasket beside the desk. It contained bits of crumpled paper, dumped cigarette ends, and a few charred matchsticks. Mindful of his orders to go over the place with a fine-tooth comb, Clarke dumped the contents of the wastebasket onto the desk and began sorting through them. Then, with a grunt that startled his partner, he held up one of the matches. "What do you make of that?" he said, holding it to the light.

What Sergeant Burt made of it was that this particular match bore a discoloration that was different from the others—a pale pinkish stain.

"Blood?" said Clarke.

"Could be," answered Burt.

"If murderers didn't make these mistakes," said Wensley as he studied the matchstick, "we detectives would have a poor time of it."

The next morning, Monday, May 22, 1927, Wensley picked up his customary newspaper and read the main headline:

TRUNK CRIME DEAD END
SCOTLAND YARD BAFFLED
300 *Statements Taken*
And No Clue

At that moment at Robinson's home, Robinson was being asked by Sergeant Clarke to dress and accompany him to Scotland Yard. After being warned that whatever he said would be taken down and possibly used against him in court, he asked to speak to Chief Inspector Cornish. "I want to tell him all about it," he said.

He did not intend to kill her. It was an accident. He didn't even know the woman. They'd only met that afternoon, May 4, at Victoria Station. She suggested going to his office. Presently, she said she was hard up for money and asked for a pound. He'd refused. She became enraged and attacked him. "I hit her on the face with my right hand," he continued. "She fell backwards. She struck a chair in falling and it fell over. I left her there and came out, closing the office door behind me." He went home, he said, and returned to the office in the morning expecting her to have recovered and left. He was surprised to find her dead. "I was in a hopeless position. I did not know what to do."

He went to a store and bought a knife—the very store where Patrick Mahon had bought the one he'd used to dismember Emily Kaye. After carrying out his grisly work on Minnie, he'd buried it under a may tree on Clapham Common. An unsuspecting friend had helped him get the second-hand trunk that he'd bought in Brixton Road down to the street. A taxi took him and the trunk to Charing Cross Station. When he searched his pocket for the voucher he realized that he'd lost it. In a state of panic, he abandoned the office and moved out of his lodgings in the expectation of fleeing from London with a little help from a friend.

These were hardly the actions of a man who'd acted in self-defense, argued the prosecutor at his trial. Rather, they were indicative of an individual who had grasped his guilt. Regarding the cause of death, Dr. Sir Bernard Spilsbury testified that Minnie Bonati had been rendered unconscious by a blow, but that death was the result of a cushion being pressed against her face until she suffocated. The story about picking her up that afternoon was also shown to be a lie. Robinson had met her weeks earlier while Minnie was a waitress at the Greyhound Hotel. He'd bigamously married her and they'd lived in the office rooms on Rochester Row.

The jury wasted no time in finding him guilty.

Seven years after Robinson dropped on the gallows, Chief Inspector Robert Donaldson could only hope that in the Brighton trunk murder he would have the same stunning success as Wensley and would not be faced with the difficulties Jonathan Whicher had run into in the Constance Kent case seventy years earlier. He need not have worried. The detective who was running the Brighton police department's investigation was no Inspector Foley.

Rather than resenting Scotland Yard's intervention in the case, Detective Inspector Arthur Pelling, whose father had been a policeman, welcomed Donaldson and immediately gave him all the details of a case in which the victim's dismembered body had been discarded in two locations.

The torso had been found in a trunk at the railway station in Brighton. The legs and severed feet had been discovered in a suitcase at King's Cross Station in London. After examination of all the parts at both places, Dr. Spilsbury declared that they matched. He stated that she had been not younger than twenty-one and not older than twenty-eight, was five feet two inches in height and weighed roughly eight-and-a-half stone (119 pounds). She appeared to be of middle-class background. She was also pregnant. So far, the arms and head hadn't been located.

In examining the woman's feet Spilsbury had described them as free of corns or other blemishes, leading him to deduce that she'd worn decent, well-fitted size 4 1/2 shoes. He surmised that, because the toenails had been expertly trimmed, she had been to a podiatrist recently. On the basis of these findings, newspapers dubbed her "The Girl with the Pretty Feet."

Pelling told Donaldson no such a person had been reported missing in the Brighton area but a survey was being taken to find out about missing women elsewhere. In what the press would call "the great roundup," 732 missing women were traced. Meantime, to accommodate Donaldson and his assistant, a twenty-six-year-old detective sergeant named Edward Sorrell, Pelling arranged for a team of a dozen local detectives and constables to be at their disposal, working out of "trunk-crime headquarters" set up in three apartments adjoining the music salon of the Royal Pavilion.

Donaldson's first step was to order re-interviews of all those who had been questioned before his arrival at Brighton and that no one be talked-to by the officer who'd done the initial questioning. During that first canvassing, the name of a missing woman turned up: Violette Kaye, also known as Mrs. Toni Mancini. But the husband had explained that his "old friend Vi" was "trying her luck in France, Germany, or somewhere like that." Besides, he said, Vi was too old to be the girl with the pretty feet. Vi was forty-two years old.

Having no reason to hold Mancini, the officer let him go.

"Maybe what Mancini said was true," said Donaldson when he learned of the incident, "but I think we should talk to him again."

Assigned the job was Detective Constable Edward Taylor, who had been the one who'd been called to investigate a malodorous trunk at the railway station and had made the discovery that had set off the current investigation. But as he was about to leave the Royal Pavilion, he received a phone call from the foreman of a group of workmen who were refurbishing a rooming house at 52 Kemp Street. "You'd better come over here right away," said the foreman excitedly. "It looks like you've got another murder."

Why no one had reported the putrid smell emanating from the house before this was beyond Taylor's understanding. Even from the street it was evident that something must have been rotting in there for a long time. Although the people who lived at the address and rented out rooms were away while the outside was being refurbished, he couldn't believe that the workmen and neighbors hadn't called in the health department. Now he placed a phone call to Chief Inspector Donaldson.

Following the stench to a cellar apartment, he was certain they were going to find the missing parts of his trunk murder and, with luck, the identifying head. But what they found inside the black steamer trunk was an entire corpse, apparently dead for weeks and crawling with finger-length maggots.

Called to Brighton for the second time in a just a few days, Spilsbury pronounced that this peroxide-blonde, older woman had been beaten to death, possibly with a hammer.

Certain that this second murder was not related to the one that had fetched him from London, Donaldson ordered questioning of the only person in Brighton who knew someone who had not been seen around for a while. The problem in talking to Toni Mancini, however, was the simple fact that he, too, had been missing immediately since his interview concerning the whereabouts of his wife. In hopes of locating him, Donaldson sent out a notice with his description to police all over the country.

On the night of July 18, Metropolitan Police Constables William Triplow and Leonard Gourd, patrolling in their car near the Yorkshire Pub in the Lewisham area of South London, spotted him. "Pardon me, sir," said Triplow, sauntering up to him. "Are you Mr. Marconi?"

The constable was corrected. "*Mancini!*"

Returned to Brighton, he told a familiar story. He did kill Violette but it wasn't murder. During a violent argument he'd thrown a hammer at her. He hadn't intended to kill her. It was a desperate act of self-defense.

If that were so, why hadn't he notified the police?

It was because he had a police record, he said. He was afraid the police would not believe him. That's when he made up his mind to acquire a trunk. After stuffing Violette into it, he told their friends that he'd moved away. Soon after, he read a newspaper headline about the discovery of a woman's body in a trunk and was terrified that it referred to Violette. To his great relief he realized that it had been a bizarre coincidence. Then came the questioning by the police about the girl with the pretty feet and his decision to skip town before they started trying to pin the murder on him, thinking she was Violette.

So who was the girl with the pretty feet? Going over the findings of Spilsbury's autopsy, Donaldson thought he found a clue as to why and how she died. She had been pregnant. Might a middle-class, unmarried young woman have sought to have an abortion? Might she have done so in a city with a reputation as a place where anything went? Dirty Brighton?

Had the woman come to Brighton in a desperate search for a way out of her dilemma? Was the job bungled? Could she have died during a botched abortion? Was that why her body was dismembered and left at railway depots? Was there an abortionist in Brighton?

Deputy Inspector Pelling had a name in mind. He was Edward Seys Massiah. Doing a thriving medical business at 8 Brunswick Square at nearby Hove, he was a man in his mid-fifties who'd come from Trinidad and become quite a wealthy practitioner. But there was no evidence to charge him as an abortionist, let alone accuse him of cutting up a body and distributing the parts by way of a trunk and suitcase left in railway stations so as to conceal a sloppy operation.

At a meeting of all his trunk-murder detectives to go over the facts concerning Massiah, Donaldson ordered that

Massiah be watched, *covertly*. Attending the meeting was a senior police officer from Hove. Perhaps he didn't know the meaning of covert. In any case, he promptly paid a visit to Massiah. As he talked and Massiah listened, the doctor busied himself by jotting notes on small pieces of paper and sliding them across the table to the police officer. In all probability, no such listing of famous names had been made since the Cleveland Street scandal, for on the papers passed to the police officer were names, addresses, and even telephone numbers of some of the most notable personages in Britain.

Shortly after, Massiah moved to London, then back to Port of Spain, Trinidad, never having been called upon to answer for the death of the girl with the pretty feet, who was never identified.

But what of Toni Mancini? Each day when he was brought to court for trial, mounted police had to use their horses to keep back throngs of women. They screamed "Hello, Toni!" and "Don't worry love, all will be well!" and "Keep your pecker up!" The trial before the Lewes Assizes lasted four days. He still claimed that he'd not killed Violette but found her dead and, out of panic and worried that his criminal past would be used against him by the police, had hidden the body. "I considered that a man who has been convicted," he said, "never gets a fair deal from the police."

The jury took two hours. Their verdict: not guilty. Mancini blinked uncomprehendingly at his attorney. "Not guilty?" he asked. "Not guilty?"

A week later he married a woman he'd met at a Brighton bar shortly after he'd shoved Violette into a trunk. The following summer they toured in a sideshow with a "sawing a woman in half" act that discarded the customary long box in favor of a trunk.

"Few people realize the amount of work that is involved in any complicated murder investigation," said Chief Constable Frederick Wensley, in writing about his 1927 trunk-murder case. "There are things that have no seeming importance by themselves until they are taken in conjunction with other information gathered later."

Sherlock Holmes had made a similar observation. "You know my method," he said to Dr. Watson in "The Boscombe

Valley Mystery." "It is founded upon the observation of trifles."

Dogged work by Wensley and other real-life detectives who'd been trained on the job in the observation of trifles had turned a burnt matchstick, laundry marks, and a lost luggage check into the solution of a murder.

Could such skills be taught in a classroom?

As Scotland Yard began its second century, some people were thinking that it might be a good idea to try.

SIXTEEN

More Bloody Business

IN MAY 1929, 10,000 MEMBERS OF THE METROPOLITAN Police marched in review before His Royal Highness the Prince of Wales in Hyde Park, and then paraded down the Mall to mark the century that had passed since Robert Peel set out to create as "perfect a system of police as was consistent with the character of a free country." In those hundred years, to strike a balance between keeping the Peace of Kings and one Queen and not offending the acute sensibilities of Englishmen or undercutting their fiercely held ideas of personal freedom, the commissioners, constables, and detectives of Scotland Yard had been subjected to probes by forty-two commissions, committees, and inquiries; the carping of the press and novelists; several riots; Fenian bombs; internal squabbles and embarrassing scandals; mutinies and strikes by the rank-and-file; bouts of self-doubt; and occasionally inept or indifferent leadership. But taking the salute of the centenary march on that splendid day was a commander of a different stripe.

Though in his sixties, General the Right Honourable the Viscount Byng of Vimy was a thoroughly modern man. The grandson of the distinguished Earl of Stafford, a hero of Waterloo, Byng was an enthusiastic proponent of the military innovation known as tank warfare. He commanded the Third Army in France. After the Great War he was universally hailed as the most successful of all the governor generals of Canada. Recalled from retirement in 1928 by Home Secretary Joyson-Hicks to take over from retiring Police Commissioner William Horwood, he was a true delegator of responsibilities, trusting of his subordinates and expecting to see results.

Although he personally disliked the telephone—the contraption rang at the most inopportune moments—he grasped its value as a tool against crime and approved a police call-box system. "Time is always on the side of the criminal," he said. "We must give the criminal less time." The Flying Squad was expanded and updated and a radio communications room was built at New Scotland Yard. Armed with the 1930s Road Traffic Act, he pioneered a traffic control system and attempted to assuage the anger of formerly freewheeling motorists by dubbing traffic enforcement officers "courtesy cops."

Having been viewed with suspicion by many critics of the police as "another military man" at the time of his appointment, he won over the detractors so well that when he announced that declining health required him to give up the job, the *Times* wrote on September 9, 1931: "Lord Byng has set the police officer of all ranks a professional standard . . . and has given an impetus to internal reforms by which London and his successors will profit."

The successor was Marshal of the Royal Air Force the Lord Trenchard. For Hugh Montague Trenchard the air force had been a life's passion. A year before the Great War he'd provided flight instruction to another advocate of aviation, Winston Churchill. But after watching Churchill "wallowing in the sky," he declared that Winston was "altogether too impatient for a good pupil." After the war, Trenchard had fought for establishment of the Royal Air Force (RAF) as a separate service and argued, as did Billy Mitchell in the United States, that future success in any war would depend on air superiority and effective aerial bombing.

The idea of running a police department was so anathema to Trenchard that it took the intervention of the King to get him to accept the post. Even then, Prime Minister Ramsay MacDonald had to promise him a free hand at New Scotland Yard. "Even if it means turning the force upside down?" asked Trenchard. "If that's necessary," said MacDonald, "we'll support you."

What Trenchard found was disappointing. Discipline was not good. Many of the beats being patrolled hadn't been revised since the days of Rowan and Mayne. The Statistical

Branch that tracked crime was "completely out of date." There was too much corruption and too much tipping. The entire department was top-heavy with supervisors. There was inadequate training. There was no map room and, worst of all, no scientific laboratory. The proverbial "new broom," Lord Trenchard attacked all of these problems.

Among his first recommendations was establishment of a Metropolitan Police College to be located at Hendon. It wasn't the first try at creating a school for police. Commissioner Edward Henry had started one for detectives in 1907 at Peel House in Westminster. Its purpose was to test the suitability of men who wished to join the Criminal Investigation Department and to offer refresher courses for those already on the detective force. It wasn't set up to train new recruits, as Trenchard's school at Hendon was meant to do. Reaction to the proposal among those who had an innate suspicion of the police was vehemently negative. Liberal Member of Parliament Aneurin Bevan said it was fascist and designed to make the police "more amendable to the orders of the Carlton Club and Downing Street." The police union looked on it with scorn.

Despite these difficulties, Hendon continued as an embattled symbol of "the class society" until World War II temporarily put an end to recruiting. After the war yet another study committee recommended changes that the postwar Labour government of Prime Minister Clement Attlee (with Aneurin Bevin in the cabinet) could embrace. Accordingly, the National Police College was created in 1948. It opened in a drab industrial hostel at Ryton-on-Dunsmore, far from London. Twelve years later, it was transferred to more comfortable digs in a spacious Jacobean house, on lush grounds at Bramshill, Hampshire, where it flourished.

But that wasn't the end of Hendon. Still in existence today as the initial training ground for those who choose to don the uniform of the Metropolitan Police, it's called Peel Centre and provides two years' training to probationers, under the tutelage of a staff of police-officer instructors, in basic practical skills of police work. After Hendon, the officers join their new divisions for ten more weeks of training by sergeants and constables on the streets of London. Twice a month they must attend area training units. At the end of a two-year probationary period they take a final examination. Those who pass may rightly and proudly call themselves constables. With time, diligence, and a little luck they can rise through the ranks and, if it's their desire, qualify to put away the blue tunics and beehive hats for the plain clothes of the detective and, perhaps, see the day come when their names are enrolled on a roster beside distinguished, even legendary, detectives of Scotland Yard's first hundred years: Pearce, Abberline, Whicher, Tanner, Dew, M'Intyre, Ward, Gough, Savage, Wensley, Cornish, and Donaldson.

As though having two trunk murders to solve had not been enough for Chief Inspector Donaldson in the summer of 1934, there was more bloody business in store for him the following year. In September of 1935 he packed up his family for an overdue and well-deserved holiday motoring through Scotland. On the way home he parked the car so they could stretch their legs and take in the view of a picturesque stream known as Gardenholme Linn, which cut through a deep ravine near the border town of Moffatt on the main road from Edinburgh. Smoking a cigarette as he enjoyed the scenery from the parapet of the bridge that spanned the chasm, he had no way of knowing that scattered below him were the butchered remains of two women or that upon his return to Scotland Yard he'd be in charge of the London end of a hunt for their identities and their cold-blooded killer.

A few days after Donaldson's pause at the bridge, another sightseer had decided to enjoy the same vista. On a holiday at Moffatt, Miss Susan Johnson gazed down into the ravine and thought she saw a human arm. Horrified, she ran two miles back to her hotel to tell her brother.

Strewn through the ravine and wrapped in newspapers were the skillfully dissected bodies of what first seemed to be a man and a woman. But closer examination by two pathologists from the Anatomy Department at the University of Edinburgh showed that they were both female. Judging the method of dismemberment, they had no doubt that it had been done by someone with surgical skills who had not only cut apart the bodies but also carefully removed the skin from the heads, extracted the teeth, and made an effort to obliterate fingerprints. In the latter, he was only partly successful. Painstaking efforts in the laboratory permitted the doctors to lift prints from one of the bodies that would make an identification of the woman unequivocal, should the police come up with a lead on who she might be.

For Scottish and English detectives who were cooperating in the investigation, the newspapers that were wrapped around the body parts provided a promising beginning. The most recent was dated September 15 and was a special local edition of the *Sunday Graphic* distributed only in the Morecambe and Lancaster area.

Had there been any reports of missing women in that area? Any previous reports of murdered women? Might there be any ongoing investigations?

Police in Lancaster had just such an open case. A lady from Morecambe by the name of Mrs. Smalley had recently been murdered. In the course of their investigation they interviewed a servant employed by a Persian-born doctor by the name of Bukhtyar Hakim, who was using the name Buck Ruxton in his practice in Lancaster.

A subscriber to the *Sunday Graphic*, Ruxton held a Bachelor of Medicine degree from the Universities of Bombay and London and a Bachelor of Surgery earned at Bombay. In 1930 he set up his practice in Lancaster. Obsessively jealous of his wife Isabella, the short, goodlooking thirty-six-year-old doctor fought with her constantly, accusing her of infidelity. He often struck her. "Who loves most," he said, "chastises most." To assist Isabella in the care of their children, he employed pretty twenty-two-year-old Mary Rogerson, who was devoted to the children and to Mrs. Ruxton. When Isabella could no longer put up with his abuse and left him (always to return), Mary invariably went with her.

Because of these stormy disputes, the Lancaster police were familiar with the Ruxtons. His wife had come in once to complain about her husband's brutality and Ruxton had been brought in for a chat. Ranting and raving, he accused his wife of cheating on him and vowed to kill her if it went on. When tempers subsided, police assumed that domestic tranquillity had returned—until Dr. Ruxton appeared at the station in high dudgeon over questioning by the police of one of his servants regarding Mrs. Smalley's murder.

After apologizing to him for any distress the questioning of the servant may have caused, the officer at the police station inquired about Ruxton's domestic situation. "Everything quiet on the home front?" he asked.

No it was not, snapped Ruxton. As a matter of fact, his wife had walked out on him a fortnight ago and taken Mary with her.

Subsequently, the young woman's stepmother reported her as a missing person. Was one of the bodies in Gardenholme Linn Mary's? When they were found, bloodstained women's garments had been scattered around the area, including a blouse with a patch under a sleeve. Taking it to Morecambe, the Lancaster police showed it to Mary's stepmother. She recognized it immediately as one she had bought in a tag sale, patched, and then given to Mary as a gift last Christmas.

Another item of clothing—quite puzzling, in fact—had been found at the murder scene. It was a baby's rompers. Mary had been employed by the Ruxtons to take care of their children. Did Mrs. Rogerson recognize the rompers as belonging to one of her stepdaughter's little charges? She did not, she replied, but there was a woman named Holme with whom Mary and the Ruxton children had spent a holiday earlier that year. She might know something.

Mrs. Holme had no doubts. She'd given those very rompers to Mary for the Ruxton children!

Ironically, as evidence mounted against Ruxton as the likely murderer of Mary and his wife, the doctor chose to stride into the Lancaster police station to demand that they help him find his wife. He also insisted that they inform the newspapers that there was no connection between the women in the ravine and his wife. Rumors that the women found in the Linn were his wife and servant, he said, were driving away his patients.

The police politely replied that they would do whatever they could to accommodate him. But when he was called by them a few days later to request that he come to the station, it was not to report on their search for Isabella. They were prepared to charge him with the murder of Mary Rogerson and to suggest to him that the other body in the Linn was his wife.

As they saw it, Mrs. Ruxton returned home and there was another violent battle that wound up with Ruxton killing her. Realizing that Mary had been an eyewitness, he killed her, too.

Denying everything, Ruxton was represented at his trial in Manchester by the same lawyer who had defended Toni Mancini in the first of Chief Inspector Robert Donaldson's Brighton trunk-murder cases. "It is suggested here by the Crown," said Norman Birkett, "that on the morning of the Sunday after your wife had come back you killed her."

"That is an absolute and deliberate and fantastic story," scoffed Ruxton. "You might as well say the sun was rising in the west and setting in the east."

"It is suggested by the Crown that upon that morning you killed Mary Rogerson."

"That is absolute bunkum with a capital B, if I may say it. Why should I kill my poor Mary?"

This time, however, the man in the prisoner's dock was not able to gaze incredulously, as Tony Mancini had done as the jury delivered its verdict.

Dr. Ruxton was hanged in Manchester on May 12, 1935, at a prison with a name that was a singularly fitting description of how he'd lived: Strangeways.

Given the reputation of Edinburgh University pathologists in the Ruxton case, it was not surprising that Lord Trenchard looked there for someone to organize his next innovation at New Scotland Yard. It was the Police Forensic Laboratory, opened on April 10, 1935, at Hendon. Headed by Dr. James Davidson, the laboratory freed the Metropolitan Police from dependence on the scientists of the Home Office. It has continued that way to the present day, the only crime laboratory in England under direct control of a police force. Serving both the Metropolitan Police and the City of London Police (still an independent department), what is now called the Police Forensic Science Laboratory is part of a nationwide forensic science network that includes the Home Office's Forensic Science Laboratories at Aldermaston, Chepstow, Birmingham, Huntingdon, Chorley, and Wetherby.

Having moved from Hendon to Whitehall in 1948, to Holborn in 1965, and ultimately to Lambeth in 1974, the laboratory's staff of approximately 200 scientists specializes in biology, chemistry, photography, documents, and firearms and uses devices that Dr. Sir Bernard Spilsbury would have wholeheartedly embraced—electron microscopes, mass spectrometry, electrophoresis, infrared spectrophotometry, chromatography, microtomy, and, of course, an array of computers. "Crime is an expanding industry," says a laboratory brochure, "and Forensic Science is endeavouring to keep pace."

The independent forensic unit and the concept for a training school for police were Trenchard's major legacies when, on Armistice Day, 1935, he handed in his resignation after four years as commissioner. Taking his place at Scotland Yard upon Trenchard's recommendation was his former colleague at the Air Ministry and, lately, governor of New South Wales in Australia: Air Vice-Marshal Sir Philip Game.

Before long, Game at New Scotland Yard and Trenchard, back on duty with an ill-equipped and ill-prepared Royal Air Force, were dealing with the blunt-reality of what Trenchard's former flying student and their mutual friend Winston Churchill was now calling "the gathering storm" across the Channel.

SEVENTEEN

Murder in a Quiet Hotel

ON THE EVE OF THE SECOND WORLD WAR THE METROPOLITAN Police force stood at 18,428 men, a little under 1,000 positions fewer than its authorized strength. With hostilities imminent, that wasn't nearly enough to cope with the increased work that wartime footing would require. It was anticipated that many members would be exchanging their police garb for military uniforms. To deal with the manpower shortfall in the coming storm the Parliament allowed for reactivating retirees, hiring full-time special constables, and creating a Women's Auxiliary Police Corps. Among the latter's first duties were registering aliens, helping with the evacuation of children and the elderly from London, and enforcement of Defense Regulations, especially in the area of air-raid precautions.

The first Nazi bomb fell on the Metropolitan District on the 19th of June 1940. Three months later began indiscriminate night-time attacks that came to be known as the *Blitz*. Later on, Hitler launched noisy V-1 buzz bombs and the silent, deadly V-2 rockets. Nearly 3,000 of these new terror weapons hit the city, killing more than 17,000 people and injuring many thousands more. During these horrendous attacks upon civilian areas, *not one policeman* moved out of the city.

When, at last, the bombings stopped and British skies had been swept clear of the enemy by the RAF, the courage and service of the police above and beyond the call of duty were duly noted by the Prime Minister. They had been in it everywhere, all the time, said Winston Churchill in a

1942 broadcast. "And, as a working woman wrote to me in a letter," he continued, " 'What gentlemen they are!' "

Of those who'd set aside policing to join the armed forces, 490 were killed in action, three-quarters of them in the RAF, and 101 were decorated or otherwise commended. Those who returned to duty in 1945 found a police force at its lowest strength in more than sixty years. They also saw a new face in the commissioner's office. Summoned to the Home Office in November 1944 and asked "Can you ride a horse?" by Home Secretary Herbert Morrison, Sir Harold Scott was at that time Permanent Secretary at the Ministry of Aircraft Production. A life-long civil servant rather than a military man or policeman, he was told by Morrison that "in the changed conditions of a post-war world the work of the Commissioner would call rather for experience of administration in a big civil department than experience in the military field." He took office June 1, 1945.

During six years of war, the crime rate had dropped. A year after the war it was higher than ever. It was also more daring and more violent. Before the war, criminals shunned carrying guns because they'd not felt the need for them against a police force that bore none. After the war the "gentlemen's agreement" seemed to have gone by the boards.

Just how vicious this turn in affairs was became evident on a street in Soho in April 1947, as Alec d'Antiquis saw his duty as a citizen and tried to use his motorcycle to blockade a getaway car carrying two men who had just held up a nearby pawnbroker. The bandits gunned the young man down in the street and sped off.

The blazing of guns in the course of a smash-and-grab hadn't been heard on a London street since the cold and misty morning of January 23, 1905, when a pair of men turned off Tottenham's High Road and into Chestnut Road, passed the rear of a police station, and stopped in front of a photographer's shop. Gazing into the window, Jacob Lapidus and Paul Hefeldt waited. Tall and powerful-looking with broad shoulders, a long sallow face, and curly black hair, Lapidus knew the area well. He'd worked at an india rubber works just across the street. From that vantage point he noted the day and time when seventeen-year-old Arthur Keyworth pulled up in a car driven by Joseph Wilson with the wages that were to be paid to employees. It was always on a Saturday around 9:30.

As expected, the car arrived. In the young clerk's bag were eighty pounds in gold and silver. Knocking Keyworth down, Hefeldt grabbed the satchel. As Wilson leapt from the car to rush to the aid of Keyworth, shots rang out. Hefeldt and Lapidus ran. Hearing the gunfire and seeing two men on the run, passerby George Smith threw a bodyblock on Hefeldt and sent him and the bag of loot flying. Four more shots. Two went through Smith's cap, a third through his coat, and the fourth into his chest. Scooping up the loot, Lapidus and Hefeldt scampered away.

From the police station scurried Constables Tyler, Newman, and Coombs to join Wilson in hot pursuit in his car. Moments later they found the bandits still on foot in Scales Road. Again their guns blazed. Four shots smashed the windshield, wounding Wilson in the neck and a constable in the thigh. A bullet also punctured the radiator, halting the car.

Springing from the car, Tyler raced after the fleeing gunmen just as ten-year-old Ralph Jayson dashed into the street from his home to see what all the noise and excitement was. Shot through the heart, he died instantly. A few moments later, Constable Tyler caught bullets in the head and throat.

By now an outraged throng of citizens had joined the chase as Lapidus and Hefeldt made a mad rush across railroad tracks, almost being run down by a train in the process. They ran wildly for Chingford Road and a tram car that had just made its usual stop. After riddling the windshield with bullets and sending the tram's terrified driver running for cover, they scrambled aboard and held three passengers, including a child, at gunpoint, then forced the tram conductor to start the car. Running behind them were more than a hundred screaming citizens. Opening fire from the rear of the tram, the hijackers wounded several pursuers.

When a pony-drawn cart bearing a police officer halted in the way of the tram Lapidus shot the pony dead. Moments later, worried that the tram was nearing a police station, they leapt off and ran. Spotting a milk delivery wagon, they blasted its driver, climbed aboard, and rattled away. A group of hunters saw them, gave chase, and fired at them with shotguns. Both were hit but kept running.

Shortly after the pursuit had begun, police stations around the area had been alerted. Now, officers—a few in the extraordinary position of having been issued pistols—had rushed to the scene and joined the chase. Among them was bicycle-riding Police Constable Charles Eagles. Soon, he found himself outside a cottage where the gunmen were believed to be holed up. From a neighbor he commandeered a shotgun, crept into the cottage, and heard what he thought was his quarry moving around upstairs. Going out again, he fetched a ladder and climbed it to have a look into a window. When he saw Lapidus pointing a gun at the window, he jumped to the ground where, to his utter horror, he discovered that the shotgun he'd taken with him was defective.

Presently, Detective Charles Dixon arrived, armed with a workable revolver. "Let me borrow it," said Eagles. "I know where they are." Moving stealthily into the cottage, he crept up the stairs. Seeing shadows moving beneath a door, he fired two shots into the door. As it swung open, Lapidus was again aiming at him but this time a single shot from the borrowed pistol dropped him. Paul Hefeldt, who'd been wounded in the desperate bid for escape, was rushed to a hospital and died of his wounds two weeks later.

In the course of this amazing and unprecedented gunplay on the streets of London, twenty people had been wounded and four killed, including Constable Tyler.

Fortunately, the similarly aborted holdup of the pawnshop in 1947 was not a repeat of the 1905 massacre. There'd been only one person killed—the motorcyclist. Like 1905, there were plenty of witnesses but, unfortunately, the gunmen's faces had been masked by scarves. Nor had anyone been able to note the car's license plate. The only lead Scotland Yard detectives had was a raincoat abandoned by one of the two men as they raced from the pawnshop toward their getaway car.

Although nothing about the coat provided a clue as to its owner, an indelible code number on its lining was traced to the manufacturer. Three batches of that type coat, he told police, had been delivered to three retailers in London. The shopowners provided sales records, most of which bore names and addresses of purchasers. Among them was Thomas Kemp, residing in the riverside district of Deptford. Yes, he'd bought a raincoat, he said. But he lost it at a cinema. Had he checked at the cinema to see if the coat had been turned in? No he hadn't. Wasn't that a bit odd? It was a fine coat, after all. Or was there another explanation for the loss of the coat? Perhaps Kemp had left it behind when he was conducting business in Soho? "All right, I'll tell you about the coat," blurted Kemp. "My wife loaned it to her brother." What was the brother's name? "Charlie Jenkins."

Not unfamiliar in the criminal records at New Scotland Yard, Charles Henry Jenkins was already on a short list of suspects in another recent robbery in which the booty tallied 5,000 pounds but there'd been insufficient evidence to charge him. In the Soho case, there was plenty. Eyewitnesses to the holdup and the murder of the motorcyclist, and others who had seen the man who'd abandoned the raincoat, identified him. Unwilling to stand alone at the Old Bailey, he implicated two accomplices—Geraghty and Holt. Because seventeen-year-old Holt was too young to be given the death penalty, he got an indeterminate prison term. Geraghty and Jenkins were hanged on September 19, 1947.

In postwar crime, theirs was noteworthy primarily because it underscored a new willingness of criminals to use guns at a time when lawlessness was spiraling upward at an alarming rate. In 1938 indictable crimes in London totaled 95,280. In 1946 that figure stood at 127,796. Known crimes of violence the year before the war were 1,679. The year after, there were 2,155. Arrests of those under the age of twenty for indictable crimes had gone up from 8,614 in 1938 to 10,367 in 1946.

The years following the war also recorded an upsurge in a more subtle sort of crime whose perpetrators wore bowler hats, business suits, and white shirts. Swindlers, embezzlers, and fraud artists, their main hunting ground was within the boundaries of the City of London. Comparable to New York City's Wall Street, the square mile of "the City" was Britain's financial center. In all the years of its rich history its anchor has been the "Old Lady of Threadneedle Street," the Bank of England. Since 1928 it had been the sole issuer of banknotes in England and Wales and the bedrock of Britain's economy. Around it thrived the stock exchanges and hundreds of other establishments in which people with cunning minds and sticky fingers might reap enormous illicit profits. In an attempt to deal with them, in 1946 there was a breakthrough—a breaking down of the ancient City walls, really. For the first time since the founding of the Metropolitan Police in 1829, Scotland Yard and the police department of the City of London joined forces.

The linkage was accomplished through creation, in March 1946, of the Metropolitan and City Police Company Fraud Department. Commonly called the Fraud Squad, its sole mission was to deal with complex and protracted cases involving businesses, banks, and investment firms in Britain and abroad. To make it work, five City detectives were sworn in as Metropolitan Police constables. It wasn't until 1964 that the law caught up with reality and permitted City police to operate on their own in the Metropolis and vice-versa.

While this "revolution" in policing was noted with interest in the financial circles, another change introduced in 1946 by Commissioner Scott at Scotland Yard caught the imagination of all animal-loving Englishmen. It was the Dog Section. Although use of canines was not entirely new in police work (as early as the fifteenth century constables had patrolled with them, and in 1914 policemen were permitted to take their own dogs on duty with them), police had resisted using them because they worried that dogs might be detrimental to public relations. To test that theory, the Home Office had launched an experiment in the years immediately before World War II, but other demands of the war had forced a suspension of the dog trials. Acquiring six Labradors in 1946 but still apprehensive about public reaction, Scotland Yard assured the people that their role "is purely detective and not offensive." They and their handlers were trained at Hendon.

Assigned to Central London, they proved especially useful in Hyde Park and were so successful that they paved the way for the use of dogs throughout the Metropolitan Police District and, in the 1980s and 1990s age of terrorism, at London's airports where a policeman with his hand grasping the leash of a German shepherd has became a common—

and reassuring—sight. "In their own way the dogs of the Metropolitan Police have performed every type of police duty," says a Scotland Yard press release, "from holding eleven violent youths in a cul-de-sac while the handler called for assistance, to finding a couple's lost engagement ring." From its beginning with five dogs, the Dog Section operates today with more than 300, one of which (and its handler) is awarded the gold Black Knight trophy at the Metropolitan Police Dog Championship Trials held each summer in London.

As interesting as these innovations were in 1946, they were dwarfed in public interest by blaring newspaper headlines that capitalized on the age-old English fascination with murder—the brutal sexual-torture death of Margery Gardner at the sedate Pembridge Court Hotel in Notting Hill Gate. In life, she had been an easygoing thirty-one-year-old divorcée with an artistic temperament. She had taken courses in drama, studied elocution, and planned on becoming a painter. But all of that ended on the night of June 24.

Although Superintendent Reginald Spooner of F Division's CID had investigated many homicides, he could only gaze with disgust at her battered, sexually ravaged body.

Presently, Spooner was joined at the crime scene on that Friday afternoon by Chief Superintendent Fred Cherill. Come to collect fingerprints, he wore his customary bowler hat. In the art of finding and identifying fingerprints there was no one better.

Arriving with Spooner, Detective Inspector Shelley Symes from Ladbroke Grove police station surveyed the scene and said, "Nice plateful for the weekend, eh?"

Dr. Keith Simpson conducted the autopsy. Reporting that the woman had not put up a struggle, he concluded that she appeared to have submitted to the sexual sadism that had resulted in her death. Blood tests by Dr. Henry Holden showed that all of the bloodstains in the room were of the same group as hers.

Who killed her? In tracing her activities of the previous night, Spooner picked up the name of Bill Armstrong, who said that he had been a colonel in the RAF. Was there such a person? A check of air force records turned up a file on an Armstrong who had been seconded by the South African

Air Force to the RAF. On his first mission his plane was hit over enemy territory and he bailed out. After the war, he went back to the South African Air Force but was kicked out. Back in England, he had been fined in April 1946 for wearing a uniform and decorations to which he was not entitled.

To find out if Colonel Bill Armstrong might have been known in other London hotels, constables fanned out through the city. In very little time they discovered that Armstrong was a vivid memory in one hotel. In February, reported the manager, screams of a woman were heard from one of the rooms. Bursting in, the manager found the man who had registered as Armstrong naked and bending over a semiconscious naked woman whose hands were bound. The couple left. The woman refused to press charges. Similar tales were unearthed at other hotels.

Who was this man, described as fair-haired and bleak-eyed? The true name of the mysterious, violent Colonel Bill Armstrong came to Scotland Yard, not by tireless legwork and a diligent searching of the massive files of known criminals, but in the Royal Mail. Addressed to Chief Superintendent Thomas Barratt, a letter began: "Sir, I feel it my duty to inform you of certain facts in connection with the death of Mrs. Gardner at Notting Hill Gate." It was not a confession of murder. He'd met Mrs. Gardner and had a few drinks with her. She asked if she might use his hotel room for the purpose of entertaining a gentleman who was prepared to pay for her temporary companionship. He lent her the keys. When he returned to the room around three o'clock in the morning, the letter said, he "found her in the condition of which you are aware." Realizing that he was "in an invidious position," rather than notify the police he packed his belongings and left. He concluded the letter by saying that he had in his possession the "instrument" that had been used by the killer and would forward it by mail. It never arrived, but the letter itself provided more than Barratt and his detectives could have hoped for: the writer's true name. It was well known at the Yard.

Born in Guilford in 1917, Neville George Clevely Heath had a criminal record dating from 1937, when he was court-martialed by the RAF for being AWOL and escaped under arrest. Kicked out of the air force, he was arrested the following year for posing as the nonexistent "Lord Dudley." Released from jail and permitted to join the army, he ran afoul of the military again while serving in the Middle East. Court-martialed and cashiered, he was put on board a ship bound for England but jumped ship at Durban. He reappeared as the fake Colonel Armstrong.

Copies of the Criminal Records Office's photograph of Heath were circulated and printed in the *Police Gazette* as a wanted man. A few days later, it was studied by Detective Souter of the Bournemouth police. Presently, he matched the photo to the face of a young man calling himself Group Captain Rupert Brooke.

While the identification resulted in Heath's arrest, it came too late for a young woman who'd fallen under the group captain's spell. The naked body of Miss Doreen Marshall was found on July 8 in Branksome Chine; she'd been murdered in the same sadistic way as Margery Gardner. Found in Heath's pocket at the time of his arrest was a receipt for a suitcase that he checked at Bournemouth Station. In it was the "instrument" used in both murders: an air force officer's riding crop.

Heath insisted that his crimes were the result of "partial" insanity. "You must decide whether Heath was insane," said his defense attorney, J. D Caswell, "not now, not when he wrote the letter [to Scotland Yard], not when he gave his statements to the police, but at the time the terrible acts were committed."

One of the earliest invocations of what was to become known and widely used as the "insanity defense," the case featured the testimony of the well-known psychiatrist Dr. William Henry Duval Hubert. "He is not an ordinary sexual pervert," he said, "but he is suffering from moral insanity, and at times he is quite unaware that what he is doing is wrong."

Others believed that Heath knew exactly what he was doing and that sending the letter and committing a second murder when he knew that he was being sought had been deliberate acts aimed at creating a foundation for his insanity plea. But it didn't work. The jury needed only fifty-nine minutes to reject "moral insanity" and convict him. An appeal to a special medical board appointed by the Home Secretary also brushed aside the insanity claim. Health was hanged on October 26, 1946.

For a brief moment—at a time in history when a war-weary world was finding its hopes for peace being dashed by the brutal reality of what Winston Churchill, in Fulton, Missouri, described as an "iron curtain" lowered across Europe by the Soviet Union—worldwide attention was riveted on another case of "murder most English."

While Neville Heath was dominating the headlines, movie fans on both sides of the Atlantic were flocking to see a film about one of America's most enduring show-business stars, Al Jolson, whose life story was the subject of the hit *The Jolson Story*, released in 1946. Its most famous—and quoted—line was "You ain't seen nothin' yet." What Londoners didn't know as they went to cinemas to enjoy "Jolie" was that a very peculiar man residing at 10 Rillington Place had been hard at work for a decade giving Jolson's catch phrase a horrible other meaning. In doing so he raised the curtain on a new-style criminal: The serial killer.

EIGHTEEN

Murder, Murder
Everywhere

"I WOULD LIKE TO GIVE MYSELF UP," SAID TIMOTHY EVANS to the police constable in late November 1949.

"And what is it you have done?"

"I have disposed of the body of my wife."

"Where have you done this?"

"Search the sewer drains below Rillington Place."

When no human remains were found police wondered why a man would confess to a crime that had not happened. Such a thing was not new, of course. Murder files at New Scotland Yard bulged with instances of deluded individuals who had rushed forward to proclaim guilt for crimes they didn't do. Evans, a low-witted, illiterate truck driver, appeared to be one of them. But he persisted in his assertion and added that he had also strangled his fourteen-month-old daughter, Geraldine. If the police would dig in the garden behind 10 Rillington Place, he insisted, they would find the bodies.

This time he was correct, but now he was telling the police a different story. It wasn't Timothy Evans who had killed them. It was the man who lived in a flat below, Reg Christie.

The police didn't believe a word of it, in part because the man whom Evans accused had stood calmly in the garden while the bodies were being dug up. If Evans knew that Christie was the killer, why didn't he say so in the first place? Furthermore, there was nothing about John Reginald Halliday Christie that suggested he was capable of murder. He was by no means perfect, but that didn't make him a killer.

A resident of Rillington Place since he moved there in 1938 with his wife, he'd been a special constable with the War Reserve Police, albeit an overly zealous one. He had been asked to resign because he was too eager to cite people for blackout violations rather than educate them in the error of their ways. Before the war he had run afoul of the law by stealing money orders during his brief employment at the post office, for which he was jailed for seven months. But in the ensuing decade, he appeared to have been a happily married man and an upstanding citizen.

At Evans's trial, Reg Christie was, in the words of the prosecutor, "a perfectly innocent man." To another barrister he "bore the stamp of respectability and truthfulness." Nor did the jury believe Evans's accusations against Christie. They convicted Evans of murder.

With his execution in 1950, peace and tranquillity settled again upon Rillington Place and the Christies returned to their routines. Among these was an annual vacation by Mrs. Christie to see her sister in Sheffield, always leaving her husband at home, apparently because he and the sister didn't get along with one another but also because he had to tend to his job with the British Road Services. Regarded as a shy man, he harbored the same authoritarian streak that had led to his dismissal as an air raid warden and so was left alone by neighbors.

He'd always been an oddball. Born in Yorkshire in 1898, he'd had a difficult upbringing. His parents showed little affection. Desperately seeking their attention as a child, he was a chronic hypochondriac and juvenile delinquent whose run-ins with police were dealt with by his parents with beatings. Caught stealing as an employee in his father's carpet factory, he was disowned. Then came the Great War. Wounded and gassed in France, he was blinded for five months and later suffered hysterical loss of his voice for three and a half years. Married in 1920, he appeared to be on his way to stability. But in 1934 he was struck by an automobile and suffered severe head injuries. Then came the trouble at the post office, jail, his short-lived reserve-police service early in the Second World War, quiet residence at Rillington Place, and Evans's outrageous allegation in 1949 that he was a murderer.

Four years later, on March 20, 1953, Christie, who was now living a bachelor's life in the absence of his wife, who'd gone to her sister's in December and never returned, sublet the flat and moved away. On the twenty-fourth the new tenants started renovations by stripping the wallpaper. As the work progressed, they were surprised to find that beneath the paper of one wall was a door. Behind it was a large closet. Inside was the horrible truth about Reg Christie.

Three female corpses, they were identified as Rita Nelson, Kathleen Maloney, and Hectorina McLennan, all London prostitutes. Autopsies showed that each somehow had been rendered unconscious by gas, strangled to death, and then raped in January. But there were more secrets to be learned about 10 Rillington Place. Stuffed beneath floorboards lay the remains of Christie's wife. According to the autopsy, she'd been strangled with a stocking four months ago, December 1952, around the time she supposedly had gone to visit her sister and shortly before the prostitutes died. Yet that wasn't all.

In the same garden where Mrs. Evans and her child had been unearthed in 1949 were Ruth Feurst, an Austrian immigrant who'd vanished early in the war, and Muriel Eddy, who didn't show up for work one day at the same radio plant where Christie had been employed during the war. The corpses had been there while the calm and cool Christie chatted with the police whom Evans had brought with his confession of murder. But, the police learned later, not only had Christie stood by as the excavating was going on for Mrs. Evans, he'd shoo'd away a dog whose rooting around in the garden at that very moment had uncovered the top of a skull. Having chased the dog, Christie calmly pushed soil over the skull and stood upon the spot, with the police none the wiser.

Arrested on March 31, Christie related more chilling details of his thirteen years as a murderer, including an admission that as he'd killed he had experienced a "quiet, peaceful thrill." None of the murders was impetuous or spur-of-the-moment. He had coldly planned them and carried them out according to that plan. He'd been in absolute control at all times. Indeed, being in such control was the thrill of it.

"This pattern can be discerned in most major sex crimes of the twentieth century," noted British crime writer Colin Wilson in discussing the Christie murders in *The Mammoth Book of True Crime 2*. A shy or nervous man, subject to depression, broods on sex until he is obsessed by thoughts of rape. Murders follow, each one succeeded by a still deeper fit of depression. Eventually, he engineers his own arrest or commits suicide. "All such cases have a strong element of illogicality," Wilson continued, "so that the normal, balanced person is inclined to fall back on the explanation as madness." Christie made insanity his plea at his trial but to no avail. He was hanged on July 15, 1953. In due course, Evans was declared innocent of the murder for which he'd been executed.

Twenty years after Christie the lexicon of criminality had a term for such crimes: serial murders. The British phrase was "pattern murders." Whatever they were called, they weren't new. World history is replete with serial killers and England has had its share, the most notable of whom, Jack the Ripper, was a piker compared to those who followed him. But Great Britain has been dwarfed in the incidence of serial killers by the United States. So prevalent had they become in the United States by the 1980s that the Federal Bureau of Investigation created a special unit to study them. Called the Behavioral Sciences Unit (BSU), its psychology-trained agents interviewed scores of convicted serial murderers in prison. The result was the technique of "criminal personality profiling" and major advancements in the understanding of the types of individuals, very much akin to Reg Christie, who commit such crimes. Chronicled in a book by this author, titled *Who Killed Precious? How the FBI Uses Psychology and High Technology to Identify Violent Criminals*, the BSU's researchers found that sexual homicide resulted from one person killing another in a context of power, sexuality, and brutality.

Although by 1991 Scotland Yard had not yet established its own special unit to deal with cases of serial killers, the FBI's pioneer in criminal profiling, Robert K. Ressler (now retired from the FBI and heading his own behavioral sciences firm), has been a frequent consultant on the process to the Metropolitan Police and other British police departments.

The key to criminal profiling is in identifying the methods used by the killer—the psychological "fingerprint" left at the scene of the crime. Another term for it is *modus operandi*, or the M.O., first elucidated by Colonel A. S. Atcherley of the Yorkshire West Riding Constabulary. Every repeat criminal, he pointed out, committed "small, irrelevant acts which had no relationship to the actual commission of the crime and which could be accounted for only by the individual."

Just that type of evidence was what Chief Inspector John Capstick of New Scotland Yard was looking for when he arrived in Ward C H III of Queens Park Hospital in Blackburn, Lancashire, on May 15, 1948. He'd come to assist in the investigation of the mysterious death of four-year-old June Anne Devaney. A patient in the hospital, she'd been taken from her bed to a grassy area near the hospital, raped, and battered to death. She was the third young girl to have been murdered in similar circumstances, although the previous deaths had been by stabbing and not in Blackburn.

Described by Tom Tullet in *Murder Squad* as a legend in his own time, Capstick had caught so many thieves in a single year as a constable at the Bow Street station that he was immediately transferred to the CID. An expert in all the tricks of his trade, he was, wrote Tullet, "quick-witted and a match for the most cunning of criminals, so much so that he was known as 'Charlie Artful.' "

Looking at the body of June Anne Devaney, he was moved to tears. "Years of detective service had hardened me to many terrible things," he recalled, "but this tiny pathetic body, in its nightdress soaked in blood and mud, was something no man could see unmoved."

Capstick's only clues were footprints of someone who'd been in bare feet or wearing stockings and who was evidently small in stature, and a bottle of distilled water that had been moved from a tray cart and left under the girl's bed. It contained fingerprints. While there could be no discounting any member of the hospital staff as a suspect, the trail of footprints suggested that the killer was an outsider. If so, any fingerprints the killer may have left on the water bottle would not match those of members of the hospital staff. Conversely, if none of the staff's prints matched the prints on the bottle, the killer had to have come from outside. Of course, many outsiders had come into the hospital as visitors. Could they be located and fingerprinted? It was an enormous task. But it was done. The result: no visitor's prints matched the ones on the bottle.

Having eliminated hospital staff and visitors, Capstick had cleared many possible suspects. But Blackburn was a city of more than 110,000 inhabitants. Of course, only adult males could be suspects. Could he check the fingerprints of all of them? There was no law against it. Nor was there a law that permitted it. Would men who were citizens of a country that had always been suspicious of police cooperate? More than likely, they'd howl with outrage. But what if the request didn't originate with the police? If someone else, perhaps the mayor, asked them, would the men of Blackburn respond?

Assured by their elected leader that the fingerprints would be employed only for comparison to the killer's, and that no one in the police would check them to see if they could be connected to any other crime, 45,000 men came in to be fingerprinted. None matched. However, not every male in the city had come forth.

According to ration-card records, some 800 males who'd lived in Blackburn during the war hadn't been contacted. How many were still living in the city? To find out, police officers went door to door. Among them on August 11 was Constable Calvert, who was assigned the houses along Birley Street. At number 31 lived Mrs. Griffiths and her twenty-two-year-old, slight-built son, Peter. Would he object to having his fingerprints taken? Wordlessly, Peter extended his hands. At three in the afternoon the next day, the prints of his left thumb and index finger were declared a match to those on the water bottle. Confronted with the evidence, he confessed.

The son of a mentally ill and thereby ineffective father, strongly attached to his mother, incapable of holding a job and unable to relate to women, he was, in the light of the later FBI research, typical of the profile of a serial rapist, child molester, and killer.

The boldness, innovative detective work, and doggedness of Chief Inspector Capstick that paid off with Griffith's conviction were required that same year after two small boys playing near a pond on the edge of a golf course at Potters Bar, about fifteen miles north of London, pulled a human hand and forearm out of the water.

Before Superintendent Colin MacDougall could go after the murderer, he first had to identify the victim. The draining and dredging of the pond provided other portions of the body of a man of between thirty-five and forty years of age who'd been dead for at least four months. The dismemberment had been done crudely, probably with an ordinary carpenter's saw. Was anyone of that description missing?

Albert William Welch, age forty-five, a railwayman, had disappeared from his Potters Bar home on November 17, 1947. Was the body his? Seeking to answer that question, Superintendent MacDougall turned to the forensic pathologists at New Scotland Yard. They sought assistance from the crime lab's photographers. Obtaining a photo of Welch from Welch's family, they made a transparent copy. Laid over a photograph of the skull retrieved from the pond, it was a fit.

As compelling as the photographic sleuthing was, MacDougall wanted more. Learning from Welch's co-workers that he had been complaining of a toothache, MacDougall had the teeth of the skull examined by a dentist. He reported evidence of an abessed root. Still not satisfied, MacDougall obtained a pair of Welch's boots. From them, the men in the crime lab produced plaster casts of the feet that had worn them, took photos of the casts, and matched them with X-rays of the corpse's feet. There was no doubt that the body was that of Albert Welsh. But, alas, with all of this forensics wizardry and intrepid sleuthing, his murderer was never found.

In 1942 the mantle of chief pathologist had been passed from Dr. Sir Bernard Spilsbury to Dr. Keith Simpson. A professor of forensic medicine at London University, he created the Forensic Medicine Department at Guy's Hospital Medical School. Assisting him were Donald R. Teare and Francis E. Camps. Like Spilsbury, Simpson believed that the forensic pathologist's job started at the scene of the crime. So, in October 1949 when Superintendent MacDougall telephoned from an apparent murder in Tillingham, Essex, to request a pathologist to conduct an autopsy, Dr. Simpson despatched Dr. Camps.

Arriving at the morgue in the cathedral town of Chelmsford hard by the windswept marshy East Coast, which was described as "one of those quiet corners of flat homely England," Camps found that awaiting his practiced eye was a torso with arms and hands of a man weighing about 190 pounds and standing five feet seven inches in height. Discovered by a boater on a sluggish tributary of the Black River, the torso had been in water for at least three weeks but, judged Camps, it had been thrown in about forty-eight hours after death. While five stab wounds puncturing the chest appeared to be the cause of death, what intrigued Camps was numerous bone fractures that had occurred after death. But first, who was he?

Although the condition of the hands was poor, Camps managed to remove the skin of the fingers and send it to the fingerprint division at Scotland Yard. There, Chief Inspector Fred Cherill used a glycerine spray to bring out identifiable fingerprints and then to match them with the print record of Stanley Setty. A forty-seven-year-old, Turkish-born swindler, he was a known blackmarketeer and dealer in dubious-quality second-hand airplanes to unscrupulous parties in Middle Eastern countries. A quick check of his London hangouts showed that he hadn't been seen by friends and associates since the fourth of October, approximately the date when the torso was dumped in the Essex marshes.

Concerning its plentiful bone fractures, Dr. Camps suggested to MacDougall that they might have been the result of the torso's being dropped from an airplane. X-rays left little doubt that the breaks were injuries consistent with falling from a great height, meaning that an airplane must have been employed in the crime. At once, MacDougall ordered inquiries at all airports for records of flights on or about October 4. The following day he heard from Elstree Aerodrome in Hertfordshire. On October 5, said airport attendant William Davey, a former war pilot by the name of Donald Hume, of 620 B Finchley Road, Golders Green, London, had arrived at the airfield in a rented automobile and hired an Auster G-AGXT sports plane. Giving his destination as Southend, he informed Davey that he would be back in a few hours. He took two bulky parcels from the car and placed them into the co-pilot's seat. "However, he didn't come back by plane that night," said Davey. Instead, he'd landed at Southend around 6:30, left the plane there, went back to London by taxi, took another cab the following morning to Elstree, retrieved his car, and said he would return the airplane that afternoon. "But he didn't do it," continued Davey. "The next day he phoned and asked us to send someone to fetch the plane at Gravesend."

"Gravesend?" asked MacDougall. "Not at Southend?"

"That's right, sir."

"May I have a look at the plane?"

Behind the co-pilot's seat, MacDougall found bloodstains.

Ordering a discreet surveillance of Hume, MacDougall turned to investigating his suspect's background. The portrait that soon emerged was of an illegitimately born thirty-year-old who'd spent his youth stealing cars for joyriding and a charlatan who joined the RAF under false pretenses. After being kicked out of service, he'd masqueraded as a pilot while running a black market in bogus Finlinson's Old English Gin. Through other larcenous endeavors during and after the war, he lived lavishly. Among his nefarious friends in these postwar illegal enterprises was none other than Stanley Setty.

Proving that they knew one another wasn't proof of murder. It wasn't even sufficient to bring Hume in for questioning. To pick him up without being able to charge him with murder was to risk giving Hume a chance to flee.

Ordering continued surveillance, MacDougall was intrigued by Hume's peculiar activities concerning the rented airplane. If he had dumped Setty's body on route to Southend, why hadn't he returned the plane to Elstree as he had promised? And why did he then abandon the plane at Gravesend, leaving it to be collected by its Elstree owner?

Workers at the Southend airport provided some illumination. When Hume came around on the afternoon of October 6, they said, he arrived in a taxi, carried a heavy bundle aboard, placed it upright in the co-pilot's seat, and took off. Three hours later, according to employees at the Gravesend airport, Hume had landed without a bundle, left the plane to be called for by someone from Elstree, and hired a taxi to return to London.

MacDougall now understood that Hume had chosen to take off at one airfield and land at another so that no one would see that in the course of his flights he'd thrown the bundles out of the plane. But that still wasn't enough to charge him with murder. He needed evidence that would place Hume in Setty's company at the time of Setty's disappearance. At this point, the routine work of a homicide investigation came up with all that was needed. While looking into Hume's comings and goings at airports, detectives combed London's taxi services for records of Hume's trips to and from Elstree, Southend, and Gravesend.

They not only located a driver who remembered taking Hume from Southend to London on October 5, but he still had the five-pound note Hume had given him for the fare. Comparison of its serial number with those of bank notes which Setty had drawn from his bank proved that the fiver had to have been passed from Setty to Hume on the day Setty was killed and butchered.

Arrested at his home at 7:45 A.M. on October 27 by Chief Inspector Jamieson, Hume proclaimed his innocence but did not deny that he'd dumped parcels from his rented plane. He did this, he told MacDougall, on behalf of three very dangerous individuals who'd coerced him into his actions. It had to have been they who killed Setty, he argued.

Although the story was convincingly told by the young, dark-haired, baby-faced suspect, MacDougall was unable to locate any of the men Hume had described in quite vivid detail. "If they are the murderers of Setty," he advised Hume, "you are still liable for a charge of accessory after the fact and I must detain you on that charge." However, he said, if the men could be located and if Hume cooperated in the prosecution, Hume might find the court lenient. Meanwhile, because Hume had expressed concern about the safety of his wife, said MacDougall, he would place detectives in Hume's home to protect her.

This was a subterfuge. The detectives would be there to look for evidences of murder and dismemberment. They soon found it. A cleaning woman who'd been working at Hume's home on the day of his first mysterious plane trip observed him leave the house with several bundles. So did a workman whom Hume had hired to refinish floors. The workman was then enlisted to help in removing the bundles.

Examining the underside of a large carpet that Hume had sent out for cleaning the day after the murder was believed to have been committed, Dr. Camps found a sizable bloodstain. He also found traces of fresh blood in the flooring and on walls. All the blood was tested and found to be human.

Was it Setty's?

At his trial, Hume did not deny the blood was human and that he had cleaned it up. He also admitted that he had suspected the bundles from which the blood had dripped contained Setty's body. But it wasn't he who'd killed him, dismembered him, and bundled him up, Hume insisted. It had been the same men who'd forced him to assist them in disposing of the remains. Unshakable under cross-examination, he clung to the story.

Lacking the sophisticated techniques of blood analysis of future decades, Dr. Camps and other prosecution pathologists could not prove that the blood in Hume's home was Setty's. Consequently, a clearly unhappy jury that believed Hume was guilty but could not convict him on available evidence reported it was hopelessly deadlocked. A mistrial was declared. Given the likelihood that no jury could do otherwise, a new trial was not ordered. Hume went free.

To escape the hangman's noose he'd concocted a clever story of three men who were the real murderers, but in relating it he incriminated himself as their accessory. Tried on that charge, he was convicted and sentenced to twelve years in prison. Released with time off for good behavior on February 1, 1958, he promptly sold the true story of the murder to *Sunday Pictorial* for 2,000 pounds.

Protected by the English law against double jeopardy, he boasted in the headline: "I Killed Setty and Got Away With It."

By the time the article appeared in June, Hume had left England for Zurich, Switzerland, changed his name to Bird, and was claiming to be a Canadian test pilot. The following year, when the money for his article was running out, he held up a bank and shot a cab driver. This time there was no hung jury. Convicted, he was sentenced to life in prison.

Although the state of the art of 1949 forensics was unable to give the jury in the Setty case convincing evidence of Hume's guilt, scientific sleuths working with Scotland Yard's homicide squad scored a swift triumph in the case of the disappearance of Mrs. Henrietta Durand-Deacon.

A well-off widow, she had vanished from her South Kensington hotel on February 18. That she had gone missing was reported to the police station in Chelsea by another resident of the hotel, John George Haigh.

Going to the police was a bad mistake. Suspicious of Haigh's glib and cocky demeanor, they ran his name through the Criminal Records file and turned up Haigh's sordid history of terms in Dartmoor Prison for swindling, fraud, forgery, and burglary.

Looking into his activities since being released from jail in 1943, detectives learned that he'd been hired by a man named McSwann to repair some amusement-arcade equipment. McSwann had vanished without a trace, as had both his elderly parents.

At present, detectives learned, Haigh was still in business as a repairman at Crawley in Sussex. Surprising Haigh by visiting his workshop, three detectives found articles of women's clothing that matched those worn by Mrs. Durand-Deacon the last time she was seen. Along with clothing they found bloodstains and a .38 caliber Webley revolver.

"You can't prove murder without a body," said Haigh with a taunting sneer. "Mrs. Durand-Deacon no longer exists." Pointing to a vat, he added, "I've destroyed her with acid. You will find the sludge which remains in the Leopold Road where I dumped it. How can you prove murder if there is no body?"

Haigh miscalculated on both points. First, the obligation of the police was to prove that a murder had been committed. To do so they did not have to produce a body. Second, Haigh was not familiar with the capabilities of forensic pathologist Dr. Keith Simpson, who at that moment was on route to Crawley from London.

Pondering the challenge that awaited him, Simpson held out little hope of finding much beyond residual sludge. Could any part of the human body survive acid? If so, he wondered, what would it be?

Greeted by Chief Inspector Guy Mahon, Simpson was escorted to the area where the acid sludge had been dumped. The ground was rough and scattered with small pebbles. "Not very promising, I'm afraid," Mahon said.

"Not at all," replied Simpson, scooping up a cherry-size stone. Examining it with a magnifying glass, he discovered that it had polished facets. "Chief Inspector," he said guardedly, "I think that's a gallstone."

Mahon gaped in astonishment. "What a piece of luck!"

"It wasn't luck," Simpson said with a smile. "I found it because I was looking for it."

Women of Mrs. Durand-Deacon's age and habits, he explained, are prone to gallstones. "The stones are covered with a fatty substance that would resist the dissolving action of sulphuric acid."

Over the next three weeks, Simpson and his associates in the laboratory at Scotland Yard discerned further evidence of murder. From 475 pounds of grease and earth scraped from the dumping site and from drums of acid removed from Haigh's workshop they sifted two more human gallstones. Fragments of eroded human bone proved to be affected by osteoarthritis, a disease common in elderly women. A groove in part of a pelvic bone showed that it was from a female. A portion of a left foot was discovered and a plaster cast was made. It fit one of Durand-Deacon's shoes perfectly. Finally, and most important, Simpson found intact full upper and lower dentures.

Beyond doubt, said Helen Mayo, the woman's dentist, the dentures had belonged to Mrs. Durand-Deacon.

Out of a mass of sludge and gallons of acid Simpson and his associates had reconstructed the body of a stout elderly woman with gallstones who was slightly arthritic and wore false teeth. Mrs. Durand-Deacon had been just such a person.

From other items drawn from the sludge and acid they could also state with certainty that when Mrs. Durand-Deacon was shot to death she carried a red plastic handbag containing a lipstick.

Confessing to killing her for her money and jewelry, Haigh also admitted murdering the McSwanns and plundering their estate for 10,000 pounds. He then declared that he'd killed three other people, names not known, in order to drink their blood.

A highly dubious confession that was investigated with no resulting corroboration, it appeared to be an attempt to lend credence to an insanity defense. It failed.

Arrogant and conceited to the end, Haigh wrote his parents boasting of his fame. "It isn't everybody who can create more sensation than a film star," he bragged. "Only Princess Margaret or Mr. Churchill could command such interest."

Haigh's execution on August 6, 1949, and the Christie case rang down the curtain on a remarkably murderous decade in the annals of New Scotland Yard, in which the age-old motives for homicide—greed and lust—still abounded but during which a new breed of killer had emerged. One who murdered often over a long period of time, the serial killer could be stopped only through a melding of the rapidly developing skills of forensic scientists in white lab coats with the skills of the intuitive, questioning, and tenacious sleuths in the plain clothes of detectives.

For other members of the Metropolitan Police engaged in the struggle to maintain the peace of the realm of King George VI in 1949 there was something new in the wardrobe. After seventy-five years, the highbuttoned blue tunic of the uniformed force was replaced with an openneck jacket worn over a white shirt and necktie. The color was the same deep blue.

What of the hat? Although there was an attempt to introduce round, slightly peaked caps of the type worn by police all over the world, the beehive-shaped helmet of the Bobby would continue to be the symbol of the Metropolitan Police through the remaining five decades of the century.

NINETEEN

Sex, Spies, and the Sixties

TO ACCOMPANY ARTHUR SULLIVAN'S JAUNTY TUNE IN *THE Pirates of Penzance* in 1879 W. S. Gilbert wrote: "When constabulary duty's to be done, the policeman's lot is not a happy one."

Seventy-two years later the lot of the newly outfitted Bobby took a dramatic turn with a revolution in the way he'd been doing his job since Rowan and Mayne first drew lines on the map of the Metropolis of London, named them beats, and sent constables out to walk them alone. In 1951 Commissioner Sir Harold Scott, facing a shortage of patrol officers, adopted a system of "team policing" that had proved itself in Aberdeen. Relegating the solitary constable and his beat to history, Scott's team policing divided the Metropolitan Police District into areas that would be policed by groups of constables in radio-equipped patrol cars under command of a sergeant. In one form or another, the system would be the basis of policing thereafter. But it did not abolish all the foot patrols. "A Police Constable on the beat is as much a part of London as Big Ben and Nelson's Column," says a Scotland Yard publication of the 1990s. "The blue uniform of the Metropolitan Police means reassurance and safety for the people of London." What team policing recognized was that in an area of 787 square miles reaching from Potters Bar in the North to Kenley in the South and from Upminster in the East to Staines in the West, encompassing a population of nearly 7 million, the police needed a highly efficient and sophisticated command structure for a force that in 1991 would total 27,215 officers. It was the inevitable extension of

Commissioner Byng's admonition when he introduced police call boxes: "We must give the criminal less time."

By 1951 the rate of indictable offenses had soared to more than half a million in a city in which new housing developments had spread the population over a much wider area. And there were more than a thousand miles of new streets and roads. All of this with a fairly static number of officers available for patrolling. In some suburbs, residents complained that they never saw a cop. To help alleviate the shortage of personnel, Scott took another leaf from provincial police departments by seeking permission of the Home Office to establish a Police Corps. Made up of young men and women, they were instructed in the handling of jobs in police stations that had been assigned to police officers, thus freeing the sworn officers for the crime fighting for which they'd been trained. It was hoped that some of the cadets would find the work interesting enough to apply for the regular force. Many did.

Having made two lasting contributions, Scott resigned his commissionership in 1953 after nine years. His successor was Sir John Nott-Bower, a twenty-year veteran of the Indian Police Service and Deputy Assistant Commissioner and Deputy Commissioner at Scotland Yard during the war and postwar period. He was to serve between 1953 and 1958 and be described by historian David Ascoli in *The Queen's Peace* as "the least memorable" police chief in the history of Scotland Yard. A contemporary quoted by Ascoli said, "He was a nice man when what we needed was a bit of a bastard." In Ascoli's view Nott-Bower was anonymous in a decade that was anything but anonymous—the 1950s.

Another chronicler of the police in England, T. A. Critchley, recorded the rise in crime. In 1955 there were 438,000 indictable offenses. In 1956, 479,000. In 1957, 545,000. In 1958, 626,000. In 1959, 675,000. Yet, confronted with three times the volume of crime in 1938, the police force of 1958 was only 9,000 stronger than twenty years earlier. "Never in their history had they, and in particular the members of the C. I .D., been so hard pressed," wrote Critchley. "The war against crime was not being won."

That is not to say that Scotland Yard was without victories. In 1956, in cooperation with the police of Belgium, detectives broke up a prostitution and white-slavery ring run by the

Messina brothers. Sicilians, Carmelo and Eugenio had emigrated to England in 1934, where they rented hundreds of flats in London and stocked them with girls from the continent and then arranged to have them married to Englishmen, who collected a fee and promptly disappeared. Safe from deportation by reason of their marriage certificates should they be arrested, the girls lived in fear of being beaten or carved up with razors if they didn't do as they were told by the Messinas. One who escaped and wrote a book about her experience claimed she serviced forty-nine men in one night.

While the smashing of the Messina sex ring made titillating reading for Britons who followed crime news—and for professional sleuths at Scotland Yard—the puzzling death of Elizabeth Barlow on May 3, 1957, in Bradford was a chilling flashback to the case of the Brides in the Bath. Famed as the birthplace of composer Frederick Delius and the spot where actor Sir Henry Irving died, and notable as the first and last city in Britain to operate trolley-buses, Bradford was the great traditional center of the worsted trade northeast of Manchester. Urgently summoned to the Barlow house in Thornbury Crescent, Detective Sergeant Naylor of the Bradford CID found Mrs. Barlow dead in the bathtub. A doctor who'd examined her reported that she'd apparently been taken ill while bathing, had vomited, and then overcome by weakness, had slipped beneath the water and drowned. The husband, Kenneth, said he'd tried to revive her. He explained that he was a male nurse at St. Luke's Hospital in nearby Huddersfield and trained in resuscitation.

But if that had been so, Naylor wondered, why were Barlow's pajamas dry? And there were other peculiar circumstances. The woman's pupils were dilated. Could the doctor explain? "I must assume," he answered, "that she was under the influence of some drug." In the kitchen were two hypodermic syringes. Barlow had an answer. He was afflicted with a carbuncle and used them to treat himself with penicillin.

Indeed, when the needles were examined by the police pathologist who conducted the autopsy on Elizabeth Barlow, traces of pencillin were found. However, Dr. David Price of the Harrogate police lab found no injection marks nor anything else about Mrs. Barlow to account for a sudden weakness. She was two months pregnant but that was no cause for a fainting spell. Might she have been poisoned? To determine that, Dr.

A. S. Curry of the Home Office Forensic Science Laboratory and P. H. Wright of the Department of Chemical Pathology of Guy's Hospital Medical School began a series of tests. Puzzled by the lack of a cause for the sudden weakness, Dr. Price decided to examine the surface of the body in minute detail under the brightest light available. Searching for signs of injections wasn't easy. The skin was dense with moles, freckles, and acne. But after two hours, he discovered two tiny marks in a fold of the skin on the left buttock. A moment later he found two more pinpricks on the right.

While this was going on police were looking into the life of the husband. What they discovered was an eye-opener. Elizabeth was his *second* wife. The first died in 1956 at age thirty-three with no plausible cause determined. They also learned that part of his duties at the hospital was administering insulin to diabetics. Furthermore, when he'd been employed at the Northfield Sanatorium he'd remarked to a patient that if anybody were to get a real dose of insulin "he's on his way to the next world." And, around Christmas 1955, he had said to a fellow male nurse, Harry Stork, that insulin could be used to commit the perfect murder because it dissolved in blood and couldn't be traced.

Informed of these remarks, Dr. Curry exclaimed, "Good Lord, you can't imagine how much that means to us."

What it meant to the pathologists and to the police was that they might be dealing with history's first case of murder by insulin injection. But if Barlow were correct and insulin could not be traced in the blood, could they prove a case of homicide? At once, the doctors began experimenting. Injecting laboratory mice with increasing amounts of insulin, they produced weakness, coma, and death. Repeating the tests on larger animals, they produced the same results. Furthermore, they found that the formation of lactic acid in muscles after death prevented the breakdown of the insulin. It was a historic discovery.

It also sealed the fate of Kenneth Barlow. On July 27, 1957, Detective Superintendent Cheshire of Scotland Yard arrested him at Huddersfield. At first, he denied everything. Then he said that he'd given his wife a shot of ergonovine to bring about an abortion. It was a lie formulated to avoid prosecution on the charge of murder. The doctors had tested the body for the drug and found none present. Despite complex scientific testimony, a jury saw exactly what had happened to Mrs. Barlow. "You have been found guilty of a cold, cruel, and premeditated murder," said the judge, "which but for a high degree of detective ability would never have been found out."

A year and a half after Barlow went to prison an incident on Putney Heath brought no ringing accolades to Police Constable Eastmond in particular and the Metropolitan Police in general. On a crisp December morning close to Christmas, Eastmond stopped a motorist for speeding, but the driver was no ordinary citizen. Brian Rix was the noted actor-manager of the Whitehall Theatre.

As the two were engaged in the sort of lively discussion that often follows such an encounter between a driver and a policeman, another car stopped. Out of it stepped a civil servant named Garratt, who proceeded to join the debate. Then came mutual allegations of assault. In due course, though Garratt was not charged with any offense, he filed a lawsuit against Eastmond for assault and battery and false imprisonment.

What precisely had occurred on the roadway is not known because the Metropolitan Police Commissioner paid 300 pounds in court, without admitting liability, and ended the case. But the settlement was not the end of the affair. It became a political issue as Parliament again debated the proper place of the police.

For the fifth time in the 130 years of the department a commission was mandated to review the constitutional position of the police throughout Great Britain, and the relationship of the police with the public, so as to ensure that complaints by the public against the police were effectively dealt with.

The result was passage of a new law, the Police Act of 1964, which for the first time attempted to put into statute the role of the Home Secretary in national police affairs and to make the Home Secretary accountable to Parliament for the affairs of all police departments, not just the Metropolitan Police.

These events were hardly a pleasant welcome to a new police commissioner. The first to have risen from the ranks, he was John Simpson. Taking over at Scotland Yard in September 1958, he was in command of 16,661 police officers and a civil staff of 3,487. In short order he was busily reorganizing and streamlining the department. "There will have to be many changes," he wrote to a friend, "even revolutionary changes." On the eve of the turbulent 1960s, they were prophetic words.

As the Royal Commission was sitting down to study the police of the nation, the Wolfenden Committee, which had been convened in 1954, published its findings and recommendations concerning laws on prostitution and homosexuality. It proposed increased penalties for street prostitution, that landlords who rented premises at exorbitant rent for prostitution should be deemed to be living off immoral earnings, that permitting prostitutes to advertise services as "masseuses" and "models" would be less injurious to society than sexual solicitation in the streets, and that homosexual acts between consenting adults in private should not be a criminal offense. Two years later, the Street Offences Act encompassed all the recommendations except decriminalization of homosexuality.

The continued legal rejection of what Oscar Wilde had called the love that dare not speak its name meant that homosexuals had to go on living duplicitously, concealing their true natures and in constant fear of entrapment. Vulnerable at law and to violence from those who hated "queers," and fair game for blackmailers and others who were eager to grasp opportunities for exploiting their plight, they were still outsiders in a society whose attitude toward them hadn't changed since Wilde stood in the dock at the Old Bailey in 1895.

Seventy years after that trial, on the evening of October 6, 1965, one of these sexual outlaws was seventeen-year-old Edward Evans. Seeking kindred companionship, he went to one of the bars off Oxford Street that discreetly catered to London's homosexual underground. Presently, he met and went to the home of a good-looking—in a rough and sulky way—twenty-seven-year-old who'd introduced himself as Ian Brady.

His real name was Ian Stewart. The illegitimate son of a nineteen-year-old Scottish waitress, he was born on January 2, 1938, but was raised in an overcrowded Glasgow tenement by a woman named Sloan who managed to afford to send him to Shawlands Academy. Unfriendly and aloof from his classmates, he was a fair student but was more interested in Superman comics and gangster movies. At the age of thirteen he was arrested for housebreaking and put on two years' probation. Repeating the offense in 1954, he again got probation. That same year he went to Manchester to live

with his mother, who was married to a man named Brady, and
promptly violated the terms of his probation by stealing lead
from the roof of his employer, a brewery, and was sentenced
to a rehabilitation facility for juvenile delinquents. Moody and
difficult, he boasted to other inmates of his crimes and said
he'd found a good way to raise money by becoming a "rent
boy" for "queers." Released from detention, he lived for a
while with his mother and went on the dole. At twenty-one,
he went to work for a chemical company and met Myra
Hindley.

Four years younger than Brady, the fairly pretty, blonde,
typical working-class girl fell for him right away. On New
Year's Eve 1962 he introduced her to sex. From that moment
on, she was his. A veritable love slave, she did not shrink
from his boasts that he was planning a series of bank robberies. Asked to buy a gun for him, she happily joined a rifle
club. When he acquired a camera with an automatic timer,
she joined him in pornographic pictures. And she accepted
without question his growing obsession with material dealing
with torture, especially books about Nazis.

Then the killing began. A neighbor of Myra's younger
sister Maureen and her husband David Smith was the first
victim. Lured into their car on July 12, 1963, sixteen-year-
old Pauline Reade was not seen again until the summer of
1987, when Myra directed Chief Superintendent Peter Topping
to her makeshift grave in a bleak stretch of Saddlesworth
Moor northeast of Manchester. In November 1963 twelve-
year-old John Kilbride, his trousers and underpants pulled
down, was also buried on the moor. Seven months later, Keith
Bennett, also twelve, was missing from Manchester. The day
after Christmas 1964, it was pretty ten-year-old Leslie Ann
Downey who vanished from a fairground in the Ancoats area
of Manchester. But not without a trace. Before going into a
grave on the moor, she was forced to pose for nine pornographic photos and recorded on audiotape performing sexual acts.

The following September, Brady was drinking at his home
with Myra's impressionable young brother-in-law, David
Smith. "Have you ever killed anyone?" he asked.

Thinking this was a joke, David laughed.

"I have," said Brady. "Three or four. The bodies are buried
up on the moor."

There was purpose in the confession. Brady had made up his mind that Smith should be a partner in the next murder. He'd also decided that the next victim would be a "queer" randomly picked up at a London bar. Thus, Edward Evans's fateful meeting with Brady on the night of October 6, 1965. Lured to a house in Wardle Brook by his sister-in-law, Smith had no idea that Evans was in the house until he heard a blood-curdling scream from the parlor. Rushing in, he gaped in horror at Brady battering Evans's head with a hatchet. Thrusting the axe into Smith's hand, Brady said, "Feel the weight of it." Again, there was purpose—to assure that the axe would bear Smith's fingerprints. Sickened by the experience, Smith returned home and told his wife what had happened. Appalled and frightened, Maureen declared, "We're going to the police."

Early the next morning, Scotland Yard detectives posing as bakery deliverymen called at the Brady house. "We have reason to believe that there is a body in this house," said Superintendent Talbot, showing his identity card. Searching the house, they found the body and a cloakroom ticket from the Manchester Central Station. There they found two suitcases filled with pornographic photos, books on sex and torture, and the nine pictures and tape recording of the last minutes of life of little Lesley Ann Downey.

On May 6, 1966, Brady was convicted of the murders of the girl, Evans, and John Kilbride and sentenced to life imprisonment for each. Myra got life plus seven years as an accessory in the murder of Kilbride. Exactly how many murders they'd committed is not known; as late as 1987 they were confessing to many more. But by then the Moors Murders were long past and new and even more shocking sensations had seized the headlines, beginning in February 1964 with the murder of Hanna Tailford.

A thirty-year-old prostitute, Tailford was found naked in the shallows of the Thames under Hammersmith Bridge. Except for her stockings on her legs and her panties stuffed into her mouth, no trace of her clothing could be located. Neither could her killer. In a city where murders were commonplace Hanna's was noteworthy only because she was nude. But on April 18 her murder suddenly took on greater importance with the discovery near Barnes Bridge at Duke's Meadows of the body of twenty-six-year-old prostitute Irene Lockwood. She had also been stripped naked. Three weeks later, striptease artist and hooker Helen Barthelemy was found dead in an alley at Osterley Park in Brentford. On July 14, the fourth nude victim was identified as Mary Fleming, discovered in a crouching position near a garage in Acton. Four months passed before the next nude victim turned up: Margaret McGowan, known also as Frances Brown. Under debris in a parking lot in Kensington, the body had lain there for more than a month. A year after the first murder, the sixth victim of a killer whom the newspapers were calling "Jack the Stripper" was Bridie O'Hara, found nude in undergrowth on the Heron Trading Estate in Acton.

Unlike the inspiration for his newsy nickname, Saucy Jack the Ripper, who'd committed his crimes without leaving a plethora of clues to assist Inspector Abberline, this Jack's murders had provided leads in abundance for Detective Chief Superintendent John Du Rose to pursue. Legendary in his own time as a superb homicide detective, he was known around New Scotland Yard and among the "ink-stained wretches" of Fleet Street newspapers as "Four-Day Johnny" in awed recognition of his unmatched record for solving murders quickly. Called back from vacation to take charge of the case, he focused on the most provocative characteristics noted in the murder of Barthelemy. Evidence that her panties had been removed *after* death and examination of the vagina indicated that her attacker had not engaged her in coitus. But sperm was found in her throat. Also lodged in the throat was one of four teeth that had been knocked out after death, leading pathologists to conclude that the killer had had oral intercourse before and after she died and, even more horrifying, that she'd been choked to death by the penis.

The condition of the body also indicated that she had not been killed where she was found and that the body had been kept in storage for four days. Where? Specks of paint on the corpse proved to be the type used in spray-painting automobiles. Might she have been murdered in an auto repair garage?

Evidence in the fourth murder, that of Mary Fleming, removed any chance that the murders were unconnected. Sperm was detected in the throat, her false teeth were missing, and her skin had been spattered with paint. Also murdered elsewhere, she'd been dumped in Acton by a man who was seen by a passing motorist who nearly collided with a van that had been used in transporting the body. Unfortunately, the irate driver of the car wasn't able to note the fleeing van's license number.

Because the next murder did not occur until months later, police reasoned that Jack's having barely missed being caught in the act had put a scare into him. When he struck again, twice, the M.O. was the same—oral copulation, broken teeth, paint. But in the killing of Bridie O'Hara, Jack had blundered. The previous victims had been transported some distance from the scene of the crime. Bridie's body had been cursorily concealed in underbrush at the Heron Trading Estate in close proximity to an auto paint shop. Had a fine mist of sprayed paint drifted on the wind to where she'd been concealed? Could the location of her body have been the spot where all the other women were murdered?

Comparative analysis matched the paint used in the shop with that on the bodies. But pinpointing where the women were killed did not direct Four-Day Johnny to immediate identification of Jack the Stripper. The Herod Trading Estate employed thousands of men. To narrow down the field, he engaged in a display of what Sherlock Holmes had called the "Science of Deduction" that would have impressed Holmes's creator, the late Sir Arthur Conan Doyle. Noting that all the victims were short, Du Rose estimated that the killer was of medium or less than medium height. Years spent with the police had also taught Du Rose that prostitutes like the victims of Jack were likely to be picked up by middle-aged men, so Jack was probably in his forties or fifties. Because the six bodies had been concealed for some time before being dumped, he concluded that they'd been brought to the estate in Jack's van at night when darkness shielded him from observation, and that Jack had taken his time in disposing of them, perhaps to guard against being seen or, perhaps, for perverse reasons known only to Jack. That Jack had easy access to the estate meant that he was likely to be an employee, presumably working at night, probably in the overnight hours. Of course, nighttime was when prostitutes plied their trade. The sexual act for which they were picked would be easily performed in the van with Jack seated as the woman bent over him.

Now Du Rose considered Jack's mind. What drove a man to do such things? Evidently, he was a sexual psychopath who was unable to engage in vaginal intercourse. Possibly, he harbored a hatred for women and wished to degrade them by having them perform oral sex. In doing so, he would not have been gentle. During the act, he would be likely to be verbally and physically abusive to the woman, speaking crude obscenities and gripping her hair and neck while he forced himself chokingly into her throat. Needing to experience the thrill again, he repeated the act after she was dead. It was not out of the question to assume that he took his time in getting rid of the bodies because he wanted to have sex with the corpses.

But why was he Jack the *Stripper*? Why bother to remove their clothing *after* they were dead? To preclude their identification? Unlikely. This was the era of fingerprinting. There had been no difficulty in identifying any of the victims. For Du Rose, the stripping of the corpses was as much a part of Jack's ritual as the killing and his obvious necrophilia.

Through this reasoning and by the routine detective work of looking into the lives of those who worked at the estate, Du Rose pared down his list of suspects to twenty, then to three. Among them was a security guard who drove a van, was unmarried, worked between 10 P.M. and 6 A.M., and patrolled in the vicinity of the paint shop. Because there was no direct evidence against him, Du Rose hoped to scare him into revealing himself by placing the estate under open surveillance, interviewing night-shift workers, and telling a sensation-seeking press that the police were close to making an arrest. It was an extraordinary occurrence; Scotland Yard traditionally kept its cards close to the vest. It was, said Du Rose, "a war of nerves."

But it did not end in an arrest. The suspect killed himself. In the suicide note he said he did so because he couldn't stand the strain any longer. Although the note contained no admissions, Jack the Stripper's murders ceased.

In putting the Street Offences Act on the books in August 1959, Parliament hoped to take off the streets exactly the kind of women who became Jack the Stripper's victims. To some extent it did so, but the law also threw open the door to an enterprise the lawmakers may not have anticipated— strip joints. Centered in London's Soho district, the clubs fit right in with a decade that was to go down in history as the Swinging Sixties. Among these flourishing enterprises was Murray's Cabaret Club where, it was said, a man on the town could meet the most beautiful available young women in London.

More than qualified to be hired by Patrick Murray for his club in the very month that the Street Offences Act became law was seventeen-year-old Christine Keeler. Somewhat of a tomboy growing up, she'd become a long-legged girl-next-door model for cheap men's magazines at the age of fifteen and then the stunning beauty who turned the heads of the Murray Cabaret Club's hot-eyed and wealthy customers, including playboy osteopath Stephen Ward.

An ebullient name-dropper with a talent for making friends in high places largely by supplying powerful and monied men with the services of high-priced but discreet call girls, Dr. Ward was vain, ambitious, and morally depraved. Among his friends was Lord Astor, who rented Ward a cottage on the Astor estate, known as Cliveden. Located in Buckinghamshire thirty miles from London, it was a perfect location for the kind of anything-goes parties that were Ward's hallmark. There, while swimming nude in Ward's pool, Christine was observed by Her Majesty's Minister of War, John Profumo. The next day at Cliveden, Profumo met another of Ward's friends, Captain Eugene Ivanov.

An officer of the navy of the Soviet Union, Ivanov was identified by Britain's counter-intelligence service as a spy. But MI5 also had him in its files as a social-climbing womanizer—a recipe for compromise. Accordingly, MI5 quietly suggested to Dr. Ward that he put his talents as a whoremaster to work on behalf of England by luring the vulnerable Ivanov into what the world's spymasters called a honeytrap. Thrilled with the notion of being a cold war secret agent as romanticized by Ian Fleming in his bestselling novels featuring the dashing agent 007 James Bond, Ward enlisted the assistance of Christine Keeler. Dutifully, Christine began sleeping with Ivanov. But what MI5 did not know was that she was also going to bed with the top official of the War Ministry, the Right Honorable Mr. Profumo. When Ward, dropping names as usual, casually let that cat out of the bag in a routine meeting with his MI5 contact, the British Secret Service realized that it had on its hands what the shadowy world of the real-life James Bonds called "a situation." Unfortunately for MI5 and the government of Prime Minister Harold MacMillan, other circles also knew about the War Minister, the call girl, and the Russian. High Society was abuzz. So were Fleet Street newsrooms.

On the afternoon of December 14, 1962, Scotland Yard—quite by chance—got involved. There'd been a shooting at 17 Wimpole Mews, within the jurisdiction of Marylebone Lane police station. The shooter was identified as a West Indian named John Edgecombe, a jilted lover. His target was Christine Keeler. Also present was another beautiful woman, Mandy Rice-Davies. The house belonged to Dr. Stephen Ward. "I love the girl," said Edgecombe. "I was sick in the stomach over her. My sickness in the stomach overcame me and I started firing the gun." Upon such stories, Fleet Street newpapers thrived, especially if they had good pictures to go with the passionate words.

Incredibly photogenic Christine Keeler was front-page news. More than willing to provide great copy—for a price—she sold her story to Manchester's *Sunday Pictorial*. Learning this, Dr. Ward convinced the newspaper that her story was all wrong and that his was better. Obviously agreeing with him, the paper went to press with Ward's account. Meanwhile, rather than testify at Edgecombe's trial, Christine skipped out of England to Spain. But by then, the shooting by a heartsick lover over a call girl was small potatoes. It had been overtaken by the scandal of a Cabinet Minister sharing Christine's affections with a Soviet spy.

Soon the rumblings were shaking the foundations of the Tory government of Prime Minister MacMillan at a moment when Britain and the rest of the world were facing tough times in dealing with the Soviet Union. Britain was acutely embarrassed by the recent revelations of the apparent ease with which Soviet Intelligence had penetrated the Civil Service. Painfully fresh in memory was Klaus Fuchs, a trusted atomic scientist who in the 1950s had betrayed his adopted country by handing over to the Soviet Union secrets of British and American nuclear weapons research. On the heels of that shock had appeared the treacheries of Guy Burgess and Donald Maclean of the Foreign Office, who'd been Soviet spies since their prewar school days. Worst of all was Kim Philby. A Foreign Office executive, he had been the Soviet Union's most important "mole" in the highest echelons of the Foreign Service for three decades.

But all of that was chiefly the concern of Great Britain's Secret Service. The business of Scotland Yard was not spies but criminals, and on that score Dr. Stephen Ward was fair game. By his own published admissions, as the operator of a call girl operation he had violated the Street Offences Act. As a result of investigations based on that law, conducted by Chief Inspector Samuel Herbert and Detective Sergeant John Burrows of the Marylebone Lane police station, he was charged with knowingly living "wholly or in part on the earnings of prostitution."

Standing in the dock at the Old Bailey, Dr. Ward listened to Christine declare, "I am not a prostitute and never have been." But he also heard the prosecutor denounce him to the jury as "a thoroughly filthy fellow" and a "wicked, wicked creature."

Ultimately, what the prosecutor, the jury, the Scotland Yard detectives, or anyone else thought of him did not matter. Before the case could go to the jury, Ward swallowed enough Nembutal pills to kill himself. However, jurors did bring in a verdict on him—guilty. They also found that Christine Keeler was a prostitute. By that time, John Profumo had resigned in disgrace, the MacMillan government had fallen, and Ivanov had made a hasty dash into the welcoming embrace of his Kremlin spymasters.

Among the observers at Ward's trial was Donald Rumbelow, a City of London policeman and the future author of *The Complete Jack the Ripper*. In a passage of that book dealing with the case of Jack the Stripper, he described one of the prostitutes who was a witness at the Ward trial as "a tough hard-faced" little woman with incongruous looking tattoos on bare arms poking out of tiny puffy sleeves. Smoking cigarettes outside the Old Bailey and wobbling precariously on high stiletto heels, she gave her name in court as Frances Brown. Her real name was Margaret McGowan, and after her moment in the limelight of the Ward trial she became the fifth victim of Jack the Stripper.

Through the prosecution of Stephen Ward the veil of cold war espionage had been partly drawn back. If there hadn't been a shooting to be investigated by police, would there have been a "Profumo Affair"? Who can say. But it seems certain that without Scotland Yard's probing of Dr. Ward under the Street Offences Act there would have been no disclosure of the existence of Christine Keeler and her amorous entanglements with a government minister and a Soviet agent.

The case had demonstrated that in the murky waters of the cold war there could be a thin line between the need to protect a nation's security and a duty to deal with common criminality. For Scotland Yard and all the police agencies of the nations of the Free World, detecting that line would be the enduring challenge of the cold war era. How often the interests of the Secret Service and the police may have met across that demarcation we are not likely to be told soon, but John le Carré provided a fascinating example of the delicate balance between Britain's spies and the Metropolitan Police in his 1979 novel *Smiley's People*. Urgently summoned from the peace and blissful quietude of his scholarly retirement at 9 Bywater Street, Chelsea, the "old spy" George Smiley appears in the cold rain of a pathway on Hampstead Heath to tidy up any loose ends in the murder of one of Smiley's cold war allies.

"Knew him personally at all, did you, sir?" asked the Detective Chief Superintendent of Police. His voice was respectfully and deliberately low. "Or perhaps I shouldn't inquire?"

Later, the man from Scotland Yard thought, he would tell his grandchildren that once upon a time George Smiley, sometime chief of the Secret Service, had one night come out of the woodwork to peer at some dead foreigner of his who had died in circumstances that were highly nasty.

TWENTY

Some Very Nasty People

ON MARCH 8, 1967, THE METROPOLITAN POLICE OFFICE opened the doors of a new headquarters in a gleaming high-rise building at Broadway and Victoria Street. Under Commissioner John Simpson's command were slightly more than 20,000 police and civil staff of nearly 6,800. In eleven acres of floor space were 669 offices, ten conference rooms, three libraries, crime labs, the Criminal Records Office, the fingerprints files, photographic section, and a new Public Relations Office. Connecting them with themselves, their city, and the rest of the world were a mile and a half of hallways, thirteen elevators, several vertical document conveyors, and countless miles of cables. If someone wanted a more direct glimpse of what was going on outside the walls there were 4,240 windows. Still, not everyone was happy about leaving Norman Shaw's "police palace" on the Embankment. "There, no one could ever find my office," groused one of the old-timers. "Now I can't find anyone else's."

Halfway between the Houses of Parliament and Buckingham Palace, the *new* New Scotland Yard was as different from its two predecessors at Great Scotland Yard and the Victoria Embankment as Elizabeth II was from Queen Victoria. The modern monarchy and the institution entrusted with the keeping of the Queen's Peace had been transformed by unsettling events at home and abroad. In the words of a detective sergeant of the Central London Criminal Investigation Department, "You have some very, very nasty people walking about."

In a glass case in the entrance hall as the new headquarters was inaugurated was an open book testifying to the dangers facing the police. In it were the names of Police Sergeant Second Class Christopher Tibbet Head, Police Constable Geoffrey Roger Fox, and P. C. David Stanley Bertram Wombwell.

While on routine patrol in the Shepherd's Bush section of London on August 12, 1966, something about an auto moving into Braybrook Street hadn't seemed right to them. Ordering the three occupants to stop for questioning, the police officers followed standard procedures. Head and Wombwell approached the car while Fox lagged a few paces behind. In the tradition of the Metropolitan Police, they carried no firearms.

The trio in the suspect car did. Leaping out with their guns blazing, they mowed down the police, killing them in the street, signaling the end of the historic assumption among the police that so long as the police didn't carry guns neither would the criminals.

Led by Detective Superintendent Richard Chitty, the Murder Squad, Special Patrol Group, Regional Crime Squad forces, and the Flying Squad launched Operation Shepherd. One of the most massive manhunts in British history, it culminated ninety-five days later at the Old Bailey with the three killers being sentenced to life terms.

Concerning the Shepherd's Bush massacre, the same detective sergeant who lamented the fact that there were many nasty people walking around, noted, "If those police officers had a firearm with them, there's a chance that at least two of them would have been alive today." While that view was shared by many, the policy on firearms was not changed. In 1970 only about 5 percent of the police force received firearms training and in the 1990s the figure was comparable.

While the police had a new home base, the day-in and day-out battle against old-style criminals was even more challenging, not only in London but everywhere in Britain. To cope with crime on a nationwide basis police departments were now highly organized in a system of Regional Crime Squads coordinated from London. Their mandate was to concentrate on detecting and apprehending persons actively engaged in criminality in the jurisdiction of more than one police force, to keep tabs on traveling criminals, to provide intelligence on prominent criminals, and to lend mobile and organized detective experience to local officers with major cases. In one year the Metropolitan and Provincial Crime Branch assisted in

4,800 investigations for police outside the Metropolis, resulting in 252 arrests for everything from burglary to murder.

On August 19, 1967, it was murder in a distant place that had Superintendent Ian Forbes packing his bags and heading for the West Midlands valley of the River Trent, where Dr. William Palmer had carried out wholesale poisoning in the 1850s and in the past few hours somebody had abducted a little girl. Summoned by the police of Cannock Chase, Forbes was a formidable figure in physique and reputation, whose record in cracking homicide cases was 100 percent—fourteen of fourteen. Although the body of seven-year-old Christine Darby hadn't been found, that he'd be dealing with a murder Forbes had no doubt. A playmate of the girl had observed a man luring her into a gray automobile. Considering that in the past two years two other young girls were abducted, raped, and suffocated to death in Cannock Chase, this was ominous.

Lying between Lichfield and Stafford, the pleasant town of 22,000 inhabitants was surrounded by remnants of hunting forests of ancient Mercian kings but was noted in modern times for its coal and iron mines and a huge overweening power station. While abduction and murder of children was repugnant anywhere, their victimization in the bracken-covered heights of Cannock Chase was especially troublesome because situated in Beaudesert Park on the former estate of the Marquess of Anglesey was a permanent campground for Boy Scouts and Girl Guides.

Shortly after Forbes arrived, searchers who'd been combing the region for hours found an article of Christine's underwear. The next day they discovered her body. Autopsy showed that she'd met the same fate as the other girls. Neither the body nor the place where she'd been murdered provided useful clues. Forbes's only leads were the scanty description of the man by eight-year-old Nicholas Baldry—from which a police artist created a picture of the suspect—and his positive statement that the car Christine had entered was small and gray.

How many autos fitting that description were there, not just in the West Midlands but in all of England? To find out, Forbes requested a search of automobile registrations. Even in today's age of computerized data banks, such a search would take some time, but in 1967 the one computer that Scotland Yard shared with the Home Office (first introduced in 1964) was being used principally to keep track of the police payroll and crime statistics. Employing it for recording and analyzing data on criminals and their methods of operation was experimental. The sifting of auto files was, therefore, a time-consuming, manual task. When it was completed Forbes and his detectives had an even more daunting challenge. The list contained the names of 1,370,000 owners or past-owners of gray autos, all of whom had to be located. By the time it was done, some of the cars and their owners had been traced and their owners questioned not only in Britain but in Malta, Germany, Spain, Italy, Canada, Nigeria, Gambia, Libya, Ghana, South Africa, Singapore, and Australia.

While the hunt for the car was underway, teams of detectives fanned out from Forbes's "murder room" command post to question residents of Cannock Chase and environs as to their whereabouts on August 19. Door-to-door inquiries totaled 39,000. Males who were talked to numbered 40,000. Statements taken down and filed came to 14,000. At the same time others on Forbes's staff distributed 24,000 leaflets bearing the details of Christine's abduction and the artist's rendering of the suspect in the hope that they might jog someone's memory of having seen Christine and her killer.

Telephone tips poured in by the thousands. Hundreds were checked out by detectives in person. Six thousand more were considered important enough to retain in hundreds of file drawers.

Employing 300 investigators, the manhunt was the largest in the history of Britain. But fifteen months after he'd arrived in Cannock Chase, Superintendent Forbes was no closer to solving his fifteenth murder case than he'd been on the day he'd piled into a car at the Broadway Street entrance of the new New Scotland Yard on route to Staffordshire, or "the Staffs" as the county had been known since the days when it was a retreat for Dr. Samuel Johnson and Izaac Walton.

Had the great detective's winning streak come to an end? Had his tenacity met its match? Did the attention given to the case by the press and the monumental manhunt scare the killer away? Was the case unsolvable? Had invincible Ian Forbes been stumped? The answers to these thorny questions seemed to be yes. Unless Forbes got lucky or Christine's killer made a mistake, they were at a dead end.

In this atmosphere of gloom a phone rang. A woman's voice on the line was tense but calm as she reported having just witnessed a man trying to entice a young girl into his car. Wisely, the girl ran. Could the woman on the phone describe the car? Certainly, the woman said. It was green with a cream-colored top. But there was more, said this remarkable witness; she'd noted the license number.

The owner of the green car was Raymond Lesley Morris. A shop worker, married, father, and long-time respected resident in the community, he was a perfect match for the drawing of the suspect. He'd also owned a gray Austin A-55. Arrested, tried, and convicted of murder, abduction, and sexual asault, he was sentenced to life in prison.

The vast organization put together by Forbes was a textbook example that the best way to conduct a murder investigation is to bring together the best talent available, as soon as possible, at the scene of the crime. It was a doctrine preached by Police Commissioner Simpson and formalized by him with the creation of a Scenes of Crime branch consisting of technical specialists in fingerprinting, forensic science, and photography. Work for them was abundant. The rate of violent crime was skyrocketing. During the first half of 1971, for example, there were fifty-four homicides in London whereas in all of 1970 there had been fifty-one. Violent attacks averaged more than thirty a day, up by 4 percent over 1970. Violent robbery cases totaled 258, a rise of 11.3 percent in one year.

The seventies also saw an increase in the incidence of the most puzzling of all violent crimes—serial murders. Between 1975 and 1981 experts from Scotland Yard joined with forces in Leeds, Bradford, Manchester, Huddersfield, Sheffield, and the West Yorkshire constabularies in a manhunt for whoever was killing women, primarily prostitutes, and sending police notes and audiotapes boasting in the singular "Geordie" accent of Yorkshire that the sender was determined to murder whores.

To "show them up for what they were" he used a ball-peen hammer, chisel, knife, or any other weapon at hand to slaughter thirteen women and wound seven.

The cost of searching for him would amount to $10 million, more than 21,000 interviews would be conducted, and 5 million hours would be clocked by the police before the world would learn that the "Yorkshire Ripper" was a thirty-five-year-old married man who lived in Bradford—Peter William Sutcliffe.

The eldest of five children and his mother's favorite, he was born on June 2, 1946, in the north country where he would troll for his victims. After dropping out of school at the age of fifteen, he drifted from job to job until he found one that he seemed to enjoy—digging graves in the Bingley cemetery.

A frequent pastime was visiting a local wax museum where he lingered over torsos depicting the ravages of venereal diseases. Sexual inadequacy had contributed to the end of his first marriage to a schizophrenic Czechoslovak girl he had met in a pub.

Described by his neighbors as a loner but a sensitive and devoted husband, Sutcliffe was depicted by Crown psychiatrists during his fourteen-day Old Bailey trial as being so paranoid-schizophrenic that he could not distinguish between who was a prostitute and who wasn't. Indeed, five of his victims whom he'd believed were prostitutes were not.

Only the arrival of a police car had prevented him from claiming another victim on January 2, 1981. Curious about a white man with a black woman in the front of a Rover, Sheffield Police Sergeant Robert Ring and Constable Robert Hydes ran a check on the Rover's license number. As they waited for the report, Sutcliffe was allowed to step into weeds at the side of the road to urinate. In the meantime, the police computer readout indicated that the plate did not belong to the car. Sutcliffe was taken in for questioning. Again, he asked to use the men's room. Upon his return he was at last asked to empty his pockets and, as he drew out a length of rope, Ring and Hydes had their first inkling that they might have caught the most wanted man in England.

If he were the Yorkshire Ripper, where was the knife and where was the ball-peen hammer? Considering these questions, the officers recalled Sutcliffe's requests to relieve himself, first at the roadside, then in the police station. Had he tricked them into giving him the opportunity to dispose of the hammer and the knife? Examination of the weeded area uncovered the hammer. The toilet cistern yielded the knife. Their possession by the police produced a confession.

In an attempt to explain his crimes Sutcliffe claimed that "voices" speaking to him in a cemetery had given him a "divine mission" to kill harlots, but the jurors at the Old Bailey didn't buy his plea of diminished mental capacity and found him guilty. "It is difficult to find words that are adequate to describe the brutality and gravity of these offenses," said the judge as he sentenced Sutcliffe to life.

Less than two years after the Yorkshire Ripper was conveyed to Parkhurst Prison on the Isle of Wight, suspicion of murder drew Detective Inspector Peter Jay on a much shorter journey to the Muswell Hill section of North London.

The previous evening, Michael Cottran, an employee of the Dynarod Plumbing Company, had been called to 23 Cranley Gardens to see about a clogged drain that had been exuding a bad odor for quite some time. Inquiring of an occupant of a ground-floor flat as to where he might find the entrance to the sewer, he was directed to a manhole. Descending into it, he recognized the problem immediately.

Chunks of human flesh had stopped the flow.

Had anyone noticed anything unusual during the night? asked Inspector Jay of the residents. There'd been a good deal of going up and down the stairs, he was told. One woman thought there was a party in the top flat, occupied by a young man by the name of Dennis Nilsen.

Finding Nilsen was not at home, Jay waited in the hallway. He wanted an explanation of the nighttime activity on the stairs. Presently, a thirtyish-looking man wearing owlish glasses ascended the steps. "Mr. Nilsen?" asked Jay.

"Yes."

Jay introduced himself.

"Oh, yes," said Nilsen, quite calmly.

"Do you mind if we have a chat?"

"No, of course not," answered Nilsen, opening the door and admitting Jay to a messy, cluttered apartment.

"I suppose you are wondering why I'm here," said Jay.

"Not really," muttered Nilsen.

In the drains of the house, Jay continued, parts of a human body had been found. Had Nilsen heard about it? Might he have any personal knowledge of the matter?

Nilsen was silent.

With all of Jay's instincts crying out that the meek-voiced man standing before him was a murderer, he tried a bit of bluster and bluff. "Where's the rest of the body?" he demanded.

Pointing toward a wardrobe, Nilsen said, "It's in there in two plastic bags."

Escorting him to the Hornsey police station, Jay asked, "Are we talking about one body or two?"

Nilsen turned in surprise. "Oh, no," he said. "More than that. Much more! There have been fifteen or sixteen altogether."

In the nearly 150 years of Scotland Yard's history, homicide detectives had listened to hundreds of murderers describe their motives—greed, rage, revenge, lust, jealousy—and they'd heard many offer mental illness and insanity in exculpation. But no one had come across the likes of Dennis Nilsen's explanation for the murders of his exclusively male victims. "I wanted to love and to be loved," he said. Not sex, he insisted. He just wanted company.

The first to die, he said, was a young Irishman he'd met at the Cricklewood Broadway pub in December 1978. He took him home, he said, but there was no sex. He didn't want sex with his guest. He invited the Irishman to stay with him through New Year's Day. The Irishman declined. Feeling hurt and rejected, Nilsen choked him to death with a necktie, hid the body under the bedroom floor, and eventually burned it in a backyard bonfire.

The second to reject him was twenty-three-year-old Kenneth James Ockenden, a Canadian on holiday. "All I wanted to do was talk," said Nilsen, but Ockenden was interested only in drinking beer and listening to rock-and-roll. "I thought, 'What a bloody guest he's turned out to be,' " Nilsen told Jay. "I was livid."

Naming victim after victim, he revealed a three-year murder spree that involved a complex ritual of cleaning the bodies and keeping them for months before disposing of them by burning, dismemberment, boiling the flesh from the bones, and throwing it into sewers. He'd done this in a house on Melrose Avenue and in the flat at Cranley Gardens—fifteen young men in all. "It's hard to know why I did all these things," Nilsen wrote while in prison. "I derived no pleasure from killing people, not as far as I can recall. I enjoyed cleaning them afterwards, though, scrubbing off all the dirt of their grubby lives."

In a bizarre footnote to the case the London newspaper *Today* reported on October 9, 1991, that author Brian Masters visited Nilsen at Albany Prison to ask Nilsen to provide an analysis of another serial killer, Jeffrey Dahmer, then awaiting trial for the murders of seventeen young men in Milwaukee, Wisconsin. In Nilsen's opinion, according to the newspaper account, Dahmer was "grossly perverted."

Although almost equaling the bloody record of Dahmer but nowhere near other serial murderers in the United States in the 1980s, Nilsen remains unsurpassed in Britain in accumulating victims. But who can say if that dubious record will be topped by a killer or killers whose deeds may still be going on? How many more young men might have died at his hands if neighbors hadn't complained about the stopped-up sewer drain of Cranley Gardens?

How many more than the five rapes and two murders for which John Francis Duffy was given seven life sentences might Duffy have committed if the police hadn't arrested him in 1986?

How many other lives might the "Stockwell Strangler" have snuffed out if Scotland Yard's Scene of the Crime Squad hadn't detected that the deaths of seven elderly men and women between April 7 and July 23, 1986, were not natural, as Kenneth Erskine arranged them to appear, but murder?

Satisfying though these successes were for Scotland Yard in the 1980s, one serial killer remained elusive. Beginning with the abduction—murder of thirteen-year-old Genette Tate on August 19, 1978, at Aylesburg, Devon, through the rape and murder of ten-year-old Sarah Harper from Morely, Leeds, in March 1986, a man believed to be slender, in his forties, with thinning ginger hair and silver-rimmed glasses, possibly in association with a woman, had killed sixteen children ranging in age from five to fifteen. In each case the victims had been taken from their northern homes and driven south to be murdered and discarded in the Midlands.

Closer to home in January 1985, Murder Squad detectives had another dismemberment case on their hands. Scattered about London were the remains of Christabel Boyce. The cause of death, said the coroner, was strangulation. A former nanny to the children of Lord Lucan, she seemed an unlikely victim of random murder or the object of violence at the hands of an extra-marital lover. So why would someone kill her? A clue as to motive surfaced in a report on the character of her marriage. She was, the detectives learned, a nagging wife who taunted her husband Nicholas mercilessly, often in front of their children. When questioned, Nicholas quickly confessed to killing her and disposing of the dismembered body in the hope of deflecting suspicion from himself. When sentencing Boyce to six years for manslaughter, the judge at the Old

Bailey noted that Boyce was devoted to his children and that "a man of reasonable self-control might have been similarly provoked and might have done what you did."

"There is a scarlet thread of murder running through the colorless skein of life," declared Sherlock Holmes, "and our duty is to unravel it, and isolate it, and expose every inch of it." In his relentless pursuit of that goal Holmes stumbled upon the existence of a "Napoleon of crime" who was organizer of half that is evil and nearly all that is undetected in this great city. His name was James Moriarty, a professor of mathematics whose genius had been misdirected from considering the dynamics of an asteroid to running an underworld of crime. Of course Moriarty, like Holmes, was fictional. But for Commissioner John Simpson and his intrepid detectives of the 1960s the malevolent presence of "organized crime" was a reality that Scotland Yard confronted on a daily basis. To deal with the rise of sophisticated professional criminal gangs, he organized a new branch within the detective division—Criminal Intelligence. Said one of the men assigned to the new unit, "It was the start of a new game—super-cops against super-robbers."

Super-cops were also required to cope with another sinister development of the sixties: widespread distribution, sale, and use of illegal drugs. To deal with the problem, Simpson created the Drug Squad. Of course, illicit drugs weren't new. Scotland Yard had been battling drug peddlers for decades, starting in earnest after World War 1. Flowing into London as never before, cocaine was the drug of choice among the West End's postwar smart set, including famous and fashionable women like popular actress Billie Carleton. But when she was found dead of an overdose in a Limehouse den in 1918, an outraged public demanded that Scotland Yard find the source of the drug and bring the dealer to justice.

Determining that the supply line began in Germany and ended in London's Chinatown, detectives learned that the head of the drug ring was a Chinese known in the underworld as Brilliant Chang. A former student of chemistry with an extensive knowledge of drugs, he dressed elegantly, spoke flawless English, and operated out of Limehouse. But his seedy Chinatown digs weren't where he lived. He had an elegant flat in exclusive Mayfair where he threw posh parties to hook the rich and famous on coke. He'd also conducted business at a posh West End restaurant. All of this Scotland Yard knew but couldn't prove, so Chang continued his drug enterprise unhindered for another five years, until a cache of cocaine was discovered in a secret compartment in his apartment. Arrested, tried, and convicted, he went to prison.

Was Chang truly the brilliant mastermind his reputation made him out to be? Author Sax Rohmer, who was fascinated by the case and doing a little sleuthing of his own, claimed that Chang had been the front man for a shadowy character known as Mr. King, who was also a wealthy Chinese businessman and the real power behind the drug ring. Whether King was or wasn't the drug lord could never be proved, but whatever his role was, the mysterious Oriental played a far more important role in the literature of crime than he could have performed in Limehouse's underworld. Inspired by the inscrutable Mr. King, Sax Rohmer created Dr. Fu Manchu, the most sinister fictional villain of all time. Or *was* he a figment of Rohmer's imagination? The author once claimed that soon after he wrote his first Fu Manchu story, the "Devil Doctor" with schemes for taking over the world actually appeared in Rohmer's bedroom. "I, the Mandarin Fu Manchu, I shall go on triumphant," he said to Rohmer. "It is your boast that you made me. It is mine that I shall live when you are smoke."

Indeed, isn't it so? Devotees of crime stories know the evil doctor. But how many can name his creator?

Whether Brilliant Chang, Mr. King, or Dr. Fu Manchu ran drugs into London after the Great War or not, Asians were involved in the drug trade of the 1960s, as were gangs of Lebanese and West Indians, by importing heroin, marijuana, cocaine, LSD, and other substances from the Far and Middle East. Catching them at their trade was a dangerous business that usually meant infiltrating the distribution system with undercover officers. In many cases the best people to do this were policewomen.

The first woman to be employed by Scotland Yard had been a Miss MacDougal, hired by Commissioner Henry in 1907 to take down statements from girls involved in sexual assaults. An official role for women in the Metropolitan Police dates from the First World War, when women's voluntary organizations formed patrols to watch out for the interests of women and girls. In 1919 some of them were absorbed into the force as regular officers, though it wasn't until 1922 that they were given full powers of constables. In 1933 a Children and Young Persons Act was passed, increasing the scope of women's duties and turning them into specialists in juvenile problems. Only the coming of World War II gave women a chance to show that they were capable of performing every type of duty, yet it was not until 1973 that they were fully integrated with equal pay and opportunities for promotion and allowed to take part in special squads.

In 1980, in an investigation with echoes of the Brilliant Chang case, Woman Detective Chief Inspector Carole Scard was key to the Drug Squad's Operation Cartoon. The target was a luxurious penthouse apartment in Wallington, Surrey, from which a major drug network was being run by a purported flamboyant homosexual known on the streets as Mr. Big.

Efforts by undercover agents to get to him had been stymied by his efficient security system, but when his flat was put on the real estate market, the Drug Squad seized the chance.

Posing as a prospective buyer, Scard was greeted by Mr. Big himself. Slim and six feet tall, he wore only a terrycloth robe as he led her on a tour of the sprawling apartment furnished with brown glove-leather settees and chairs and the latest in video equipment. An incessant talker, he bragged of the many properties he owned and, to her astonishment, volunteered that he'd served time in prison for murder. Full of himself, he inadvertently let her know that he was deeply enmeshed in dealing drugs. Then he made a pass at her. "And he was supposed to be gay," she thought. Doing her best to produce a terribly disappointed and regretful smile, she said, "I'm sorry to disappoint you, but I'm afraid it's the wrong time of the month!"

The more he talked, the more convinced she became that he was the boss of a vast drug ring. "So, what about the flat?" he asked. "Will you be taking it off my hands?"

"I'll have to talk it over with my husband, of course," she replied.

At that moment the doorbell rang. "Ah, that will be my best friend," said Mr. Big, opening the door.

As the friend came in, Scard recognized him immediately as one of London's leading drug gangsters against whom she had gathered evidence in an undercover operation. Certain that he recognized her, she thought, "Carole, you're dead."

"This young lady is interested in buying my flat," explained Mr. Big.

"How very interesting," said the gangster with a tight smile. "You look very familiar. Have we met? Perhaps in one of my nightclubs? I own several in the West End."

"Not likely," she said, easing past him into the hallway. "I don't go out much. I'm a homebody. I haven't been to a nightclub for years."

Badly shaken, she returned to Scotland Yard to report that she was convinced that a raid on Mr. Big's flat would turn up the evidence to put him away on drug charges. That is, she added, if the "best friend" hadn't by now remembered who she was and warned Mr. Big of the danger they were in.

Because obtaining a warrant to raid Mr. Big's flat required time, the squad had to wait, hoping that Operation Cartoon hadn't been blown. For Carole Scard, it was a restless night and nervous hours at her desk the following morning. Trying not to dwell on her close call and the possibility that Operation Cartoon was in peril of being ruined, she was catching up on paperwork when her phone rang.

She recognized the voice immediately. "You owe me one," he said. "Oh, I remembered you yesterday, honey," he continued. "I'd never forget your face, darling." What she owed him for his not blowing her cover, he said, was a promise that he wouldn't be on the list of those to be rounded up along with Mr. Big's gang. "I saved your life, you know. One word from me and you'd've taken a flier out the window. Is it a deal?"

If letting off a relative smallfry was the price for nailing the rest of the gang, said Scard's superior officers, it was a deal they could live with. With warrants in hand, they raided the home of the gang, arresting six drug dealers. But when they moved in on Mr. Big's sumptuous flat, they were disappointed. He wasn't at home. Had he been tipped off after all? Did he, on reflection, deduce that the pretty young woman who'd visited him was a cop? Did he realize that he'd talked too much? Was he gone to ground? Might he have fled the country?

A few days after the raids, Scard and her companions on the Drug Squad learned his whereabouts. His corpse was found in his car in the Hackney Marshes. Although it appeared to have been a suicide, the autopsy proved otherwise. He had died of natural causes.

Looking back on the case and others she'd handled, Scard spoke with utter contempt of Mr. Big and all those who dealt in drugs. "A killer may murder once or more times," she said, "but the leaders and members of drug rings are nothing less than mass murderers who promote long-term misery. They are devoid of human feelings and are motivated by only one thing—greed. They're not remotely concerned with the trail of death they leave in their wake."

The war against drugs did not proceed without setbacks. In an investigation for the television program "The World in Action" and in a subsequent book, *Scotland Yard's Cocaine Connection*, reporters Andrew Jennings, Paul Lashmar, and Vyv Simson claimed in 1990 that they had evidence that the Metropolitan Police had engaged in a coverup of drug-related corruption in its ranks. Alleging political influence at Scotland Yard, they questioned how free the police were to do their work unchecked. "It is a constitutional fiction that the Met (Metropolitan Police) is independent of the politicians," they charged. Rather than answer allegations of corruption, they asserted, Scotland Yard "hired an expensive firm of image consultants to try and paint over the cracks."

In the face of criticism a quarter-century after the Drug Squad was formed, with the war against narcotics far from won and as overwhelming as their task appeared to be, members of the Drug Squad labored on with all the enthusiasm, cunning, and bravery demonstrated by those like Scard who had joined its ranks when Commissioner Simpson created it.

While those pioneers were being enlisted to combat the drug gangs, a group of detectives had joined another of Commissioner Simpson's daringly innovative special teams. Their objective, they were told, was to combat growing traffic in forged and stolen art.

Scratching his head, one of the detectives grumbled, "I don't know a Botticelli from my backside."

He soon learned the difference. And he learned that in the rogues' gallery of British criminality there had been and always would be individuals who were prepared to think BIG.

TWENTY-ONE

Grand Capers

ON THE NIGHT OF JUNE 30, 1960, IN THE THIRD YEAR of Sir John Simpson's tenure at Scotland Yard, glittery first-nighters in the stalls and galleries of a West End theater fell under the spell of the most lovable rascal in Victorian literature. "You've got to pick a pocket or two," crooned Charles Dickens's corrupter of youths in the premiere of Lionel Bart's enchanting new musical *Oliver*! Sending Oliver Twist out on his first job, Fagin makes a plea to the waffish leader of the pack. "If you happen to pass the Tower of London," he begs the Artful Dodger, wistfully, "have a look at the Crown Jewels, won't you, boy?"

Similarly greedy eyes had been cast toward the ceremonial regalia of the Kings and Queens of Britain by Sherlock Holmes's archenemy, Professor Moriarty, in the second of Basil Rathbone's cinematic incarnations of the Deductive Sleuth of Baker Street (*The Adventures of Sherlock Holmes*, 1939). "Somewhere in London at this very moment something tremendous is happening," laments a puzzled Holmes to Dr. Watson. It is to be, he speculates, the crowning act of Moriarty's infamous career.

Crowning?

"Watson," exclaimed Holmes, "we're wasting time!"

The Crown jewels of England had been coveted by thieves long before Moriarty and old Fagin and appropriated twice. First to grab them was Oliver Cromwell as he wrenched power from Charles I in 1649. Regarding them as symbols of tyranny he had the crowns destroyed, but with the restoration of the monarchy, new regalia were created for the coronation of Charles II.

Ensconced in the formidably guarded Tower of London, the new crowns, orbs, state swords, scepters, spurs of chivalry, and other objects were cared for by Talbot and Dolly Edwards. Residing in an apartment above the jewel room in Martin Tower, from time to time they exhibited the objects to worthy visitors. Accordingly, when a clergyman whom the Edwards knew and trusted appeared at the Tower with two friends in April 1671 and cajoled Mr. Edwards into letting them see "the ensigns of the king," Edwards admitted them to the jewel room. But as soon as they were inside, the clergyman hit Edwards on the head with a mallet. Stuffing the regalia under their cloaks, the trio made a dash to escape.

Unfortunately for them, a guard sounded an alarm, sending mounted militia in hot pursuit. An hour later the jewels were recovered, the thieves were in custody, and the clergyman was identified as Colonel Thomas Blood. An Irish rebel who'd been a Cromwell cronie, he had tried several times to kidnap members of the royal family in hopes of again toppling the monarchy.

Rather than reaping the wrath of Charles II, Blood charmed the king into forgiving him, restoring his estates, and conferring upon him an annual pension of 300 pounds. Whether successors to Charles II might have been as magnanimous is unknown. Since then, no one has tried to steal the royal trinkets.

Although the Crown jewels remain the booty of all booty and loot of all loot, lesser targets have been nonetheless tempting and lesser crooks have been nonetheless challenging to Scotland Yard. Whether the crime was a single-handed smash-and-grab or a grand caper executed by a gang, the legendary Flying Squad was ready, as on August 8, 1963, when word was flashed to London from Buckinghamshire police that the Glasgow-to-London mail train had been stopped and robbed near Cheddington at an overpass known as Bridego Bridge.

It was an ideal location. The mauve brick bridge spanned a quiet country lane and was surrounded by shielding woods with the nearest farmhouse a quarter-mile away. More important, there was a signal tower that could easily be ascended by a member of the gang in order to tinker with the lights, changing green to red and bringing the oncoming express train to a halt. Having done so, the gang uncoupled a baggage car containing sacks of money, shot their way into it, and carried off no less than 120 bags stuffed with millions of pounds in currency.

That afternoon, Detective Superintendent Malcolm Fewtrell of the Buckinghamshire police traveled to London to brief George Hatherill, deputy chief of Scotland Yard CID, and others on what he knew. There'd been at least fifteen men involved, he said, and the getaway vehicles may have been an army truck and Land Rovers. He also reported that as the robbers fled, one of them warned the workers in the money car to "do nothing for half an hour." It was a significant clue. What it told the police was that the gang was not planning an immediate escape from the area, but expected to go to ground within a thirty-minute drive of Bridego Bridge. Based on that reasoning, a search was launched to cover every inch of ground within a thirty-mile radius of the stickup site. At the same time the press was informed that the police were especially interested in hearing from anyone who'd seen an army truck or a Land Rover in the vicinity of the robbery— the hope being that if the gang members learned that their vehicles had been identified they would be reluctant to move from their hideout.

If the robbers were holed up in the immediate vicinity of the robbery and they were not locals, it seemed reasonable to assume that they'd rented a house or other suitable building. Accordingly, detectives set out to inquire of real estate agents about recent rentals, but what promised to be a time-consuming task was cut short on Monday, August 12, by a telephone call from an inquisitive farmer concerning a recently bought property known as Leatherslade Farm, where he'd noticed a five-ton army truck in a locked garage. Since putting out information about the vehicles believed to have been used in the robbery, many such reports had been received, so there was nothing unusual about the farmer's report. Like all the other tips, it had to be checked out. Two constables were despatched.

What they found was, in the words of Buckinghamshire CID Detective Superintendent Fewtrell, "one big clue." The truck was there as were two Land Rovers. Within the farmhouse were stores of food, sleeping bags, blankets, *and* a heap of empty post office mailbags and torn-up money wrappers.

Without a doubt this was the hideout. But where was the gang? Where had they gone? In all that they'd abandoned, had they been stupid enough to have left fingerprints? From Scotland Yard at dawn the next day arrived Detective Superintendent Maurice Ray and a team of experts with all the equipment that was needed to find and lift latent prints. Starting work at once, they quickly realized they had a treasure trove to take back to Scotland Yard for comparison to the fingerprint cards in the Criminal Records Office.

If the files provided matches with the prints of the men who pulled off what the newspapers were now calling the "Great Train Robbery," odds favored that the crooks were known to Detective Chief Superintendent Thomas Marcus Joseph Butler of the CID.

Slight, balding, bachelor, fifty-year-old Tommy Butler was a veteran of the Flying Squad with a phenomenal knack for remembering names and faces of crooks. Therefore, when Maurice Ray matched a set of prints found on a box of salt and a cellophane wrapper on a first-aid kit at Leatherslade Farm with the file on Charlie Wilson, Butler was not surprised.

What the Criminal Records Office did not know about Charlie, Butler did. The files described his criminal record, which was considerable. But Butler knew Charlie's human aspects. Married (wife's name, Pat) with three kids, tall and strong with angular features and bright blue eyes, he was warm-hearted with family and friends, had a sense of humor, and was fiercely loyal to gangster associates who afforded themselves of his talents as a violent enforcer for their West End protection rackets. Charlie lived in Clapham and that's where he was arrested.

Methodically and patiently and acting on Maurice Ray's fingerprint discoveries and scene-of-the-crime evidence turned up by the Metropolitan Police Forensic Science Laboratory team led by Dr. Ian Holden, Butler cast a net. By September he'd pulled in five of the principals of the gang and had sent out "wanted" notices for five more and suspected four others. By the end of the year, 120 police officers working on the case had taken down 2,350 written statements, 1,700 exhibits were ready as evidence, and nine of fifteen known gang members were in police custody and awaiting a date in court in Aylesbury, Buckinghamshire.

One of the longest and most complex prosecutions in English history (the judge's summation alone took six days), the case was turned over to the jury on the afternoon of March 23, 1964. Two days later it came back with guilty verdicts that ranged from robbing with violence to obstructing the course of justice.

But that was not the end of the Great Train Robbery. Two of the robbers escaped from prison. Charles Frederick Wilson broke out of confinement in Birmingham and fled to Canada with his wife and three daughters, living there under the name Ronald Alloway until the international police force (Interpol) tracked him down in Rigaud, Quebec. Arrested on January 25, 1968, he was returned to England handcuffed to Tommy Butler. The second escapee, Ronald Biggs, had fled to Rio de Janeiro where he was safe from Butler because Brazilian law didn't permit extradition.

Of the gang, only one had slipped through Butler's dragnet. He was Bruce Richard Reynolds. An intellectual thief, he'd been one of the ringleaders and was identified from fingerprints on a Monopoly board. Immediately after the robbery he'd fled with his wife Franny to Mexico and then hopscotched to Canada, the United States, Germany, and the South of France until the need for money forced him back to England to replenish his purse from his share of the loot.

In the meantime, Tommy Butler was so determined to track him down that he postponed retirement from Scotland Yard. Although five years had passed and his triumph had been recognized in his promotion to head of the Flying Squad, he trawled his sources in the criminal underworld of London for any inkling as to Reynolds's whereabouts. Doggedness—some members of the Flying Squad said obsessiveness—paid off in November 1968 when a tipster reported that Reynolds might be found in a rented house called the Villa Cap Martin at Torquay on the coast of Devon. Accompanied by men of the Flying Squad, Butler knocked on the door of the neat white house overlooking the sea at six in the morning of November 8.

When Franny opened the door, she gasped in amazement, then spun round and dashed upstairs with Butler at her heels. Striding into the bedroom, he recognized his man. "Hello, Bruce," he said. "It's been a long time."

With a shrug Reynolds replied, "*C'est le vie.*" Persuaded by Butler to plead guilty, he was sentenced to twenty-five years.

That left only Ronald Biggs at large. A cheeky crook in his Brazilian safe haven, he cooperated in an account of his flight written by Colin Mackenzie titled *Biggs: The World's Most Wanted Man*. Ironically, the first installment was published in London by the tabloid newspaper *Sun* on the very day that Tommy Butler died at the age of fifty-six.

What of the loot? Out of the $7,386,715 (2,631,684 pounds), the equivalent of less than a million dollars was recovered. As calculated by author Piers Paul Reid in *The Train Robbers*, after expenses, each member of the gang received a share in the amount of 150,000 pounds—not much of a payoff when divided by the time the gangsters served in prison. For those paroled after twelve years it came to under 3,000 pounds a year, less than the income of an honest middle-class Englishman in 1963.

Despite Butler's tenacious police work, it's the grand total of the proceeds of the Great Train Robbery that's remembered and by which all succeeding robberies were to be measured, as in the hijacking of a bank truck in the Islington section of London on May 1, 1967. The booty was $2 million worth of gold bullion in the form of 144 bars weighing 1.9 tons—hauled away by six to ten gunmen.

In 1971, an armed gang got away with $1.1 million in cash from an armored car.

That same year, bold bandits pulled off a bank burglary by taking a leaf from a Sherlock Holmes story, and did so only a stone's throw from Holmes's legendary lodgings in Baker Street. Their target was Lloyd's Bank Baker Street Branch. Inspiration for the crime came from "The Red-headed League." Published in 1890, the story involved a gang of robbers who lured gullible flame-haired Jabez Wilson away from his pawnshop in order to tunnel their way from his cellar to the bank vaults two doors away.

In the story the burrowers surface to find Holmes, Watson, the bank manager, an inspector, and two police officers waiting for them. The 1971 tunnelers, said prosecutor Robert Harman at their 1973 Old Bailey trial, "got clean away."

Almost.

Thanks to tips and dogged legwork, detectives of the Flying Squad tracked down Thomas Stevens, Reginald Tucker, Lee Street, and Anthony Gavin, all of whom pleaded guilty to possession of explosives and stealing from a bank.

Their deed was neatly done, Harman explained to court. To discover the layout of the bank a gang member rented a safe deposit box, enabling him to regularly visit the vaults and take measurements with his umbrella. Having obtained the data, they began digging in the cellar of an empty shop some forty yards away. Completing the seventy-five-foot tunnel on the weekend of September 11, 1971, they looted the vaults of money and safe-deposit valuables in excess of 1.5 million pounds.

Three years before the gang copied the plot of "The Red-headed League," *Punch* artist Bill Tidy exhibited prescient irony with a May 1968 cartoon showing disguised bandits robbing a post office. "Hurry up," says one of the crooks while a pair of police constables ignore them, their backs turned. "They still believe we are re-enacting an old Sherlock Holmes adventure."

Exceeding the 1963 Great Train Robbery was the stickup of a Mayfair branch of the Bank of America in 1976, in which eight men grabbed $13.6 million, only to be caught within forty-eight hours with most of the cash recovered.

Six years later, on April 4, 1983, a lone guard was eating breakfast at the headquarters of the Security Express Company in London. It was Easter weekend. In nearby vaults lay cash receipts of shops and supermarkets. Seven million pounds.

Looking up from his meal, the guard found himself staring down the muzzles of six guns, as did several other employees when they reported for work. Taking their time in the quiet of the long holiday, the thieves made a clean getaway.

Their success was short-lived. Rounded up by Scotland Yard detectives, property developer Terrence Perkins and garage owner John Knight, the ringleaders, were sentenced to twenty-two years and three accomplices got six-to-eight years.

Seven months later, six masked men eclipsed the Great Train Robbery by barging into the Heathrow Airport vaults of Brinks Mat Ltd. On November 26, 1983, they doused a guard with gasoline, an act that left no doubt in the minds of other guards that if they did not cooperate, their captors would engulf their gasoline-drenched coworker in flames.

The gang made off with 26 million pounds in gold bullion and two boxes of diamonds, causing gold prices on the international market to climb to $18 an ounce.

Because of the complexity of the robbery plan and the ease with which it was carried off, investigators suspected that the thieves had an inside accomplice. They also appreciated that because the stolen gold bars were marked, they could not be sold intact. To profit from their booty, detectives reasoned, the thieves would have to melt down the bullion. Then they would have to find a buyer.

Presently, the Criminal Intelligence Branch collected information pointing to a suspect. Lacking sufficient evidence to make an immediate arrest, the investigators elected to put the man under surveillance.

At Scotland Yard there was no one better at that sort of work than Detective Constable John Fordham. A member of the Criminal Intelligence Branch, he was accompanied by another surveillance officer, Neil Murphy, in observing the home of a chief suspect. Unarmed and dressed in camouflage clothing and wearing balaclava helmets and face masks, they awaited the execution of a search warrant by others. Their task during the raid was to ensure that no one escaped from the house.

A veritable fortress, the house was guarded by three vicious Rottweiler dogs. Sensing Fordham's presence, barking and snarling, they attacked. Attempting to draw them off, Murphy retreated and radio'd for assistance.

By the time help arrived Fordham lay dying in the snow. He had been stabbed ten times in the back and chest. "He has done me," he gasped. "He has stabbed me."

The "he" to whom Fordham referred was the chief suspect in the robbery and the owner of the house, Kenneth Noye. Arrested, he claimed that he had believed that Fordham was an intruder and that he had acted in self-defense.

Although Noye and an accomplice in the gold robbery, Brian Reader, were acquitted of the murder after an eleven-week trial at the Old Bailey, Noye was convicted of masterminding the robbery and was given a sentence of fourteen years. Reader was given nine years. Another gang member, Garth Chappell, received ten. Two others, Brian Robinson and Mickey McAvoy, also got ten years. A sixth member of the gang, John Fleming, was being held for extradition in the United States. Still sought were at least ten others, as was more than half the gold.

Daring and lucrative as it was, the Brinks Mat heist did not remain very long in the record book as the biggest caper in history. It was matched on July 12, 1987, when three men posed as potential customers of a safe-deposit center in Knightsbridge and got away with 125 boxes estimated to contain at least the equivalent of the gold heist.

As spectacular and colorful as these crimes had been and as romantic as the culprits seemed, the motivation for them had been personal greed. The gangs differed from the thieves who had been pursued by the Bow Street Runners only in the amounts they stole. But in 1950, one of the most spectacular capers in the colorful history of crime-with-a-flair signaled the arrival in England of a bold new breed of criminal with an entirely new motivation in that the objects they stole had no intrinsic value.

Dating back even further than the Crown jewels, the Stone of Scone had been resting beneath the coronation throne of English monarchs, which was quite an antique in its own right, believed to be the oldest article of furniture in the city of London. A 336-pound rectangular slab of yellow sandstone, the Stone of Scone had been central to rites of coronation for the kings of Scotland at least four hundred years before it was removed to Westminster by Edward I in 1296. Scottish legend put an even earlier date on the stone, citing it as the one on which Biblical Patriarch Jacob rested at Bethel when he beheld a vision of angels. It then made its way, according to Celtic tradition, to Egypt, Sicily, and Spain, thence to Ireland 700 years before Christ, and, at last, to Scone in Scotland.

Understandably, its disappearance from Westminster Abbey on December 25, 1950, astonished Britain, not only for the daring of the deed but because of the prodigious feat of hauling it out of one of the most secure public places in England on a morning when the ancient abbey was to be the focus of Christmas celebrations. Just as breathtaking was the fact that the theft occurred within easy strolling distance of Scotland Yard.

For the police, who stole the stone was no baffling mystery. Nor was the motive. The culprits had to be Scottish nationalists who'd been threatening to carry it back to its place of origin as a gesture of opposition to English sovereignty over Scotland. The most likely suspects appeared to be Glasgow University students Ian Hamilton, Alan Stuart, Gavin Vernon,

Alistair MacDonald, and David Rollo. However, proving their complicity in the theft was another matter.

There was also a thorny legal question. Was the taking of the stone really a theft? A sound case could be made that the English government had violated a treaty of 1328, in which the stone was supposed to have been returned to the Scots.

As to the stone's whereabouts, there was little doubt at Scotland Yard that soon after its removal from the abbey the stone had been whisked northward, well beyond the jurisdiction of the English police. Unable to find it and unwilling to seek arrests, they bided their time.

At last, having made their point, the people whom many Englishmen considered thieves and many Scots regarded as national heroes, handed over the stone on April 11, 1951, amidst the ruins of Arbroath Abbey in Scotland. Eight days later, Vernon, Stuart, Hamilton, and Kathrine Matheson, a schoolteacher, announced at a press conference that they had taken the stone and returned it on the promise of the British government that they wouldn't be prosecuted.

While some Englishmen may have found bargaining with thieves morally reprehensible, the deal that restored the Stone of Scone to Westminster Abbey a year before the coronation of Elizabeth II was not the first instance in which a valuable object was stolen and held for ransom. In 1878, Adam Worth, a burglar who knew art when he saw it, "kidnapped" "The Duchess of Devonshire," a priceless painting by Gainsborough, from the art dealers Agnew and Agnew. To get the painting back, he demanded in a letter to the police that his friend George Thompson was to be released from jail where he was being held on a check-forgery charge. But when he learned that Thompson had already been released on a technicality, Worth had a change of mind. Now, to rescue the Duchess, Agnew and Agnew were asked to come across with money. Meanwhile, the painting was smuggled to the United States, where it remained until Worth and the Agnews finally came to terms in 1901. But whatever Worth got for his trouble was a hollow victory. He was dying from tuberculosis.

Nearly a hundred years after Worth stole the Gainsborough in a bid to free a friend from jail, and twenty-four years after the Scots swiped the Stone of Scone as a political gesture, Bridget Rose Dugdale thought she could achieve her goal by taking their lead. In a bid to win the release from prison in

England of four convicted Irish Republican Army compatriots, she barged into the mansion of Sir Arthur Beit outside Dublin on April 26, 1974, and threatened the millionaire with guns and explosives while she and her accomplices pillaged his collection of paintings by Vermeer, Goya, and Rubens, valued at $20 million.

Herself the daughter of a millionaire, the former university lecturer sent a note to a Dublin art gallery threatening to burn the paintings unless her IRA friends were transferred from prison in England to one in Northern Ireland. She also demanded money: the equivalent of $1.2 million. Instead of collecting, she was arrested and the paintings recovered at her hideout in southeast Ireland. Quite by coincidence, two days after her arrest, police in London received an anonymous tip that resulted in the recovery of Vermeer's "The Guitar Player," valued at $4.8 million, after it was abandoned in a churchyard by an unknown individual who'd also demanded transfer of the same IRA prisoners and may have gotten cold feet after hearing about the arrest of Dugdale.

While these politically motivated capers were sensational, no one had been killed or even seriously hurt. The same could not be said for activities of other individuals and groups who burst upon Great Britain in the 1970s with old aims and hellish new ways of pursuing them.

TWENTY-TWO

Terror on Parade

THE VOICE ON THE PHONE HAD AN IRISH LILT. "THIS IS THE IRA. Car bombs outside Harrod's."

Abandoning her lunch in the cafeteria of the Chelsea Police Station and rushing to a patrol car, Woman Police Constable Jane Arbuthnot muttered, "The bloody killers!"

The world-famous department store on Brompton Road was her beat, patrolled by bicycle. Just yesterday, Sunday, December 18, 1983, in the hope of easing Christmas season traffic congestion, she had been ticketing illegally parked cars outside the store. "It makes you feel like Scrooge," she had said to her sergeant, Noel Lane, a fellow as genial as his jolly name.

Speeding to the store in Lane's car at the noon hour Monday with only six shopping days left until the big day, she and Lane knew that the pavements in front of the store would be thronged as they had been yesterday.

As the police car wheeled into the Brompton Road, a lacework of 11,000 tiny white lights sparkled from the splendidly proud and domed Edwardian architectural landmark. Beneath one of the green awnings gracing the store's eighty Christmas windows a Salvation Army band serenaded shoppers with a sprightly blaring brass rendition of "God Rest Ye, Merry, Gentlemen."

Lane squeezed his vehicle past a double-parked car.

Arbuthnot jogged around the blue Austin 1300. Yesterday she would have ticketed it. Today there was no time to be doling out penalties to scofflaws. What mattered immediately was assisting the swarm of officers from other arriving police units in getting the people off the street and possibly out of the store so that steel-nerved experts of the Anti-Terrorist Squad could set about the business of finding and neutralizing the bomb.

If there was one.

If this wasn't a false alarm.

Bomb? Or bomb scare? No one could be certain. The murderous Provisional wing of the IRA had shown itself capable of sending either sort of greeting.

A decade of mayhem proved it, starting on October 31, 1971, with bombs that severely damaged top floors of the Post Office Tower and an army drill hall a quarter-mile away from Parliament.

On February 22, 1972, they hit Aldershot Army Base. On March 7, an IRA bomb exploded at the exact site of the May 1884 Fenian bombing of Scotland Yard, and, seven minutes later, a car bomb was detonated at the Old Bailey.

In August 1973 the Provos set off incendiary devices in Harrod's and other stores in Oxford Street. That December they struck an annex of the Home Office, bars, hotels, a railway station, and theaters.

June 1974 saw an attack on Parliament, damaging the 900-year-old Westminster Hall.

During four days of August 1975 bombs ripped through a bar in Chaterham in Surrey, a store in Oxford Street, another in Kensington Church Street, and a London bank. In September, there were five bombings in as many days, including an assault on the London Hilton Hotel.

Targeting individuals was not beyond them. On March 30, 1979, they planted a bomb in the car of Airey Neave, Conservative party spokesman on Northern Ireland, blowing him to bits as he left the House of Commons.

Continuing the terror campaign into the 1980s, the Provos concealed a nail bomb in a parked van, detonating it by remote control as a busload of Irish Guards drove past on October 10, 1981. "The attack," said an IRA statement, "is attributable to the state of war which exists between the British government who occupy Ireland and the oppressed Irish people who strike through the Irish Republican Army."

On July 20, 1982, in perhaps the most horrifying assault on British soldiers in London, a remote-controlled car bomb killed troopers and horses of the Queen's Household Cavalry as they paraded from their barracks near Hyde Park for the changing of the guard at the Horse Guards in Whitehall. A short time later, another bomb exploded under a bandstand in Regent's Park as the Royal Greenjackets were giving a lunchtime concert for tourists and Londoners. "There may be more attacks of this kind," warned Scotland Yard, "and they may be in the near future."

Now it was Harrod's at Christmas time. Inside were 230 departments on five floors covering twenty acres. There were six restaurants, five bars, a legendary food hall, a lending library, a bank, a pet shop, a beauty parlor; on the fourth floor, scores of wonder-struck children filled the expanded toy department, eager to whisper their hearts' desires into the ear of Father Christmas.

As Constable Arbuthnot reached the curb and stepped from the blacktop Brompton Road onto the sidewalk she could hardly miss noticing Inspector Steven Dodd. One of the tallest members of the Met, he had married one of the smallest women officers on the force. Recipient of a commendation from the commissioner for subduing a gunman, he towered over the holiday crowd.

Before the inspector and the woman constable could speak to one another, the timer of the bomb in the double-parked Austin sparked thirty pounds of explosives.

In an instant Arbuthnot was dead, hurled across the road and slammed into iron railings. Dodd would die of wounds as he lay in a hospital operating room.

In the blast and a hailstorm of shredded window glass Mrs. Caroline Cochran-Patrick, a twenty-four-year-old mother of two, died along with Philip Geddes, a young reporter for the *Daily Express*, and his girlfriend, Jean Beaton. They'd come to Harrod's from a mass at nearby Brompton Oratory. Parts of the dismembered body of Kenneth Salvesan, an American living in Kensington, would be found on the store's roof. Seventy others fell wounded.

Since 1883 and the advent of the Fenians, the task of dealing with the "Irish problem" belonged to the Special Branch. With the upsurge of IRA terrorism in the form of bombings in the 1970s it became clear to Commissioner John Waldron that the situation required a centralized team to carry out countermeasures. Drawing primarily on veterans of the Special Branch, he formed the Bomb Squad.

A crucial test of this expanded capacity for dealing with the

IRA presented itself in mid-February 1972. Special Branch intelligence operatives in Northern Ireland reported that an IRA action was being planned, probably to coincide with a referendum on Northern Ireland autonomy scheduled for March 7. Significant public buildings in Central London were likely to be the targets of car bombs.

The IRA plan called for four automobiles to be stolen in Belfast and transported to the Irish Republic, where they would be repainted and fitted with false registrations and then spirited into Britain. In London they were to be rigged with explosives and taken to the targets: New Scotland Yard, the Old Bailey, an army recruiting office in Great Scotland Yard, and the British Forces Broadcasting offices in Dean Stanley Street in Westminster. With timers set to detonate the bombs at 3 P.M., March 8, the ten men designated to carry out the plot planned to head to Heathrow to catch an early morning flight to Dublin.

Patrolling the vicinity of New Scotland Yard, two special patrol constables observed that the number on the plates of a Corsair parked near the Yard did not jibe with the year of the auto's manufacture. Neither did the car bear a tax disk. Moments later, Bomb Squad experts rushed from the police headquarters, popped open the Corsair's trunk, and found it packed with sticks of gelignite.

Immediately, Bomb Squad Commander Bob Huntley notified all British ports of exit to be closed, including Heathrow.

Meanwhile, an anonymous caller to the *Times* provided the locations of the other car bombs. Rushing to Dean Stanley Street, Bomb Squad members found and defused a Vauxhall Viva. But at Great Scotland Yard, something went wrong. While being tested the bomb detonated, injuring sixty-one people. Seven minutes later, the car bomb at the Old Bailey exploded, causing 162 casualties.

By night's end the plotters, thereafter to be known as the "Belfast Ten," were being questioned. In the morning they were all under arrest. Tried at Winchester Crown Court in the autumn of 1973, eight were sentenced to life in prison and one to a term of one to fifteen years. The tenth, a young girl, was acquitted on grounds of diminished responsibility.

The IRA terror continued. Investigation of bombings that killed seven people at Guildford and Woolich in 1974 led the Special Branch to descend on the London home of the Maguire family.

Convicted in 1976, Patrick Maguire; his wife Anne; brother Vincent; son Patrick, Jr.; Sean Smyth, an uncle; Giuseppe Conlon, another relative; and family friend Patrick O'Neill were given long prison sentences. Principal evidence against them had been confessions obtained during intense interrogation.

That same year, six men from Birmingham were sentenced to life on charges of killing twenty-one people in two bombings. Police testified that all had confessed in jail after being informed that traces of nitroglycerine had been detected on their hands.

In all of these cases the accused proclaimed innocence, to no avail, until 1991, when Britons heard the stunning news that appeals by the Maguires, the Guildford Four, and the Birmingham Six had been upheld by the courts.

In the case of the Maguires the judges ruled that confessions had been coerced and that nitroglycerine tests in their case also had been flawed, an assertion that embarrassed officials at Scotland Yard did not contest. Meanwhile, the elder Patrick Maguire had died in prison.

"What I would like," said his son as he walked out of court, "is for someone to tell me why I have had to suffer for sixteen years."

Freedom for the Birmingham Six was ordered by the appeals court after prosecutors said they could no longer vouch for the evidence, again admitting that tests for nitroglycerine had been faulty.

"The police told us from the start that they knew we hadn't done it," declared one of the six, Patrick Hill. "They told us that they didn't care, that they were going to frame us."

Seven months after the release of the Birmingham Six those in the West Midlands police who had arrested them were, themselves, arrested on charges of perjury and conspiracy to pervert the cause of justice.

Dismissal of the convictions of another group, the Guildford Four, was also ordered on evidence that confessions, the primary reason for their prosecutions, had been illegally extracted by the police.

While Britain reeled with these reversals, Home Secretary Kenneth Baker, in recognition of the obvious, said, "I believe that it is now necessary to undertake a review of the criminal justice process."

At the same time, the government announced formation of a Royal Commission to study the need for changes in criminal law, trial procedure, and police practice.

In the turbulent, explosive, and dangerous period when the Maguires, the Birmingham Six, and the Guildford Four were being rounded up, the commissioner of police was Sir Robert Mark. Born in Manchester in 1917, the son of a garment maker and retailer, he became a Manchester policeman in 1937, served in the army in World War II, and returned to policing. In 1957 he was appointed Chief Constable of Leicester, a stepping stone to Scotland Yard in March 1967 as an assistant to Commissioner John Simpson.

In the London to which Mark moved there were few people who believed that there was anything to love about architect Eero Saarinen's design for the American embassy. Topped by an immense eagle with widespread wings, it sprawled along the west side of historic Grosvenor Square, which for two centuries had been the home of the leading political figures of Britain and focus of the grandeur, fashion, hospitality, and taste of an empire that had ruled the world but in 1968 no longer existed.

"Rule Britannia" had been supplanted by the superpower whose stars and stripes floated over the square, in the heart of which stood another symbol of British decline and American ascendency—a statue of President Franklin D. Roosevelt by sculptor William Reid Dick.

Opened in 1959, the U.S. embassy was viewed by many people as outsized, grandiose, and bombastic—terms which a throng of protesters converging on Grosvenor Square on March 17, 1968, attributed to the United States itself.

Though it was St. Patrick's Day and though there were Irish amid the noisy crowd surging toward the embassy, the cause that drew them was not the old "troubles" of Ireland but the war in Vietnam. Under the banner of the Vietnam Solidarity Campaign, they flooded into the square by the thousands. Shouting and toting placards in the name of peace, their purpose was not to stage a demonstration but to storm the embassy and take it over.

In order to do so they would have to push through a cordon of Metropolitan Police whose only recourse was to link arms and stand as best they could while abiding goading taunts of "pigs," "fascists," "imperialists," and the rest of the crowd's colorful vocabulary.

Inevitably, the thin blue line was breeched. Surrounded and under physical attack, the besieged police had no choice but to defend themselves.

The situation quickly took on the makings of another Bloody Sunday. In a pitched battle that was by far the most violent in the 139 years of the Metropolitan Police, 145 officers were injured enough to require treatment. Scores more were punched and kicked and knocked to the ground.

There was one more casualty. Three days after the riot, Sir John Simpson was stricken with a heart attack. The first head of the Metropolitan Police to die in office since Robert Mayne, he had been, in the words of David Ascoli, "a great policeman and a devoted public servant" whose innovations were his legacy—the Scene of the Crime Squad, the art-theft specialists, Regional Crime Squads, the Drug Squad, Special Patrol Groups, modernizing the department, and reforming working conditions.

"Without a contented force," Simpson had said, "the public cannot be given the protection to which they are entitled nor will there exist between the police and the public that mutual trust and respect which is itself a vital element in the war on crime."

Appointed to the commissionership upon Simpson's death, Sir John Waldron, approaching sixty years of age, found himself called upon to deal with some of the most tempestuous years in London's history. In the words of a confidential Scotland Yard report written in 1971, persons were "intent upon grasping every opportunity to challenge, denigrate and, if possible, overthrow the form of society which finds acceptance by the majority of the population."

Self-proclaimed revolutionaries in their early twenties, they were, according to the report, "unemployed, with no permanent addresses and willing to attach themselves to any cause, however hopeless or impractical, which they consider will aggravate or cause embarrassment to authority." Very nasty people indeed.

"If a policeman reacts at all and replies with force," said Waldron, "this is just what the demonstrators want." How to deal with them? Waldron advised "tact and restraint."

That did not mean the police should be unprepared. Stung

by the events at Grosvenor Square, Waldron set out to remedy the obvious flaws in crowd control. Riot training was instituted. In recognition of the rise in terrorism the Bomb Squad was formed.

The next year, 1972, an old bugaboo of the detective force landed on Waldron's crowded desk. There was, reported the *Times*, "disturbing evidence of bribery and corruption among certain London detectives." A *Times* reporter, the newspaper claimed, had offered a telephone book with the names of "bent" policemen by a member of the force who'd boasted, "We've got more villains in our game than you've got in yours." He added, "I know people everywhere. Because I'm in a little firm in a firm."

Involving corruption by dozens of detectives charged with cracking down on the pornography industry and illicit drugs, the scandal stirred public outrage, disgust, and deep doubts about the ability of Scotland Yard to clean its own house. Demands were made for an investigation by outsiders. "It was a humiliating moment for the force," observed police historian David Ascoli, and a "devastating comment" on Waldron's inability to deal with the crisis. Waldron announced plans to retire.

Succeeding him on April 17, 1972, Sir Robert Mark faced the dual challenges of cleaning out the crooks and restoring the public's confidence. Of that task he wrote: "No one could possibly doubt the need to preserve belief in, and support for, the desperately undermanned police force of a capital city which had long managed somehow to contain problems, ever increasing, some of them giving rise to public anxiety."

Scotland Yard, he observed, imparted an aura. "No one really wanted, or perhaps thought it possible, to separate fiction from reality. It had gone on for so long that everyone concerned tended to accept it as unchangeable and, in any case, better than anything that might replace it, much the same view, in fact, that many take of British justice and Parliamentary democracy."

In a lecture to the Royal Society of Medicine he addressed himself to the general population, raising age-old questions of the proper place of police in a free country. "You must make up your minds what you really want. Absolute unrestricted freedom for the individual with all that this implies? Freedom to rob? Freedom to steal? Freedom to intimidate minorities by threats and violence? Do not think I am exaggerating when I say that this is a part of the price you will pay increasingly for the continued enjoyment of liberty without responsibility."

Ahead of Mark, his police and the people of London lay not only the terrors of IRA bombers whose targets would range from army barracks and Horse Guards on parade to holiday shoppers at Harrod's and in Oxford Street. The streets of London were also the stage for all the causes and grievances of the 1970s whose champions were quite likely to turn their anger and frustrations on the police.

"Dissent is the very essence of democracy," said Mark. "The role of the police is not to suppress it but to ensure that it does not express itself unlawfully, and if it does, to contain it by lawful means. This is a lesson that policemen often take years to learn. It can be a bitter lesson because the more dissatisfied the dissenter, the more he will sometimes vent his displeasure on the police."

These were trying years. In 1975, Mark recalled in his memoirs, *In the Office of Constable*, twenty-nine bombings and other types of terrorist acts had killed ten people and injured another sixty-nine. At the same time the CID arrested 103,252 criminals, 16 percent more than in 1973 and double the total of 1967. Violent crime was rising at a rate of 8 percent a year. But what alarmed Mark most was the age of those going astray of the law. Of those who were arrested for robbery, 62 percent were twenty years of age or under. Half the burglars were under seventeen.

"The difference between the fictional impression of crime and its reality," Mark noted, "is not generally understood by the public who like their criminals suave, their heroines elegant and attractive and, generally, a happy ending," he wrote. "But it is seldom like that in real life."

Two cases of real-life crime during Robert Mark's tenure as commissioner rivaled fiction for suspense and action. Around New Scotland Yard the events are recalled simply as "Balcombe Street" and "Spaghetti House." The latter was, Mark recalled, "the most difficult and potentially explosive of all the various problems with which I had to deal in my twenty years as a chief officer of police."

In Central London in 1975 the Spaghetti House seemed to be everywhere. Known for inexpensive, tasty Italian cuisine, the chain of restaurants proved to be a profitable enterprise, as their managers attested when they gathered late each Saturday night at the chain's Knightsbridge branch to tabulate the day's receipts.

In the wee hours of Sunday, September 27, as the tally of 13,000 pounds was being prepared by Giovanni Mai and eight others for deposit in the night safe of a nearby bank, Mai heard a noise behind him. Turning round, he stared down the twin barrels of a sawed-off shotgun in the hands of a grim-faced black man. Two of his companions held handguns.

"We'll take that," said the shotgun holder as the gunmen scooped up the cash. "Everybody down to the cellar," he said. Pointing toward a door, he appeared to know quite a lot about the layout of the restaurant. But as the trio shepherded their captives below they seemed surprised to find that the descent was by way of four short staircases.

The split-second of confusion was all that Mai needed to dash through an exit. Speeding along Knightsbridge, he reached the Berkeley Hotel. "Your phone," he gasped to the desk clerk. "I must use your phone!"

As police surrounded the Spaghetti House, they recognized that armed robbery had turned into exactly the hostage situation for which they had been preparing for two years. First, they sealed off the area. ("With minimum inconvenience to ordinary traffic," noted Mark in his book, obviously reflecting Mark's having served for a time as assistant commissioner for traffic.) Second, the Home Office was asked to provide a psychiatrist who had made a study of hostage situations, Dr. Peter Scott.

When contact was made with the hostage takers, their leader identified himself as Franklin Davies. A Nigerian, he was known at the Yard as a man who had just served ten years in prison for armed robbery. Consequently, when Davies asserted that he and his accomplices were members of the Black Liberation Front (BLF), the claim was, in Mark's words, "received with the derision" it deserved. After speaking to Davies, a genuine member of the BLF disassociated the group from the gunmen.

With politics out of the picture the following hours saw the development of what had become the typical scenario of a hostage situation. Requests for water, cigarettes, and sanitary supplies were met by the police. Demands for freedom for all blacks who were in police custody, a meeting with the Home

Secretary, safe passage for themselves, and an airplane to take them to Jamaica were refused.

The standoff lasted six days. Except for what Mark called "a halfhearted attempt" by Davies to kill himself, no shots were fired and no one was injured. With the gunmen in custody, Mark received a letter from Buckingham Palace. "Her Majesty," wrote the private secretary to Elizabeth II, "has told me to congratulate you, and all members of the Metropolitan Police who were involved, on taking such difficult decisions so calmly and so well, and in bringing about such an eminently satisfactory result."

Like everyone in Britain, the Queen had watched the drama unfold via television.

Several weeks later, TV trained its cameras on a second hostage crisis, this one in sedate, sophisticated Mayfair. On December 6, four terrorists drove past Scott's Restaurant in Mount Street, spraying it with fire from automatic weapons. The gunmen were members of the IRA.

Their arrival was not unexpected. Analysis of previous IRA operations had persuaded Scotland Yard that there was method and pattern in their madness and led the analysts to deduce when and where the next action might occur. Based on this presumption, a force of 700 uniformed and detective officers was deployed in Mayfair.

Despite a leak of details of the planning meeting to the newspaper *Evening News*, which printed the story in late November, the terrorists drove into the trap.

Moments after their attack on Scott's Restaurant their bullet-punctuated, high-speed dash to escape ended with the terrorists abandoning their car and weapons. Holing up in a building in Balcombe Street, they seized hostages.

A replay of the Spaghetti House standoff, the siege went on for five days, eighteen hours and fifty-five minutes. In the end, the hostages were freed unharmed and the terrorists were taken into custody.

In the aftermath, Mark was asked by a reporter what he would do if hostage takers grabbed a politician or cabinet member. With a hint of a smile Mark replied, "Ask them if they would like a few more."

TWENTY-THREE

Murder at the Savoy
and Other Illustrious
Addresses

SOME MURDERS ARE REMEMBERED BECAUSE OF THE VICTIMS. Some stand out because of the nature of the crime. Others are too bizarre to be forgotten. A few achieve notoriety for the place where they were committed.

Such was the killing of Catherine Russell. At Scotland Yard her death is also enshrined because of the carelessness of the murderer.

Like Polly Nichols and other victims of Jack the Ripper nearly a century earlier, and the unfortunate women who ran afoul of Jack the Stripper in the 1960s, twenty-seven-year-old Catherine was a prostitute, albeit considerably more upscale than the others, allowing her uncontested entry into one of London's most historic and poshest hotels.

Built during the zenith of the Victorian era by Richard D'Oyly Carte next to his Savoy Theater on the Strand, the Savoy Hotel accommodated the toast of English society and visitors from abroad. Designed by T. E. Collcutt, it was the first hostelry to provide electric lights and elevators and was managed by Cesar Ritz, whose name became an adjective for luxury. Discriminating palates had been satisfied by chef Auguste Escoffier.

When Catherine arrived on the evening of October 1, 1980, the hotel had lost none of its grandeur. Crossing the opulent entrance court, she breezed past the entrance to D'Oyly Carte's theater in the company of a suitably well-dressed man who was five years her junior. Registering at the hotel barely an hour and a quarter earlier, he had given his name as D. Richards of Birmingham. His true identity was Tony Marriott

245

of Highland Avenue, Horsham, Sussex. His room at the Savoy was on the eighth floor.

Around 10:15 P.M. Marriott hurriedly left the room and the hotel without stopping to pay his bill.

The departure did not go unnoticed. Hearing noises coming from the room, possibly a woman's screams, an employee of the hotel had decided to investigate. Nearly bowled over as Marriott came out of the room, the employee glimpsed what had appeared to be blood on his clothing.

Cautiously entering the room, the employee found Catherine. Partly undressed and sprawled beside the bed, she had been stabbed fifty-five times.

Rich with fingerprints, a bloody clasp-knife lay nearby. The door latch yielded even more. So did a pocket diary discovered under the bed. More important, the little book bore the name and an address of its owner.

Might the diary have been left behind by an earlier guest?

Not at the Savoy. Vacated rooms were cleaned meticulously, including vacuuming *under* the beds.

The manhunt for Marriott was brief. It ended the following evening. Recognizing him as being a wanted man, the landlord of a public house in Southend-on-the-sea, Essex, called local police.

Sex with Catherine had never been his goal, Marriott told questioners. He had invited her to his room at the Savoy because he wanted to murder a prostitute. "The real problem, I feel, is that I seem to develop a resentment of normal sexual relationships," he said. He stabbed Catherine even before she had undressed. In a blood frenzy he continued even after he knew she was dead.

At trial at the Old Bailey his defense attorneys offered evidence of a record of persistent psychopathic disorder that generated abnormally aggressive behavior. Persuaded, the jury found him guilty of manslaughter.

A year before their quick resolution of Catherine Russell's savage murder the Metropolitan Police had celebrated their 150th anniversary. In that time the fledgling 1829 force that was created by Peel, Rowan, and Mayne had grown from a handful of men to a department of 22,196 men and women officers and 15,491 civilian staff.

The commissioner, the fifteenth since Rowan and Mayne, was David McNee. Born the son of a railwayman in a tenement in the center of Glasgow, Scotland, he left school at the age of fifteen. After wartime duty with the navy, he joined the Glasgow police, serving as a beat officer, was in the CID, and was a member of the Flying Squad. As chief constable of Starthclyde in 1976, he was invited to succeed retiring Robert Mark in what McNee saw as the "most important and renowned chief officer post anywhere, head of the greatest police force in the world, and working at a headquarters which was an international byword."

Depicted by the London press as a teetotaling, Bible-punching martinet with the nickname the "Hammer," the new commissioner took command in March 1977. The metropolis in which he was expected to keep the Queen's Peace accounted for nearly half the robberies in England and Wales, 75 percent of crimes involving firearms, 55 percent of all drug addicts, more than 600 protests and demonstrations per year, and the bulk of Britain's terrorist bombings and shootings.

Coincidental with McNee's appointment as commissioner a new chief took over as head of the CID. As the sixteenth successive assistant (crime) commissioner who would bear the considerable responsibility for dealing with the terrorism of the IRA, fifty-three-year-old Gilbert Kelland had been born on St. Patrick's Day.

Quiet since the Balcombe Street debacle, the IRA stirred from dormancy in 1978 with bombings in several cities, including two carbomb blasts in Central London. The new campaign continued into 1979 with the blowing-up of Lord Louis Mountbatten's boat, killing the Queen's uncle, and the bombing of Airey Neave's car as he left Parliament.

But acts of terror were not confined to the IRA. Following the shooting of Yemenite diplomats in 1977, two Syrians died in a car bombing. In January 1978 the London representative of the Palestine Liberation Organization was assassinated. In July a grenade attack was made on the Iraqi ambassador outside his embassy, and a former prime minister of Iraq was gunned down at the Intercontinental Hotel.

As horrifying as these acts were, they paled in comparison to a drama that began on Wednesday, April 30, 1980. At 11:25 A.M., six anti-Khomeini terrorists barged into the embassy of Iran in quiet, genteel, residential Kensington, site of the home of the Prince of Wales and known as London's "royal suburb."

Calling themselves the Group of the Martyr, they demanded independence for the Iranian province of Khuzistan.

Among twenty-six persons taken hostage was Police Constable Trevor James Lock. Assigned to the embassy as a member of the Metropolitan Police's Diplomatic Protection Group, he was forty-one years old and had been a policeman for fifteen.

What the terrorists did not know as they invaded the embassy was that Locke's embassy assignment permitted him to carry a gun. Holstered under the right-hand patch pocket of his blue tunic, the presence of the .38 Smith and Wesson revolver was obscured by the bulge of several notebooks.

Frisking him, a nervous terrorist patted the thick pocket. "What is this?" he demanded.

Locke lifted the flap of the pocket. "Books. Maps."

With a satisfied nod, the jittery terrorist moved aside, searching others.

Outside the embassy, the by-now-familiar hostage-situation operations of the police were on television for the entire nation to see. Amassed police. Guns. Stalemate. But there was a dramatic difference between this standoff and those of Spaghetti House and Balcombe Street. In this instance messages from terrorists were shouted from windows by P. C. Locke while a pair of pistols were held to his back.

Hopes that rose with the release of some hostages were dashed when the terrorists killed one of the Iranians and dumped his body outside a door, vowing to kill others.

The time had come to take action. McNee proposed to the Home Secretary a plan calling for use of the elite antiterrorist Special Air Services regiment in a full-scale military assault.

Meeting with the SAS commander, McNee said, "Don't forget that Trevor Locke is in there in uniform."

As the assault swung into action outside, in the room where Locke was being detained the frightened leader of the terrorists dropped his pistol. Locke sprang upon him.

Sprawling to the floor, the terrorist groped for the fallen gun. Piling atop him and pinning him, Locke drew the revolver he had managed to conceal for six days.

Jamming it under the terrorist's chin, he growled, "You're the leader, aren't you?"

"It was not me," the terrorist pleaded. "It was the others."

With a clank and a hiss, a yellow tear gas canister rolled

into the room. Others followed. For an instant Locke thought they looked like lemons. Then, out of the blinding, choking smoke, he heard an English voice. "Trevor, move over!"

As Locke rolled to his right rapid gunfire ripped into the terrorist.

Muffled behind a gas mask, a man in black shouted, "Trevor, make for the corridor."

Dashing out of the room, Locke found himself being lifted by the armpits and passed from one pair of rescuers to another until he was out of doors and gulping fresh air. Still in his clasp was his Smith and Wesson, unfired.

Together with Locke at a press conference, McNee told the throng of reporters, "You write about bravery, now look at it."

Like Kensington, St. James's Square ranks at the top of the list of London's most fashionable addresses. A block north of the exclusive clubs of Pall Mall and south of Piccadilly's venerable Fortnum and Mason, traditional provisioners to the monarchy, the square in February 1984 was the location of the Libyan embassy.

Renamed the Libyan People's Bureau by the government of Colonel Muammar el-Qaddafi, the embassy had become a subject of grave concern to the Metropolitan Police. On April 6, a full alert had been issued by Scotland Yard warning that hit squads formed by opponents of the terrorist dictator were planning to take over the embassy. On the tenth, a cable from a pro-Qaddafi group, the Revolutionary Students' Force (RSF), was intercepted. Sent from London to Tripoli, it threatened to open "directly attributable action" and "the pursuit of the stray dogs" who opposed Qaddafi.

Following public hangings of anti-Qaddafi students in the Libyan capital, furious members of the RSF called for a protest at St. James's. On April 17, seventy-five of them arrived at the northeast corner of the square and gathered before the embassy.

Between them and the building ranks of police stood behind aluminum crowd-control barricades. Among them, primarily for the purpose of traffic control, was twenty-five-year-old Woman Police Constable Yvonne Fletcher. At five feet, two inches she was the tiniest member of the force. Born in the village of Semley, Wiltshire, she had announced at the age of three that she wanted to be a policewoman. She had served at Bow Street and considered the historic police station her home. Her boss, Chief Superintendent Brian West, considered her one of the best. In that, he got no argument from P. C. Michael Liddle. Her fiancé, he was also on duty in front of the Libyan People's Bureau.

At 10:18 A.M. loud music suddenly blared from the embassy. Seconds later, gunshots fired from windows of the first floor sprayed the people in the street.

Struck in the back, Fletcher fell dead. Knocked from her head by the impact, her hat spun across the pavement. A saucer-shaped cap with a gleaming black visor and black-and-white checkered band, it would lie there during the longest siege in the history of Scotland Yard's struggle against terrorism.

Eleven days after Fletcher's murder the crisis ended with the severing of British diplomatic ties with Libya and expulsion of everyone in the embassy, including, presumably, Fletcher's killer.

"We have become used to seeing our policemen and women respond magnificently to any challenge but we must never take their professionalism for granted," said Prime Minister Margaret Thatcher as she dedicated a memorial where Fletcher died. "Our police uphold the law without regard for their own feelings and their own safety, never knowing what the day may bring."

TWENTY-FOUR

Dial 999

To THE WORLD THE LONDON POLICEMAN IS KNOWN AS A Bobby. Londoners call him "Old Bill." The police as an institution is known as the "Bill." A newcomer to the force is a "sprog." A Scene of the Crime Officer is a SOCO. An informant is a "grass." If he is an especially important source he's a "supergrass." A HORTI is a summons to a miscreant motorist to produce his driving papers at the station. A jail is the "Nick." To be placed under arrest is to be "knicked." To the general public the Metropolitan Police Office is the "Met." The entrance is called the "back way."

Why? According to Bill Waddell, curator of the Black Museum, when Sir Robert Peel's fledgling policemen reported to their new headquarters they discovered that it was more convenient to enter by the rear door. The back way has been the way in ever since.

In the New Scotland Yard that rises above Broadway between busy Victoria Street and the tranquillity of St. James's Park the back way is a narrow marble-walled lobby guarded by a wary constable with a sharp eye for suspicious guests who might turn out to be a member of the IRA. At an information desk a guest must sign in and be given a tag to be worn at all times within the building and a paper pass to be returned when leaving. Duly authorized, the visitor still must await the arrival of an escort.

Emblazoned on the wall opposite the waiting area are these words:

STATEMENT OF OUR
COMMON PURPOSES AND VALUES

The purpose of the Metropolitan Police Service is to uphold the law fairly and firmly; to prevent crime; to pursue and bring to justice those who break the law; to keep the Queen's Peace; to protect, help and reassure the people in London; and to be seen to do all this with integrity, common sense and sound judgement.

We must be compassionate, courteous and patient, acting without fear or favour or prejudice to the rights of others. We need to be professional, calm and restrained in the face of violence and apply only that force which is necessary to accomplish our lawful duty.

We must strive to reduce the fears of the public and, so far as we can, to reflect their priorities in the action we take. We must respond to well-founded criticism with a willingness to change.

Beneath this credo stand two glass cases. In one burns an eternal flame for Metropolitan Police martyrs whose names are inscribed in a book along with the dates and manner of their deaths in the line of duty. The second case commemorates the death of Constable Keith Blakelock. Assigned to protect firemen responding to a blaze at the Broadwater Farm Estate in the North London suburb of Tottenham, he was hacked to death by rioters in October 1985. In charging several men with the murder the police alleged that one of the attackers wielded a machete in an attempt to chop off Blakelock's head.

The slaying marked a horrifying escalation of violence in a decade of the worst riots in Britain since the police did battle with Chartists and others a hundred years earlier. Beginning in 1976 with gangs disrupting the annual festival of London's growing West Indian community and a repeat of the rampage in 1977, civil disorders had broken out in major cities.

Sparked by a variety of causes, including the disappointment of fans at sporting events, the era of violence was described in July 1981 by Prime Minister Margaret Thatcher as "most worrying."

A common characteristic of the disturbances was attacks on police. In Commissioner Robert Mark's view the police were doomed to be the losers. "The simple but unpalatable truth is that our system of justice is not fitted to deal with political or racial violence on a large scale and that no one knows what to do about it," he wrote in his memoirs. "The police wind up bewildered and resentful. They are faced from time to time with a deliberate breakdown of law and order and can do little about it unless they are prepared to take the law into their own hands which might win the immediate battle but involved them in a war they must inevitably lose."

Others asserted that the police contributed to the problem. A study of police practices begun in 1979 by the Policy Studies Institute at the request of the Metropolitan Police supported the charge. Surveying West Indian men ages fifteen to twenty-four, investigators found that 63 percent said they had been stopped and questioned unjustifiably by police at least once in the previous year. The study group also disclosed that one of its own members, a young black man, had been arrested observing a protest march and falsely accused of attacking an officer. Other officers then told lies, he claimed, to save their colleagues from perjury charges. Racist language was found to be common in police ranks.

In what Commissioner Sir Kenneth Newman called "the most comprehensive scrutiny of a major police force ever conducted in Europe," the report also accused police of having an unofficial policy of restricting the proportion of women officers to about 10 percent of the force.

The institute also alleged heavy drinking among officers. One in twenty was likely to have taken a bribe. Promotions to the rank of inspector depended on success in passing examinations and was "very little related to proven ability, performance or standards of conduct."

Made public in 1983, the report's revelations of Scotland Yard's shortcomings again stirred ancient embers of doubt as to whether Britain could ever attain the ideal of Sir Robert Peel's perfect system of police.

As disturbing as the indictment was, no item in its bill of particulars proved so deeply undermining of public confidence in its system of law and order as an event on July 9, 1982. It inscribed in the annals of Scotland Yard a crime and the name of a perpetrator without peer in the 153 years of the Met.

At half-past six that Friday morning as Michael Fagan, dressed in shabby clothes and barefooted, gazed at the Royal Standard atop Buckingham Palace, he was several hours ahead of the tourists who would gather for the colorful Changing of the Guard. Then, the forecourt of the palace would bristle with red-coated troops. Rich in the romance and history of the monarchy, the old guard would form up in the courtyard at 11:00 while the new guard mustered at its barracks in preparation for a proud march to the palace. Accompanied by a regimental band of the Guards Division and the battalion's own Corps of Drums they would arrive at the Palace at 11:30 to march through the North Center Gate. But for now, the forecourt and the palace were quiet. Within, the Queen was still asleep.

Climbing over railings, Fagan dropped to the ground.

No alarm sounded.

Nor did one go off as he walked to the palace.

By means of an unlocked window he entered the Stamp Room. Here an alert signal was triggered. Nobody responded to it.

Having had a look around, Fagan exited through the window to another, also unlatched. Finding himself in the office of the Master of the Household, he made his way through the state apartments. Despite his unusual appearance he passed a cleaner unchallenged and sat for a while on a throne.

Next on his tour was a room for the Queen's dogs. The prized Corgis might have signaled trouble, but they were already out for their morning walk.

Opening another door, Fagan crept into the Queen's bedroom. Gently parting the bed curtains, he found Elizabeth II awake.

Sitting beside her on the bed, Fagan inquired about the royal family. Calmly engaging the intruder in conversation, Her Majesty pressed the button of a silent alarm. No one answered.

As Fagan rambled on, she picked up a bedside telephone to whisper to an operator to send a policeman. It would be a long ten minutes before a constable responded.

Meanwhile, unrelated to any alarms from the Queen, a maid and a footman came in. Politely but firmly, they escorted Fagan out.

Informed of the intrusion, Deputy Assistant Commissioner of Police John Radley reported the incident to Brian Cubbon of the Home Office. However, Home Secretary William Whitelaw was not told until Monday morning.

Also notified on Monday by CID Chief Gilbert Kelland of what had happened, Commissioner McNee rushed to Scotland Yard from a visit to the Tooting police station. With a "sickening sinking in the pit of the stomach, disbelief linked with dismay," he felt a deep sense of shame that the Metropolitan Police "had failed to protect Her Majesty."

Equally appalling to McNee was the fact that since 1979 he had been striving to launch a review of policies and practices intended to improve protections of the royal family and their residences. For numerous reasons the project had never been begun. "Alas," he thought as he rushed to his office, "it was too late."

As soon as the news broke, McNee noted with remarkable understatement, "a great hubub arose" with a clamor for heads to roll. The ones most mentioned were those of the Home Secretary and the commissioner. Neither was asked by the Prime Minister to quit. "You don't sack the general," he said, "for the failure of one of his soldiers."

Believing that matters could not be worse, McNee received a phone call a week later from Sir Philip Moore, private secretary to the Queen. Might the commissioner come to the palace?

At the meeting Moore told McNee that the previous Wednesday he had met with a journalist on the *Sun* who had informed him that a male prostitute had regularly associated with the Metropolitan Police commander who was the Queen's personal policeman.

McNee was stunned. To his knowledge there had never been any suspicion or the slightest indication that the commander was a homosexual.

"What are you going to do about it?" Moore asked.

"Leave it to me," McNee answered.

Back at Scotland Yard he called for Gilbert Kelland. "Look into it," he ordered. "Find the person making this allegation and question him."

After interviewing the youth in a flat at Cleveland Square, Paddington, Kelland phoned McNee. "It's a true bill," he said. The term was CID talk. It meant the youth was telling the truth. Admitting a relationship with the prostitute, the Queen's police officer resigned.

A further shock rocked Scotland Yard during its investigation of Michael Fagan. His visit to the Queen's bedchamber, he said, was not the first time. He'd also sneaked into Buckingham Palace in early June and walked away with a bottle of wine.

Tried on a charge of breaking and entering and theft of the

wine, he was acquitted by jurors who believed he'd had no criminal intent. Because trespassing was not a crime but a violation of civil law, he was not prosecuted for the subsequent early morning call upon the Queen.

Asked why he broke into the palace, Fagan told the court he wanted to show how easy it was for someone to get into the royal home. "I wanted to show that the Queen isn't safe."

Although it is widely assumed that the Queen is protected primarily by the military units that take part in the Changing of the Guard, the responsibility for the royal family is in the hands of the Royalty and Diplomatic Protection Department of the Metropolitan Police. Commanded by a deputy assistant commissioner, the unit works closely with the Anti-Terrorist Squad and the Special Escort Group. An elite motorcycle squad formed in 1953 to accompany Marshal Tito of Yugoslavia around London during a state visit, it is made up of officers selected from the ranks of the Met's Traffic Patrol.

Coping with street traffic had become a police responsibility in the Metropolitan Police Act of 1839, but the Traffic Department did not come into existence until 1919. In 1991 its 800 men and women bore responsibility for nearly 3 million licensed vehicles and 8,600 miles of roads and motorways.

Older than the Traffic Department by at least eighty-one years, the Mounted Branch traces its roots to Sir Henry Fielding's office in Bow Street in 1758. Incorporated into the Met in 1836, the horse police played a major role in quelling Chartist and other riots, and continues to be used in crowd control.

Almost as old as the mounted police, the Thames Division goes back to 1798 and the opening of the first Maritime Police Office downriver from London Bridge at Wapping. Patrolling fifty-four miles of Thames from Dartford Creek to Staines Bridge, its police boats operate from two riverside stations and one that floats at the Waterloo Pier. In 1990 the sailor-police rescued 545 people.

If a bird's eye view of the Metropolis is needed, the Met calls upon its own air force. The Air Support Unit, it is based at Lippitts Hill in open country near Epping Forest and provides helicopters for situations ranging from ground traffic control to searches. Carrying out 3,557 assignments in 1990, the airborne force logged 1,628 flying hours.

To maintain law and order in a metropolis sprawling across

799 square miles, Commissioner Peter Imbert in 1991 headed a police department consisting of more than 28,000 officers, 17,000 civil staff, and 1,400 part-time special constables.

Property consisted of 1,943 premises including 196 police stations, 3,800 motor vehicles, 25 Thames patrol boats, 3 Bell 222 helicopters, 379 bicycles, 389 dogs, and 180 horses.

The Met operating budget totaled 1.4 billion pounds.

Out of a 1990 population of 7.5 million, 28,000 Londoners were reported to the police to be missing. At year's end only 407 remained unaccounted for.

Calls to 999, the London emergency telephone number, totaled 1,044,276—an average of one every thirty seconds—while a second number, Crimestoppers (0800 555 111), received more than 3,000 tips resulting in 242 arrests. A third, the Metropolitan Police Crimeline (071 230 2301), commenced in 1989. It was made available to encourage calls from witnesses to crimes whose details are featured on the BBC's "Crimewatch UK" and London Weekend Television's "Crime Monthly" television programs, similar to the "America's Most Wanted" TV program.

"During 1990 it was a sad fact that more crimes than ever were reported," said Commissioner Imbert in his annual crime review.

Included in that jump in statistics was a 10 percent rise in reported cases of domestic violence. Of these, 81 percent were cleared up, compared to 59 percent for other categories of violence against the person.

More than 90 percent of crimes in 1990 were against property, including 173,200 burglaries. Under the Theft Act of 1968, a person is guilty of burglary if "he enters a building as a trespasser, with intent to steal, assault or rape someone therein, or to cause damage, or having entered the building he steals or assaults someone." According to Scotland Yard statistics, the crime occurred on an average of one every thirty seconds.

Swamped by the number of burglaries and admitting that "it would be impossible to solve all the crimes," Scotland Yard had devised a screening system to sort through break-ins most likely to "respond to investigation, allowing manpower to be concentrated on those cases liable to yield positive results."

For those whose burglaries had been screened and determined to be unlikely to "respond," the system provoked bitterness. In an article headlined "Why I No Longer Have Faith in the Police" in the *Evening Standard* of October 4, 1991, Sophia Watson wrote that after four burglaries in two months at her home in Notting Hill she had begun to wonder how seriously the police regarded the crime.

"They arrived within the hour," she wrote of the latest burglary of her home. "They are sad, look about, suggest that the back door has been broken into, write down a few notes and ask what was stolen. The policewoman pats the dog and discusses his diet. The policeman begins to look miserable and says that the problem with their job is that so many people hate the police and really all they wish to do is help people and catch burglars."

Noting that her Notting Hill home had not been robbed or harmed during the carnival riots of the 1970s, she implied a racist motive to the police, wondering whether, if she had called from Mayfair "to report the theft of a Van Dyke rather than from Notting Hill to report stolen silver plate, the crime would not have been allowed to slip by."

In 1990 it was not the carnival at Notting Hill that brought out the riot police. The battleground was the scene of so many Bloody Sundays. Angered by the Thatcher government's imposition of a poll tax, protesters battled police in Trafalgar Square on March 31, in what Commissioner Imbert's 1990 Crime Review called "one of the most serious outbreaks of public disorder my officers have ever been confronted with" and "one of the most vicious and sustained attacks" upon police officers in many years. During the riot, 542 police officers were injured.

Continuing this litany of crime in his annual report, Imbert found some encouragement in the Met's war against drugs. Arrests and seizures were up significantly, he said, with a "substantial number" of major drug trafficking networks destroyed. Despite the successes, he admitted, drugs still were readily available in London.

"It is now as easy to buy crack at King's Cross as it is to get a railway ticket," wrote novelist and ex-drug addict Will Self in the September 1991 *Evening Standard Magazine*. "You only have to stand outside the main entrance to King's Cross for five minutes to start spotting the street people who are involved in drugs." He called King's Cross "New Crack City."

• • •

The corner of York Way and Goods Way behind one of London's busiest underground, bus, and railway stations also teemed with prostitutes. Strolling there on the night of Wednesday, October 2, 1991, painfully thin and chain-smoking twenty-two-year-old Nicola Evans had been selling her body for twenty pounds a throw for two years. Recently, she had been beaten up by pimps. She also owed a hundred pounds in fines for soliciting.

To three undercover vice policemen in a van nearby her face was familiar. But Nicole was not their target. They were looking for men who might attempt to pick her up.

The offense was "kerb crawling." Under the Sexual Offences Act of 1985 it carried a maximum penalty of four hundred pounds. To be charged a suspect had to be shown to be "persistent" in soliciting a woman for the purpose of prostitution from a motor vehicle in a manner likely to cause annoyance to the woman or nuisance to people in the neighborhood.

To justify a claim of persistence the Metropolitan Police policy required vice squad officers to observe two approaches by a kerb crawler.

At eleven o'clock the three policemen in the van at King's Cross observed a man leave his car. Well-dressed and wearing eyeglasses, he had the looks and bearing of a gentleman as he spoke to a woman known to the officers as a prostitute. A moment later he approached Nicole.

Leaving the police van, a plainsclothes constable crossed the street. "I beg your pardon, sir," he said, approaching the man. "I must ask you to identify yourself, sir," he said as he drew from an inside pocket a small wallet to identify himself as a police officer.

The man being questioned had no difficulty recognizing the validity of the identify document, known as a warrant card. He'd seen many of them, not as a suspect but as a lawyer.

Neither did the constable have any difficulty in recognizing the name given to him by the man he had stopped. He was Sir Allan Green, Queen's Counsel, Director of Public Prosecutions, and head of the Crown Prosecution Service.

Educated at Charterhouse and St. Catherine's College, Cambridge, Green had been called to the Bar in 1959. Concentrating in criminal law, he became a junior prosecuting counsel at the Old Bailey in 1977. His celebrated prosecutions included East German spies Reinhard and Sonja Sculse and serial killer Neville Heath. As DDP he had decided that the Crown would not oppose the appeals of the Maguire family, Birmingham Six, and Guildford Four.

Married and the father of two grown sons, he resided in a Georgian home in exclusive Chalcot Square, Primrose Hill, North London. Barely six months before he went kerb crawling at King's Cross, his knighthood had been bestowed at Buckingham Palace.

"The career and reputation of one of Britain's most senior law chiefs was in tatters last night after he was brought down by the oldest crime in the book," declared *Today* on Friday, joining Britain's sensation-hungry newspapers in publishing front-page headlines describing the incident, made public along with an announcement that the DDP had resigned and that Green "bitterly regreted what has happened."

Recalling Sophia Watson's account of her frustrations over police inability to catch the burglar who had invaded her home in Notting Hill, a reader of the *Evening Standard* discerned in the Green case a "clue" as to why it was impossible for the police to deal effectively with crimes such as burglary.

"No one would deny that kerb-crawling in residential areas is a considerable nuisance which should be discouraged by all reasonable means," said J. Mackenney. "But it is hard to see what public good is served by devoting substantial police resources to pursuing prostitutes and their clients in areas such as the derelict streets behind King's Cross."

Scotland Yard's answer to such criticism was to point to numerous complaints registered by women residing in the King's Cross area who were not prostitutes and resented being approached by kerb crawlers who assumed them to be. Such citizen complaints had resulted in enactment of the kerb-crawling law, said a Met spokesman.

"It must be understood that the police do not decide what the law shall be," declares the Metropolitan Police Office in one of its press releases.

While the scandal of the Director of Public Prosecutions dominated newspaper headlines, the lawyer who had represented the Birmingham Six during their appeals appeared on BBC Television with a scathing indictment of Britain's criminal justice system.

Offering a radical remedy, Queen's Counsel Michael

Mansfield suggested revisions that would emulate the legal systems of the United States and France. He called for institution of a more equitable system of bail, elimination of traditional trappings of the court room (wigs and gowns), and abolition of the prisoner's dock.

"The dock is the embodiment of prejudice," he said. "There's the judge up on high and the accused in the dock surrounded by the police. Is that the way to treat someone we are told should be assumed innocent?"

Writing in the *New York Times* of June 2, 1991, Craig R. Whitney saw in the overturned prosecutions of suspected IRA terrorists a growing crisis of faith among Britons concerning their treasured system of justice. What he discerned among the people of England and Ulster, he wrote, was a badly shaken faith brought on by a series of miscarriages of justice and of innocent people sent to jail. "What most of [these cases] show is what many common criminals in nonpolitical cases have been saying for a long time," he continued. "They say that behind what may seem to be the genteel image of the unarmed British bobby is a police force that is not above 'putting the boot in' to get confessions out of people they think are guilty, a prosecutorial system more geared to securing confessions than to insuring that justice is done, and a judiciary that is slow to recognize that there is any problem."

As pointedly embarrassing as these criticisms were for the institutions of British justice in general and the Metropolitan Police in particular, another incident in October 1991 provoked more red faces at Scotland Yard.

Despite the rigorous security safeguards in effect in the "back way," a mentally disturbed twenty-five-year-old woman had slipped unchallenged through the lobby. Taking an elevator to the seventh floor, she helped herself to several items of police equipment and departed just as easily.

Even more humiliating to Yarders, the theft was only discovered when the woman's family returned home to find her wearing full riot gear.

With the property restored, the Met chose not to prosecute.

Although it seems unlikely that the woman's larcenous tour of the Yard will be enshrined in the Black Museum, it ought to be. Never mind that it was not a bloody murder. Overlook the fact that the crime fell far short of those of Constance

Kent, Charley Peace, Dr. Cream, Crippen, the Yorkshire Ripper, Haigh, and Heath. Forget that it wasn't solved through intrepid sleuthing in the grand tradition of Inspectors Whicher, Abberline, and Dew.

The woman who robbed Scotland Yard ought to be remembered simply because her crime was one of those bold deeds that are strewn throughout the colorful and illustrious story of Scotland Yard and the pages of this book.

Although there is no way of knowing for sure which member of the Metropolitan Police first decided to keep souvenirs of his cases, credit for recognizing their intrinsic value belongs to Sir Harold Scott. During nine years as commissioner (1945-53), he decided to inspect the rooms in the basement of New Scotland Yard where relics of the history of the Metropolitan Police had been stored.

"The place was known outside the Yard as the Black Museum," Scott wrote in a memoir, *From Inside Scotland Yard*. He found that it was black in more ways than one. There was the blackness of some of the crimes commemorated there. But he found it black in another sense. The way to it was through dark and dingy underground passages. The museum itself was dusty and disordered. "It was hardly more than a rubbish dump," he recalled. "The only relief in seeing some exhibits was in the thought that these crimes had been detected by the police."

Dismayed, Scott ordered the museum to be "spring-cleaned and properly organized" with exhibits logically grouped, labeled, and displayed. His intent was to use the collection for training by showing new officers "the tools and methods of criminals and the countermeasures and discoveries of the police."

Removed to the *new* New Scotland Yard in 1967, the Black Museum has been used in that manner since then. Opened only to members of the Met and carefully screened guests, primarily visiting police officials, it is guarded by its curator as scrupulously as Beefeaters protecting the Crown jewels in the Tower of London.

Unfortunately, in keeping the British public and tourists from being admitted to the Black Museum the Metropolitan Police have missed a golden public relations opportunity. In shutting out ordinary citizens Scotland Yard reinforces the allegations of its critics that police are an instrument of an elitist class-based social and political establishment rather than providing a means by which they might encourage an appreciation of the Met in times when the police force comes under withering scrutiny.

After all, the history of Scotland Yard belongs as much to the British nation as to the police.

While there are legitimate concerns about the security of New Scotland Yard because of the IRA's continuing reign of terror, in which a terrorist might decide to plant a bomb among exhibits, any such threat would evaporate if the Black Museum were moved out of New Scotland Yard.

An ideal location might be the site of the original police headquarters in Great Scotland Yard. Close to such landmarks as Piccadilly Circus, Trafalgar Square, the Horse Guards, and 10 Downing Street, the location would prove convenient to interested citizens, schoolchildren on an educational outing, and the 19.2 million tourists who visit the Metropolitan Police District each year.

For evidence of how a public Black Museum can be organized and run the police need only to walk a short distance from New Scotland Yard to the Clive Steps, King Charles Street, to see the success of the recently opened Cabinet War Rooms museum.

As the visitors to that underground wartime command center are carried back to a crucial moment when London withstood the Nazi threat, exhorted by Winston Churchill to make the crisis "their finest hour," so, too, would visitors to an open-to-the-public Black Museum be enthralled and inspired by the history of Scotland Yard.

And what mementoes! The wooden alarm rattle carried by the police until 1885. Charley Peace's knife and violin. A tipstaff, rather like a scepter, which was carried by superintendents of police in the midnineteenth century, with a crown head that could be unscrewed to reveal a cavity in the shaft where the officer carried his warrant card. A top hat worn by a Bobby at the time of the coronation of Victoria displayed beside examples of all the hats worn by constables through the years, from Bow Street Runners to today. An array of forged passports, checks, postal money orders, bank notes, and coins. A smuggler's shoe with a hollowed-out heel. The silver-headed walking stick concealing a glass tube for smuggled drugs. Half a button, the clue that sent a murderer to meet the hangman. Guns. Daggers. Bludgeons. Jack the Ripper's knife. Dr. Cream's lethal pillbox.

There, too, would be a woman's hair curler discovered in the red clay of a shallow grave dug in a coal cellar that convinced Inspector Dew that Hawley Harvey Crippen had murdered his wife. Possibly, the visitors would catch the ghostly voice of that unfortunate woman, Belle Elmore, singing words that bestowed upon her the theatrical fame she had sought and which exemplify the history of Scotland Yard: *"You can't beat a British crime."*

INDEX